Gangland to God

by
DAVEY FALCUS

First British edition 2007

ISBN No. 978 1 904726 80 1

Published by Verité CM Limited,
8 St John's Parade, Alinora Crescent,
Goring-by-Sea, West Sussex BN12 4HJ
Tel: 01903 241975 fax: 01903 521959
email:enquiries@veritecm.com
Web: www.veritecm.com,
www.verite.co.uk and www.trinityvision.co.uk

British Library Cataloguing Data

A catalogue record of this book is available
from The British Library

Typesetting by Eric Escott

Designed and printed by Verité CM Ltd.

Acknowledgements

There are many people I would like to thank for their help and support in enabling me to reach this point in my life—so many that it would probably fill another book, so if you are not mentioned, don't take it personally, there just isn't enough space to list everybody.

First of all I would like to thank my wife Kathryn and my children for being such a support to me, and at times my reason for living. I would especially like to honour the following people: My adoptive mam Joan, who poured such love into me and told me about Jesus. My adoptive dad, Derek who knelt by my bed and taught me to pray— I'm sorry I was such a disappointment to you and put you through such hard times. Brenda, Steven and Jane, sorry for all the distress I caused and thank you for not holding it against me. My gran, Hannah and grandad Jack, especially Hannah, who never stopped praying for me and never gave up hope. Auntie Wynne and Uncle Ron, my godparents, who faithfully fulfilled their obligations and took me to Sunday school.

I would like to thank Liz Arthur who gave us a place of refuge when we were in need and for leaving the bible that was to lead to my salvation, Linda and Glenn Fabian, our first Christian friends, and their children Scott, Peter and Daniel and all our friends at Holy Family, Killingworth who were such a support to us especially Geoff and Julie Smith, Lesley Christie and Mavis Bertram.

I would like to thank Evangelist Dougie March who helped disciple me in those early days. Pastor Alan Finlay and the congregation of Longbenton Community Church, especially Dr Ian and Helen Longfield who have been such a source of strength and support to us and Jim and Gail Harrison for their love and friendship. I would also like to thank David Campbell who encouraged me to write my story and helped me in the early days of this book.

I would like to thank Douglas Jarvie for all his help and support and for his company on many adventures around the world.

I would like to thank Apostle Harry Das for recognising the calling on my life and ordaining me and to Rev Randy and Dorothy Vickers for giving me my regular spiritual MOT's.

I would like to pay tribute to my friend the late Patrick Hinton for being such a support and encouragement and Canon David Wood for his teaching and enthusiasm.

A special thank you to those who have supported us and our ministry—especially Greg Davies, Ken and Mary Connop, Richard and Jenny Coleman, Martin Clarke and of course our dear friend the Rev Dr Robert Ward. And to my dear friends John and Susan Wright for being such an inspiration and sharing my testimony all over the world!

Thanks to the congregations, past and present of our churches in Killingworth and Ashington and those who have caught the vision and supported our prayer network and Church leadership groups.

I would also like to thank my friend Chris Powell for encouraging me not to give up on this book and patiently waiting for its completion.

I would like to honour the evangelist J. John, the man God used to impart His Holy Spirit to me and light the fire.

Finally, to My Lord, my Saviour, my God and my Friend the Lord Jesus Christ who has never left me and never stopped loving me.

Dedication

I dedicate this book to my Gran Hannah, to my wife, my children and my grandchildren and all those who are lost and searching.

Contents

1
The Visit—1976

"David, we're off to the shops" my Dad's voice boomed up the stairs, "mind you behave yourself—and no rooting around" he added.

"Right" I answered back.

I heard the kitchen door shut and footsteps on the driveway, a couple of seconds later, I heard the slamming of car doors and the engine of my Dad's Ford Cortina starting up. I lay back on my bed and relaxed as I heard the car pull away. I gazed up at the ceiling.

"Dad's always on my case" I thought, feeling sorry for myself.

I closed my eyes for a while and drifted into a waking dream, it was a most peculiar experience, I can only try and describe what happened. As I drifted into the dream or vision, I heard a knocking on the front door. In the dream I got off the bed and went downstairs to the door. When I opened it I saw a man standing there, he was casually dressed and I guess he looked to be in his mid thirties. He had a tidy goatee beard and dark shoulder - length hair parted in the centre with dark, piercing eyes.

"Hi David, is your Dad in?" he asked.

"No, he's just gone to the shops" I answered, surprised that the man knew my name.

Must be one of Dad's friends, I thought.

"Will he be long?" the man asked.

"No, not really" I replied.

"Look David, I'm a friend of your Dad's, do you mind if I come in and wait for him?" the man asked.

"Yeah, no problem" I said letting him in.

As we sat chatting for a while in the living room, the

man asked me about school and if I liked it, what did I like at school—that sort of thing.

I chatted to him for a while trying to figure out who he was. He seemed familiar, but I couldn't put my finger on it.

After a while he said "Look David, it's not your Dad I've come to see, it's you"

"Me? Why?"

"Look son, I've come because your Dad is worried about you and has been praying about you," the man said.

"Who are you?" I asked.

"Jesus," he answered.

"Jesus!" I said, startled.

"David, I'd like you to help me" he said, "would you like to help me?"

"If you are Jesus why do you need my help?" I asked, totally amazed at the man's revelation.

"Look, if you're Jesus then make the sun shine right now!" I said trying to get my ten-year-old mind around what was happening.

Suddenly the sun began to shine outside, I was gob-smacked,

"Yes, of course I'll help you, what do you want me to do?" I asked fully convinced.

"It won't be for a few years, but I want you to behave yourself and be good for your Dad" he said.

Then, leaning over me and looking straight into my eyes, he said:

"Son, because you're going to help me, evil will target you."

I saw the look of concern on his face and the fire in his eyes.

"Can you not stop it?" I asked.

"Son, I'll be there to shield you, but I will never interfere with your free will" he replied.

I didn't understand what he was saying at the time but I do now. He was saying 'I will protect you, but I can't stop you making your own mistakes and decisions, I have given you a free will.'

Then I said to him in a ten year old's way "Will I get magic powers?"

He said, "No son, My grace is sufficient for you."

We sat and talked for a while and then he got up to leave; as he was leaving he once again asked me to be good for my Dad.

I waved to him from the window as he left and as he walked along the path he disappeared before my eyes, completely vanishing!

Then I awoke, back on my bed and I could hear my Dad banging about downstairs, putting the shopping away. I went to tell him about what had happened, full of excitement, but he just looked at me as though I'd lost the plot!

And he said to me "My grace is sufficient for you, for my strength is made perfect in weakness". 2 Corinthians 12 v9 (NKJ)

2
Early Years

What follows is a true account of my life and testimony though a few names and places may be changed to protect people's confidences and identities.

I didn't have the best start in life, I was born in Brampton near Carlisle, Cumbria on the 30th May 1966, two months before England won the World Cup. I was the product of an adulterous affair, my father was already married with a family and visited my mother on his 'business' trips. My father's business trips were of a criminal nature since that was how he made his living.

My mother was young and unable to cope and so I was put into foster care before being adopted at six weeks old a by a couple from Newcastle upon Tyne, Derek and Joan Falcus. Derek was in his mid thirties at the time, a structural engineer by profession, and his wife Joan was a nurse. We lived in a small flat in Bavington Drive, Fenham, which is in the infamous West End of Newcastle upon Tyne.

The first few years of my life were very happy. We were a very close family, my grandparents on my adoptive mother's side, Hannah and Jack, were always around and I loved them very much, they lived nearby in Aldwick Road. Hannah was a devout Christian who prayed every day and attended St John's Anglican Church on Grainger Street in Newcastle city centre.

My early recollections of this time are all happy, every day seemed to be sunny back in the sixties—this was the time of the Animals, the Beatles, George Best, and Jimi Hendrix.

When I was two years old we moved to a new house

in the Westerhope area on the outskirts of the city. The house was a new semi-detached with a garage and three gardens. This was to be my home for the next twelve years or so. Life was very happy at Priory Way, so much so that Derek and Joan decided to adopt again, this time they adopted a girl—Jane Roslyn. It was quite an experience to have a new sister. I remember being very excited by the prospect; at that time I was a happy, normal little boy. I was fairly quick at learning and I was taught to say my prayers at an early age. My adoptive mother, Joan, was a bible-believing Christian and she used to tell me stories about Jesus.

People who say that television programmes don't influence or do any harm to kids should take note of this!

Every Saturday afternoon the family would go to my Dad's parents' house for tea. I would enjoy the day because my grandad Harry would always watch the wrestling on TV, which I also enjoyed. The wrestling was followed by Batman, which I loved—I liked all the fighting and action sequences, Batman was always crashing through doors and windows…!

One day aged four during a game of 'Batman and Robin' I decided to emulate my hero, so I ran and dived head-first through our glass front door!

My Mam who was doing the ironing at the time heard the crash, dropped her iron and came running! Thanks to God I had no scratches at all and seemed unshaken by the experience, but my mam was panic stricken as she sat picking the glass from my hair!

My Mam adored me, she spent hour after hour fussing over me, pouring love into me, teaching me to read, I loved her dearly, she was the whole world to me. She was kind, gentle, and a very gracious woman, who taught me manners and respect for my elders, everyone who knew her loved her.

Her father, Jack Dodd, was another who doted on me. 'Granda Jack' as I would call him would often come and take me out for the day, which would usually include a visit to Scotswood Social Club as part of the itinerary!

There was great community spirit in Scotswood in the late sixties, everyone left their front doors open without fear of burglary. You would see row after row of houses with clean scrubbed doorsteps, the women always seemed to wear headscarves and flowery overalls—the 'Hilda Ogden' look! They used to hang around in groups, discussing the latest scandal and gossip, it seemed everyone knew everyone else's business! Most of the community worked in the huge Vickers Armstrong armaments factories on the famous Scotswood Road. When the men weren't in the factories they'd be found in one of the road's fifty-four pubs, typical of the hardworking, hard drinking Geordie image and of course much to the disapproval of the flowery apron brigade!! The women would be waiting on their doorsteps for their husbands to get home with their wages, preferably before they were all spent in the pubs and clubs!

My Grandad was a great character who was always laughing and joking, he worked in the nearby Dunston Power Station. After he retired his favourite port of call was the Scotswood Social Club where he would enjoy a pint with the lads and like most men in Scotswood he was often in trouble with Gran for dodging mealtimes. It was quite amusing at times, as we walked up the road we would pass row after row of these woman who seemed rooted to their doorsteps. They would be standing waiting for their husbands to come home knowing fine well that they were in the club. We would get a disapproving look as we passed, occasionally one would call out:

"Is mine in there, Jack?"

Then as we would reach Grandad's house my Gran

would be waiting on the step with arms folded!

"Where've you been Jack?" my Gran would ask, "Ya dinner's been on the table for hours!

"Have you been to that club again?"

My Gran and Grandad were precious, I loved them both dearly, they were so loving and kind.

I was actually quite bright as a child, my sense of security probably played a large part in this—a happy child will always learn more quickly than an unhappy one. My first school was Westerhope Primary School, which I started in 1970 at the age of four. My first teacher was a woman called Mrs. Shields; she was in her late fifties, a tall, thin woman with a rosy complexion. She would wear long skirts and polo neck sweaters with a cardigan over the top. She was a lovely person and became very good friends with my mother.

So for the next year or so things passed along quite pleasantly, I remember times being very happy, especially the family holidays at Scarborough, though our idyllic little world was soon to be turned upside down.

Over the next few months my Mam became ill and would have long spells in hospital, so my Gran and Grandad were around to help my Dad. Then in the space of a few months my world caved in. First of all my Dad's parents died within a few months of each other, then my Grandad Jack died one weekend whilst on holiday in Scotland and then to top it all, my mam lost her fight with tuberculosis and died aged 42 years old in Newcastle General Hospital—a place where she had worked. It had been traumatic watching my mam dying, I remember the last time I saw her; she was so weak and tired and had a grey complexion. She had an oxygen mask on and was smiling—"Be a good boy for your Dad".

The death of my adoptive mother left a scar that never really healed. On the night of Mam's death I was granted what I now believe to be a very special favour and I can only describe what happened. I was in bed and it was dark, suddenly the whole room was flooded with light. I lifted my head from the pillow to see what was happening and looked across the bedroom to where my sister was sleeping. There was a figure standing over her—it was my mother, but there was something different, she was shining so brightly, light was coming from her. She bent over and kissed my sister and whispered to her. Jane mumbled something in her sleep then she turned to me:

"David I want you to be strong and brave, I'm going away and won't be coming back."

"Why Mam? Where are you going?" I asked.

"I have to go to be with Jesus, darling" she whispered,

"Will I see you again?"

My Mam turned round and was talking to someone but I couldn't see who it was, then she turned and said to me:

"Yes, but not for a lot of years, not until you're an old man."

"I don't want you to go Mam," I cried.

"I'm sorry son but I have to go"

For a while she sat rocking me in her arms,

"I'm sorry darling, but I have to go now, be a good boy for your Dad. Mummy loves you very much, good bye darling."

"Goodbye Mam" I said as she kissed my forehead, then she was gone. The light went out of the room and the room returned to darkness, immediately I heard a light tapping on our bedroom door, it was my Dad,

"David, Jane, are you awake?"

"Dad, Mam's just been here..." I started.

"David, I've just had the hospital on the phone... Mam died earlier tonight that's what I've come to tell you" and with that we both cried, but in my heart I knew that mum was alive with Jesus and one day I'd be with them.

3
Life without Mam

My Mother's death left a huge hole in our lives; life was never the same again. All the deaths had left us absolutely shell-shocked; Dad completely changed and was never the same person. On occasions I would catch him crying, at other times he would try to drown it all with a bottle of whisky, life at times was unbearable. Dad tried his best but bringing two children up on his own was beginning to prove too much. The first year after Mam's death Gran came to live with us, she was in her late sixties at the time and things were difficult for her as well.

My Gran was a remarkable woman of faith she had a really gentle nature, she was a Bible-believing Christian and was to be involved with St John's Church on Grainger Street, Newcastle for more than 75 years, till her death on 22nd January 1998 aged 94.

I believe that my Gran's prayers over the years were to contribute more to my salvation than I will ever know. Gran was always involved with one church function or another and would often take Jane and myself to the various parties and jumble sales held there. Occasionally we went to the services, which I hated. My Mum's aunt Wynne continued to take us to Sunday School up at St Wilfred's Church on Newbiggin Hall Estate, until we were seven. Saturdays were the highlight of the week, every Saturday morning Gran would take us to the Odeon picture house. We loved it; we joined in all the competitions and loved the films, which helped to provide us with a break from the misery of our own lives. Dad was becoming increasingly distant coping with things in his own way. I tried hard to please him, but he never seemed to notice. I was clever at school and in 1972, just after my sixth birthday, I had a poem published in a book called "Children as Writers". I won the under eights section of a national competition even though I was only five when I wrote it. I had a temporary type of fame as different newspapers came to school to take my picture.

I won a small amount of money and was presented with a scroll for my efforts, it was a nice feeling to be known and popular—something I hadn't known before, but would definitely know again. I enjoyed all the attention, the headmistress, Mrs Edith Murray, made such a fuss over her star pupil, as did my class teacher Mrs Pinkney.

It was around this time that Dad took me out of Westerhope Primary and enrolled Jane and myself at Simonside First School at the bottom of our street, it was a lot closer to home whereas I had to walk about a mile and a half over the golf course to the Westerhope School. In my opinion, Westerhope was a far better school, but Dad knew best. All my friends were at Westerhope and once again I would be losing people I knew. Simonside First School was a modern comprehensive with an adjoining middle school—it was later to become a college for unemployed adults, but in 1972 it was the school I attended.

I found it difficult to settle at first as I didn't know anyone and since the death of my Mam, I had become something of a loner. I missed my Mam, desperately needing love and attention, but after my Gran went home to Denton Burn that was the end of that. As Dad got over his grieving he became hardened and bitter, less tolerant than he had been before. He seemed to be a totally different person, which is not surprising when you consider that in the space of a year or two he had lost his mother, father, father-in-law and more importantly, his wife. Also a couple of years before, his older influential brother had died.

My first few weeks were hard. I had a few fights, mainly

because I was considered to be a "poshie" as I lived on the nearby private estate whilst most of the kids lived in the adjoining council houses. I became a bit of an outcast, I was thoroughly miserable and life became even more unbearable when the kids found out that I was clever as well.

I might as well have walked around with a bell shouting "unclean, unclean!!" as in the days of the plague. In the space of two years, my life had turned completely upside down. At times the pain got so bad I wanted to die,

In a desperate bid to find acceptance at school I began to steal, firstly the loose change out of my Dad's pockets, then from the local sweetshop, supplying my peers with all sorts of things. I found that I quite enjoyed stealing and it was to become a habit for the next twenty years or so. I began to be accepted.

It was around this time that I discovered the delights of alcohol. For years I had watched Dad come in from work and hit the drinks cabinet, he would pour himself a generous glass of whisky and knock it back. Boys often want to be like their fathers and in that respect I was no different, so one day after school I decided to have myself a drink.

My mind was awhirl with excitement as I approached the drinks cabinet and I wondered what to have. I got a stool to stand on to reach up to the cabinet and I slowly pulled the door down until it was flat and served as a shelf. I looked at the choice of different bottles and tumblers and decided on whisky, so many times I had seen Dad down a glass of whisky in one. I reached inside the cabinet and took out a glass and a bottle of Bells whisky. Grinning with impish delight I poured a small amount of whisky into the glass. I could smell a pleasant aroma from it as I hesitantly swirled the liquid round and round in the glass like some wine connoisseur, then in one brief moment I swigged it back! I began to cough and splutter. I found the taste repulsive—it was not what I had expected. Then I remembered that Dad often mixed his drinks, the neat whisky had not really agreed with my seven-year-old palate. Next to the bottles were some old beer mats with cocktail recipes on them, so aged seven I made my first cocktail—a "Bloody Mary". I found that I preferred Vodka to whisky and that it mixed better. So now every night after school it became the norm to come home and mix myself a cocktail and have a cigarette. I had also started smoking due to the influence of an older boy up the street and my petty thieving ensured a steady supply of cigarettes, which at the time were freely available at a vending machine outside the nearby bingo hall, priced two shillings. Predictably it wasn't too long before Dad realised that I was thieving his booze and I was suitably rewarded with a good hiding.

Because of my increasingly disturbing behaviour, Dad decided that I could not be trusted and that I needed supervision—no longer would I have the freedom of a latchkey kid. Dad began to advertise for someone to pick Jane and myself up from school and make some tea for us until Dad finished work. Various people applied for the job, the first lady was really nice, she was called Sheila and her husband ran a working men's club in North Shields. Sheila would bring her dog Cindy with her, a German shepherd. I became really attached to the dog and loved to take it for walks, though in reality it took me for walks such was its size!

After six months or so Sheila left to help her husband out in the club taking the dog with her. Once again I was losing someone I was attached to, but by now I was used to people coming and going. I was becoming a very angry and bitter person, I was hardening up inside and had a deep mistrust of adults, adults always died and left me.

It was during this period of my life that my godfather, uncle Ron died from tuberculosis, the same as my Mam. Ron's wife Wynne was my grandad Jack's sister; I loved them and spent time on holiday with them in their caravan in Scotland. Uncle Ron was a war hero. During world war two he had flown Hurricanes and Spitfires at Tobruk and El Alamein, and had been decorated on numerous occasions. He would often tell me tales of the war and gave me memorabilia including cap badges and SS belt buckles. As the years went by my relationship with Dad deteriorated and we became increasingly distant. I loved my Dad, he was my hero but I simply could not please him no matter what I did, so in the end I gave up trying. Various housekeepers came and went but by now I could not have cared less. My behaviour was becoming more and more bizarre and I began to see the housekeepers as sport. I would go out of my way to be rude and upset them, to see how quickly I could get rid of them.

One of the housekeepers began to take liberties with me and along with her older daughter would beat me up. Dad eventually found out and took action but by then the damage had been done and these incidents only fuelled my belief that adults simply could not be trusted. I now totally rebelled; I hated the world I lived in and with good reason.

4
Off the Rails

It was a shock to the system, even though I should have expected it, when Dad suddenly announced that he and Brenda had decided to marry. I suppose that looking back, I should have been thrilled, but I wasn't, just the opposite in fact. The truth was, I was so full of insecurities that I believed things were bound to fail. I thought that mothers were things that died and left me, my mind was so twisted at the time.

I had hardened my heart to love; it was as if I had built a shell of bitterness and hatred around myself to protect me from any more deaths or disappointments. I'd had years of practise at discouraging housekeepers and though I now regret it, I suppose I saw Brenda as another housekeeper, the enemy, someone to be got rid of.

I know that Brenda knew I had a few behavioural problems, but I don't think that she realised the full extent of them. In fact Brenda didn't know what had hit her, living with us was a real baptism of fire! It was 'Welcome to the house of fun.'

Brenda is a nice person and I get on with her today, but back then it was war!! I was the ten year old from hell or so it must have seemed at times. Around this time Brenda read books like 'The Omen' and 'The Exorcist' I'm sure at times she must have thought I was something out of those books.

Brenda had a son called Steve who is exactly a month older than me, so I also acquired a step brother who I got on very well with, as we had a lot of common interests. Brenda and Steve had lived in Gateshead prior to living with us, her husband had died two or three years earlier. At the time of their marriage Brenda was 34 and my Dad was 45. Brenda was working in a draper's shop on Coatsworth Road and lived in an upper flat in the Bensham area of Gateshead, opposite her parents.

Life should have been great, but it wasn't and our holidays away seemed to be the only relief from the fighting. Scarborough, situated on the North Yorkshire coast is a place I have always loved, and every year when I was young we would head off there and stay at the Green Gables Hotel. Green Gables was quite a size, complete with indoor pool and games rooms—I loved the place, it was a real gem to me. It was a place that I associated with happiness, it was also a place where I'd spent time with my Mam. The old mansion style of hotel was set in its own grounds in the south bay area of Scarborough and run by a man called Mr Hopper.

I remember the thrill of going to Marineland, the water park, to watch the dolphins and also the model battleship wars in Peaseholme Park. Scarborough was a place that held excitement for me.

Back home, things became unbearable. One by one, to my horror, Brenda began to find all my little hiding places. There was nowhere safe to hide things anymore. I would arrive home from school to find that Brenda had found yet more of my stashes. One day it was pornographic magazines, the next it was an air pistol under my mattress. In the end Brenda was so paranoid that my room was 'spinned' every day while I was at school. It was terrible— nowhere was safe anymore, not even the garden. One day she found some sheepskin coats, which I had stolen from a car, hidden in the hedges.

I regularly robbed cars, mainly for cigarette money and I had developed all the attributes of a thieving magpie. I was always on the alert for easy pickings, nothing escaped my notice.

More often than not, Brenda's purse would take a hammering if she left it lying around and for that I would be suitably rewarded with a good hiding. It must have been around 1977 that I decided I would make petty crime my hobby. I found it exciting—things were quite lax in those days. People weren't as guarded about their possessions as they are now and most people were ripe for picking, so not only was I stealing from my parents, but I was stealing from cars, shops, houses and garages and I was also breaking into local factories on the nearby industrial estate. Camping out also gave me great scope for all-night wandering about and I would often pitch our tent in the front garden and encourage my pals to camp out with me.

But I was becoming dangerous, I was the kid that mothers didn't want their children mixing with, but I didn't care— I was having a whale of a time, smoking, drinking, stealing, staying out all night and I was still only eleven!

I suppose that my only other hobbies at this time were sport—football, athletics and boxing. I always loved these and in this I was no different from most eleven-year-old boys. I have been a lifelong Manchester United supporter, which is strange in a city that has such fanatical support for the local team, Newcastle United. I suppose that made me a bit of an outsider, but George Best and Bobby Charlton were my footballing heroes and I am still a supporter today.

I boxed at boys' clubs in the West End of Newcastle—I suppose that it was a way of venting frustration and releasing pent up violence in a controlled way. During one bout, I remember knocking out an opponent's front teeth! Boxing also helped me to meet one of my all-time heroes, Muhammed Ali. Ali visited the West End Boys' Club at the height of his fame. It was a great thrill to shake those enormous hands, Ali truly was a hero of mine and at the time he was probably the most famous man living on the planet. At the time of writing, Ali is sixty years old and suffers from Parkinson's disease and it is upsetting to see him now. I choose to remember him at his peak as probably the ultimate athlete who brought joy and entertainment to practically the whole world. There was a lump in my throat as I watched him light the Olympic flame a few years ago, his arms shaking at the effort to lift the torch, the whole world was watching and willing him to lift it and ignite the flame. Ali was a true champ, but like Reg Kray I consider Jesus Christ the greatest of all champs. In his autobiography Reg says:

"I met Rocky Marciano, Joe Louis, Sonny Liston and many champions, but the greatest champion I ever met was the Lord Jesus Christ."

It was 1977-78, and a crucial stage in my life. Bands like the 'Sex Pistols', 'Damned', and 'The Clash' were emerging from the suburbs of London and challenging the authorities.

I remember being blown away the first time I heard 'Holidays in the Sun' by the Sex Pistols. I was standing in the kitchen of a friend's house when it came on the radio, the impact was tremendous and bang I was totally hooked. It was an exciting time in music and I jumped on the bandwagon. People like John Lydon, Sid Vicious and Joe Strummer became my new heroes. They were singing about everything I believed in—anti-authority, anti-police, anti just about everything. I loved the lyrics, which were peppered with four letter words and thrashing guitar chords. My favourite songs were anthems like 'Anarchy in the UK,' 'Pretty Vacant,' 'White Riot,' and Sham 69's 'Borstal Breakout.'

I joined a punk band called Danger UXB and we started to write songs. I played the bass guitar and for a long while I really got into the punk scene. I began going to concerts seeing bands like the Sex Pistols, The Clash and local bands such as the Angelic Upstarts.

My mind was a mess, I shaved my head, wore tartan bondage trousers, Dr Martens and an array of vulgar t-shirts, shirts, fluffy jumpers, crombies and donkey jackets, usually with slogans painted on the back. I also began to sniff glue. I just wanted to get out of my box and I didn't care how I would achieve it.

The first time I sniffed glue properly was in 1979, a few friends and myself bought a tube of glue from the local supermarket. We had heard from others on the estate that it was an experience not to be missed—but you had to have the right kind of glue. So after a couple of false starts we discovered that it had to be Evo and with evil giggles we squirted a little bit of glue into our individual bags and inhaled it. After a few puffs we found ourselves totally out of it. It was an amazing experience, the toxins went straight to the brain and our gang became hooked on it. It became the norm to either buy or thieve some glue from the local DIY store and bunk off school, there were loads of us at it, girls as well as boys, and we were constantly high as kites, it was like 'trippin' on Acid and I would have all kinds of weird experiences

Some of the kids in our gang only did it occasionally but my pal Mark and I were at it all the time, we went really overboard. I was desperate to fill the aching void and glue helped provide a temporary distraction. After a while my Dad cottoned on to the fact that I was spaced out and I was constantly stinking of glue.

I don't think my Dad ever understood why I was doing it all and probably thought that it was to get at him. He seemed completely oblivious to the pain that I was feeling, my behaviour already disgusted him and now here was something else.

He ranted and raved about it

'Didn't I know how stupid it was?'

'Didn't I know that it could kill me and that kids had died because of it?'

I knew all of these things but to tell you the truth I couldn't have cared less what happened to me, the glue sniffing and punk music were helping me to escape the reality of my situation.

I believe I had opened a door to the dark side of life and demonic forces were moving in on my life just as Jesus had warned. I believe that if you expose yourself to glue, gas lighter fuel, LSD or other solvent substances, then you can attract the attention of malevolent spirits who would seek to control and destroy you. The high rate of suicides and self-harm connected with solvent abuse only re-iterates this claim. I became fascinated with evil and started to read books on Hitler and the occult. I believe now that it was demons within me that encouraged research into these morose subjects as a way of enticing me in to their web of deception. They would continually feed my mind with negative thoughts or perverse ones; I regularly came across pornographic magazines that had been dumped in the woods near our home. These images left me with a distorted view of women and I began to see them as objects of my lusts and fantasies instead of real people.

We lived on the outskirts of Newcastle, the countryside was nearby and there were lots of fields and small wooded areas. Nearby were some woods, which were surrounded by water from a small river. These were known as 'The Islands' and were like a safe haven for us. Much criminal activity went on at these 'Islands' and a lot of stolen booty was hidden there. It was like a sanctuary from the Police, anybody approaching could be seen up to half a mile away. We dug underground hideouts and in one massive hole a workman's hut was placed, then covered over with soil leaving only an entrance, which was covered by a board.

We began to steal cars and motorbikes. My best friend
at this time was a lad called Mark whose brother, Kev,
was a couple of years older. Kev's gang began to lead us
astray, we were quite happy with this as we were easily
impressed at this age and of course we were looking
for excitement. One bloke in particular from Kev's gang
really sticks in my mind. Sean was quite an oddball, he
was not your average criminal and was very, very, clever.
Sean understood practically everything possible about
alarm systems on cars and buildings, and would be able to
bypass almost any system. He was a sort of 'mad professor'
type and would invent gadgets to bypass alarms and then
sell them to the criminal fraternity. Sean had a weakness
for high performance cars, especially Porsches and would
target them.

Night after night would be spent searching for expensive
cars to steal. I loved the buzz I got when I was taking off on
a stolen motorbike or car. It was probably the excitement
that drove us to do it, with the possibility of a chase by
the Police, which only added to the thrill. The chases by
the police occurred just about every night of the week,
as we would sometimes steal up to six cars a night. On
occasions we would spin off the road or flip over the
cars and have to abandon them, we were in effect, a mini
crime wave all on our own. It was so bad at times that the
police refused to chase us, even if we pulled alongside
and started to taunt them.

I began to stay out all night and go with Kev and Sean
and two others of their gang, Mark and Steve. During the
day I would take my glue and head off down the fields to
the 'islands' and get spaced out. The sun always seemed to
be shining and the birds singing—it was a perfect escape
from my turbulent world, then as the sun went down I
would return to reality as the effects from the glue began
to wear off and I would stagger home for my tea and try

to convince my parents that I had been to school. Home at that time was hell for me but I brought it all on myself, sometimes I would be missing from home for days. My parents were beginning to despair—drastic action was needed.

5

In the Care of the Local Authority

It was inevitable that I would end up in care. I had pushed my parents too far. I was extremely selfish but I couldn't help myself, I was on a collision course, a course of self-destruction. My long absences from school had brought me to the attention of the local authority truant officer who, after numerous visits to the house, referred me to the school psychologist, Roger Matthewman, who I enjoyed playing head games with. He eventually sent me off to Arthur's Hill clinic, next door to Bethshan Church, in the West End of the city and it was here I first met my social worker Colin.

Colin was in his early forties, he had a beard and was a 'Clement Freud look-alike', who smoked a pipe and was one of the most laid-back people I've ever met. Colin thought the best course of action was for me to go into voluntary care, an idea that really appealed to my parents, so my bags were packed and off I went. A place was quickly found for me at Gloucester Way, a children's home/assessment centre in Cruddas Park. I was told that if I learnt to behave then eventually I might be allowed home at weekends and if things really improved, then at some stage I might be allowed home full time.

I found that in the home I was allowed to smoke, I had my own room and financially I was better off because as well as my pocket money and clothing allowance, there were various funds for things like visits to the pictures and bonus schemes for good behaviour. I didn't take long to settle in and get into the swing of things.

Gloucester Way itself was comprised of three council

houses joined together and was quite a size. It was situated in the middle of poverty-stricken Cruddas Park, now referred to as 'Bandit Country' after all the riots, shootings, petrol bombings and also has a history of drug gang warfare between the various crime families. The area is notorious and was featured on the TV show "The Cook Report", it is considered by many to be a no-go area and in places it resembles Belfast or Beirut with many burnt-out buildings. Most people live a hand to mouth existence in fear of the drug gangs.

Most of the kids there were older than me and nearly all had been in trouble of one sort or another. There were about eleven kids in all, aged between thirteen and eighteen years old and six members of staff who worked a shift system. Nearly all of them came from broken homes and like me, most were into petty thieving and glue sniffing. Apart from the odd fight, we all got along okay. Bed times were comical; as soon as the sleep-in staff went off to bed it was like musical bedrooms. The girls in the home tended to sleep with the boys in rotation as well, and this was often the source of much arguing! More often than not on the rare occasions that I did go to school, I would be falling asleep.

My bedroom was situated over the veranda, at times it was like Piccadilly Circus with a constant stream of traffic. People who wanted to go out burgling or whatever, would come through my room and hop out of the window onto the veranda and away. I would often awaken at five in the morning to see someone clambering through my window with bags full of stolen loot or some girl who'd been out partying all night. Life at Gloucester Way was most definitely an eye-opener, so in addition to lying, stealing, drinking, smoking and glue sniffing, I was also sleeping with girls and I was still only thirteen!

My behaviour at school had deteriorated to the point

where I was to become the latest inhabitant of the school's "Special Unit" or "The Hut" as it was more commonly known. The "Hut", was a portacabin in the middle of the school field, and was the last resort prior to expulsion. The "Hut" or "Cooler" was filled with delinquents like myself who simply could not be trusted to behave themselves in the normal lessons; we were the kids the teachers refused to teach.

A drunken lunch time brawl with the RE teacher was the latest in a long line of events that was to seal my fate, most of my teachers were fed up with the mental abuse that I dished out, many were on tablets unable to cope with the pressures. The headmaster simply loathed the sight of me—I was trouble with a capital T. During one chemistry lesson I snapped one of the tall lab taps, it came right off in my hand with water everywhere. On another occasion I was having a sly cigarette at the time and blowing the smoke out of the window, the teacher suddenly got a whiff of the smoke and saw that it was coming from my direction.

"Right Falcus" he screamed "Headmaster's office, now"

I got up and stormed off and as I flung back the door, it hit a freestanding fire extinguisher, which crashed over and went off!

I was also to blame for much of the gang fighting between the local schools. I was among a group that would ambush kids from the other schools at lunchtime. A lot of this violence spilled over from the lunch times into after school fights.

Most of the fighting took place in the nearby Marley Dip, a piece of wasteland that separated West Denton, Blakelaw and Slatyford with Newbiggin Hall over at the back of it.

Night after night there would be pitched battles between "West Denton Wild Bunch" and "Blakelaw Aggro

Boys." Knives, bottles and baseball bats were used in the running battles. Occasionally there were serious injuries like someone put in a coma and once or twice there were even fatalities. The death of one fourteen year old boy brought it all to a head. I remember with horror, the first time the murder squad called at our home to quiz me about the incident, they seemed pretty sure that I'd been there. I wasn't so sure, and if I had been then I was too spaced out on glue to remember a thing.

But really I loved it, it was exciting and I always seemed to be in the thick of it, the 'Law' seemed to be at the door every five minutes for one thing or another. It seemed at times that no matter what went on the Police would assume my involvement, often I was arrested and questioned for things I had no knowledge of and on more than one occasion I was hauled in by the murder squad.

Back in the 'Hut' my days were spent reading comics or dirty mags, very rarely did I put pen to paper. The two teachers, George and Dave, spent most of the day sizing up the local 'crumpet' that passed the school en route to the shopping centre and on occasions I would be sent off on an errand down to the shops by one or other of them, mainly to kill time or call to the Bookies! The previous 'Special Unit' teacher, Nicholson, had drunk himself to death. Each day he would arrive at school with a large bottle of orange laced to the hilt with vodka! Another teacher who knew we were nicking cars was always on the look out for 'cheap' car parts and accessories for his motor!!

School was just one big joke to me, however one teacher was to make an impact on me. Alan Findlay was my maths teacher, totally fed up with my messing around, he relegated me to bottom set in maths, to which I responded by being top in the year after the exams. Years later I was to become friends with Alan in very different circumstances.

I stayed at Gloucester Way until just after my 14th birthday and then Dad decided that I could go home. It wasn't that I had changed; I just wasn't getting caught anymore. My time at Gloucester Way was a sort of learning experience, an education in how to get away with things. All in all, the nine months I spent there were an education. I remember one young lad who came to the home while I was there. He had come from another home, Hartburn Walk, and he stayed for a week while the rest of Hartburn Walk were on holiday—he went on to play football for England.

So now I was back home, things were okay for a while, but only for a while. It wasn't long before things were back to normal with me running riot, stealing cars and motorbikes and once again I began staying out all night— sometimes I would be missing for days at a time. During one period I was missing from home for 36 days. All the while I was out stealing cars and then to keep me in the money, I would go from pub to pub, fiddling slot machines. A friend showed me how to clock up the credits on the fruit machines using a coin, thread and sellotape, it was an earner for a while. Gradually the companies got onto the scam and made the machines more difficult to fiddle. A pal of mine called Fryer, had the workings of a machine in the house and was constantly playing cat and mouse with the fruit machine companies and always seemed able to crack the new security measures.

During my long absences from home I would often stay with friends or in a tent on one or other of the 'Islands'. The police were regular visitors to our house, I was well known to them and they had a real hatred of me. Apart from regularly bunking off from home, they knew I played a large part in the theft of motor vehicles in the area. Often I would be seen riding around the estate on stolen motorbikes. More often than not I would invite the police to chase me, but catching me was another matter altogether! Of course I was arrested on a number of occasions, one week I was arrested three times for thieving cars!

I always seemed to be locked up for one thing or another, whether it was in a Police Station or in a remand centre. Our gang was notorious and the police hated us, sometimes we would be accused of things we didn't do, but it was swings and roundabouts. Occasionally it would mean a beating—one or two officers preferred to dish out a good hiding rather than be saddled with a load of paper work. We knew that if we were caught by certain officers, then a hiding was guaranteed as they really hated us taunting them.

One day my Dad decided to give our Stephen and myself driving lessons, I didn't have the heart to tell him I could already drive and that I'd been driving for a couple of years! So off we went into the country to an old unused airfield to practise.

"You're picking this up rather quick" my Dad said quite amazed at my handling of the car.

"Yes it's easier than I thought," I answered quite tongue in cheek.

Our Steve gave me a knowing glance, he knew I was thieving cars and knew fine well I could already drive; he also knew that I regularly invited a chase from the Police just for the excitement.

One chase sticks in my mind, it wasn't long before my sixteenth birthday, Easter Sunday 1982. It was a nice sunny day and ideal for a spot of joyriding. A lad called Steve, and myself stole a Ford Cortina from the nearby Blakelaw Social Club car park. We then took it on a tour of the area in search of something faster and more exotic. Finding nothing suitable, we parked it up for the night and went home.

The following day was nice and sunny so we set off again, this time we went over to the Gosforth area of the city, a well-to-do suburb. First of all we looked in the car parks at the rear of the High Street, then in the multi-storey car park at Regent Centre Metro station; finding nothing, I drove out. Just my luck—I drove straight past a police car. The policeman either recognised me or was vigilant enough to realise I was too young to drive a car, or maybe he was just in the mood to pull anybody. However, as I was only fifteen with no licence, I had other ideas about stopping! The siren and the lights went on, I banged my foot hard on the accelerator and took off down the Great North Road like a bat out of hell.

I dodged in and out of cars, swerving around a roundabout as my speed approached 100 mph. The fact that I was in a built up area where the limit was 30 mph had no bearing on me. I was having a ball, my senses and scruples had long since departed. I howled with laughter as I shot across a mini-roundabout and up the kerb onto a grass verge, then back onto the road again. Steve, the lad in the car with me, started to cry,

"Shut up" I yelled at him, I was having a real buzz and kept making whooping noises.

I bundled car after car out of the way. Eventually I hit a roundabout at the bottom of Kingston Park Estate. I rounded a bend at 90 mph and tried to handbrake turn the roundabout. I lost control as the car went into a spin and ended up spinning off the road and hitting a fence.

Suddenly half a dozen police cars surrounded me. I quickly decided the next course of action was to get out and run for it. I leapt out of the car, bounded over a nearby fence and began to run over the field. Eventually I ran out of steam, it was a hot day, the sun was blazing and I was sweating like a pig. I was wearing a leather motorbike jacket, which was a ton weight. I decided to fight with the chasing Police officers instead, it seemed a better option at the time so I stopped running and turned on the policeman who had almost caught me.

"C'mon then?" I panted, totally out of breath. I put my fists up in a half hearted effort, but I realised I was too exhausted for that so I went quietly much to the copper's relief.

"Okay, you've got me, I'm knackered" I said.

"You're nicked son," the copper said, wiping the sweat from his brow. By now other officers had caught up with us and were now fighting between themselves over who was arresting me.

After much deliberation, I was eventually taken to Newburn police station and banged up. "Hello Davey son, back again eh? What've we been up to now?" the old desk sergeant beamed as he saw me entering the station with the other coppers.

"Up to his old tricks again—thieving motors" the arresting officer grinned. "How many bails you on now son?"

"Too many" another copper laughed.

"Well Davey, you know the drill by now, empty your pockets. Name? Address? We then went through the mundane drill of being booked into a Police Station.

"Well my boy it's off to the 'Big House' for you" the sergeant laughed as he finished his writing "Take him away."

The Police Station had recently been painted and the smell of fresh paint hung in the air as two policemen led me away. The law had had enough. I was on bail for a number of offences, so they decided to put me up before a special court the following day, which was Easter Monday. I was locked in the medical room, as the cells were full of drunken people who had over-celebrated the bank holiday. The Police were really ******* off with my antics.

"Maybe we should unlock the medical cabinet for him!!"

"Plenty of tablets in there Davey, why don't you take a few eh?" the officers quipped as they locked me up.

I sat on the examination table resigned to my fate. I looked in my coat for my cigarettes and lighter that I had secreted away. To my delight I found a marker pen stashed away in the lining of my jacket. A smug sort of satisfaction crept over me as I stared at the gleaming white newly-painted walls.

"Right you ********" I thought with a glint in my eyes, I then proceeded to scrawl all over the walls—the usual anti-police slogans: 'All cops are *********, etc. I had just stood back to admire my artwork when I heard footsteps and then the keys turning in the lock.

The old desk sergeant brought me some chips for my supper from the nearby Chinese takeaway; he stopped dead in his tracks when he saw his walls! His mouth was open but no sound was coming out as he gazed at my handiwork. Then he began to shake and his face went bright red, it was obvious that Krakatoa was about to explode!

Then off it went, the chips hit the deck and he rushed at me like a bull running for the matador's red flag, steam coming from his ears!

"You little *******," he started "You're for the ******* high jump" he ranted as he set about me.

"I've just had this ******* place painted!" he screamed frothing at the mouth and grabbing me round the throat.

"You are definitely going to prison, I'll make damn sure of it," he said glaring at me.

"Yeah whatever" I said relaxing back on the examination bed with a feeling of satisfaction and not really giving a damn.

Then he stomped out of the room banging the door

shut behind him, I decided to put my feet up and get some kip.

About four in the morning I had a rude awakening, it was the sergeant again.

"C'mon Rembrandt, you're being transferred" he said sarcastically.

"Where am I going?" I asked, rubbing the sleep from my eyes?

"You're going down to Market Street, then you're going to court and then my friend… you're going to ******* jail," he said with a real glint in the eye.

"We've had more than enough out of you". Hopefully that will sort you out!

I was then led out into the dark, put in a police car handcuffed to two coppers and shipped down to Market Street police station, which adjoins the City Magistrates Court. After the usual procedures of signing in and transferring property, I was lead down to the cells and banged up. I was woken again at six thirty for a wash and then breakfast followed. Breakfast in a police station is a real treat! Let me assure you of that—a pre-packed sort of sausage and egg. The sausage could quite easily be used on a squash court as could the rubber egg and you can never tell whether or not they've ******* in the tea!

Market Street was a real toilet of a police station, the cells were stinking, there was a hard bench to lie on and the blankets were so infested with various sorts of lice that they could run around the cell by themselves. The only entertainment was to read the roll of honour of previous tenants scratched on the back of the cell door. The light is left on so it is hard to sleep.

At about ten o'clock or so I was transported up the stairs to the cage area just beneath the court and from there, up into the courtroom. In this case I was remanded to Low Newton Remand Centre at Brasside, County Durham.

Low Newton is situated just outside Durham city next to the top security prison Frankland. Low Newton was for juvenile offenders aged fourteen to twenty-one, though I believe that it's now used more for women. During busy times there are usually three to a cell. Apart from the half hour exercise and meal times, you are usually locked in your cell for the rest of the day unless you have classes or something. I have always loved to read and that is exactly how I spent most of my sentences.

Time seems to pass slowly in prison and it gives time for reflection, but I wasn't for turning yet. I should have been finishing off my schooldays but here I was in prison.

My Dad came to visit me whilst I was on remand in Low Newton and for much of the time sat at the visiting room table with an exasperated 'not knowing what to do' look on his face as he shared the latest news from home.

After a week or two I was taken back to court. I was bailed for a month or so, then at my trial I was found guilty, fined, banned from driving for four years and received 24 hours at an attendance centre at Mill Lane in the west end of the city. I was required to do three hours every Saturday afternoon, scrubbing floors and doing physical exercise.

After I came out of Low Newton, my parents decided that there was no way I'd be allowed to return home, so a month before my sixteenth birthday, a place was found for me at Gill Street Hostel which used to stand in Benwell in the West End of Newcastle. Once again I was in the care of the local authority. I just want to say at this point that my recent incarceration in Low Newton had no effect on me except to enthuse me and no sooner was I back out than I was stealing and drinking again. There were one or two familiar faces at the hostel and we quickly renewed old criminal partnerships.

I was also leading a very promiscuous life and was

sleeping with a lot of women around this time having several different girlfriends on the go at one time, but always with an eye open for new additions. Once again the familiar scenario of musical bedrooms was being played out just as it had been at Gloucester Way and once again I managed to sleep with the majority of the female population within the walls as well as the neighbourhood nymphomaniac who lived opposite the hostel, who spent most of her days servicing the staff as well as the inmates! Christine, a blonde woman in her early forties was very generous with her favours and it was not unusual to see a steady supply of various tradesmen disappearing up the back stairs to her upper terraced flat. Often I would pass the Postman or the Gasman on the stairs as they made their way out, where there would be a nod and a wink.

I stayed at Gill Street for six or seven months but my behaviour and violence brought me into constant conflict with Social Services who basically wanted rid of me at the earliest opportunity.

6
The Waterloo

It wasn't too long before Social Services got their wish and I was out of their hair. I set up home with one of the girls from the hostel, her name was Julie and she was a year or so older than me. We moved into a flat just behind the Dodd's Arms pub, which used to stand on Elswick Road before it was burned down during the riots in the late eighties.

After this, Social Services would not touch me with a barge pole, whenever I was in court for anything and there was a possibility of being bailed they would refuse to take me and so I'd be sent off to prison. Nobody wanted me, my parents, my adoptive parents, not even good old Social Services. I was an outcast in a world that didn't care. I realised that it was survival of the fittest and stuff everyone else.

Julie was working in a shop called Countdown and I got a job at St. Anne's Convent just along the road from where we lived. It was one of those government-training schemes and didn't last long.

My relationship with Julie didn't last much longer either, neither of us were ready to settle down and my sleeping about was getting too much. Eventually I got a flat in Fawdon and moved in there by myself—party time really started now. Drugs were not as available as they are now but it was round about this time that I got to know about the pleasures of Marijuana. I was first introduced to it by a pal called Geordie in the "Waterloo" and found its intoxicating effects very pleasurable.

"What's that smell George" I asked as he sat down with

the longest cigarette I'd ever seen! "It's the Bob Hope," he said.

"Bob Hope?" I queried mystified.

"Dope man" he said "You kna what I'm talking aboot, Grass? Gange? Marijuana?

"Ooh aye," I said not really having a clue about it, "Aye Geordie, drugs, I thought you were supposed to inject it?" I naively continued.

Geordie raised his eyes heavenwards and shook his head:

"Naa man you daft bugga, you smoke it!!! Do you want a shot of it?"

"Go on then, give us a bash, can't do me any harm!!"

I enjoyed the relaxing high that it brought and I soon became skilled at spliffing up and many happy hours were spent stoned out of my box listening to the thumping bass lines of Bob Marley's 'Buffalo Soldier'. So this was my real introduction to narcotics and like everything else I dived headlong into it with reckless abandonment.

At the time I did not realise that I could become dependant on it and I believed all the ******** about it doing no harm—less harm than cigarettes, all that nonsense. Let me assure you after twelve years or so of smoking it, you find you can't cope without it and yes, it does lead on to harder things, take it from one who knows. One of the side effects of marijuana is that you become totally paranoid, some people get so paranoid that they cannot leave the house because of the fear they're feeling, nightmares are also common. The truth is that you're opening doors for the demonic to come in, but at the time I just wanted to get stoned and party.

I had been drinking in the city centre since I was fourteen but "The Waterloo" was my first regular bar. It is no longer standing, but was situated at the bottom of Westgate Hill in the centre of Newcastle. It was a very colourful place with lots of interesting characters. Almost anything could be obtained from the Waterloo—at a price—drugs, stolen property of every type, weapons, prostitutes, you name it, it was available.

The clientele were a tightly knit group of villains nearly all related to one another or inter-married, my natural father was related to some of these people. Relationships were so close in there that non-regulars would feel intimidated within minutes of entering and would knock back their drinks in one and leave in search of friendlier pastures. When a fight kicked off in the Waterloo it really did kick off. Often some unwitting strangers would fancy their chances and this would often result in them being thrown through the front windows and out onto the pavement. It was not a place for strangers to work themselves, as the whole bar would turn on them.

The 'Waterloo' was my introduction to 'gangsterism' as there were some real gangsters who drank in there, people who were household names in the North East. The 'Old School' men who commanded respect like my friend George and Arthur T and Lenny C., respective heads of their families. 'Panda' the armed robber was another notorious villain, made famous by the "McVicar" film and by one or two much-publicised shootings. There were also the more recent characters such as the Nigerian brothers, Snowy and Stevie who I was later to work with.

Another man who commanded respect was my friend 'Fred the Head'. Freddie is respected by the criminal fraternity all over the country. He is a legend in the prison system and is mentioned in a number of biographies including Ronnie Kray's biography. Freddie had a fight in Broadmoor with Roy Shaw, the King of the bare-knuckle arena. Ronnie Kray said "It was the best fight I ever saw!"

Freddie also fought with many other notorious villains including Mad Frankie Fraser, the head torturer of the

Richardson Gang. Years later I was a partner with Freddie in quite an amusing scam.

These were the men I looked up to and respected along with other members of the local crime families. Over the years I worked with all the families, these were the men who controlled the 'underworld' in the North East of England, the "Hardmen" the "Godfathers" this was the "Geordie Mafia"! The Police keep a record of known associates on your files and one policeman quipped that my known associates read like an alternative 'Burkes Peerage,' a 'who's who' of the criminal underworld!

I decided that this was the life I wanted, I was attracted to the free and easy lifestyle of doing as I pleased and was impressed by all the wrong people and I slotted quite nicely into this subterranean culture.

I would sell most of my stolen swag in the Waterloo. It became my second home; it was a place where you'd be terrified to miss a session in case you missed something. When I wasn't in the Waterloo, I would be out robbing and stealing. After the bar closed, if there wasn't a lock-in, we'd head off to the Casablanca nightclub next door—a sort of downbeat club frequented mainly by villains and homosexuals. In its heyday, it was known as "Changes" and was owned by the comedian and TV personality, Bob Monkhouse. Another of the places in Newcastle that I would frequent was the afro-carribean disco bar 'The Playground' which was opposite the 'Waterloo' and this was another place we frequented. Like the 'Waterloo' there were often a lot of fights in 'The Playground' and I used to be there every night smoking dope and listening to the reggae music. On my nights out I would carry either a knife or a gun, as trouble never seemed to be far away. It was around this time that I first met my pal Viv Graham who worked on the door of "Wheelers" nightclub next to the Tyne Bridge on the Gateshead side of the river. Viv at the time was an 'up and coming' ex-boxer who was beginning to make a name for himself as a 'fighting man' on Tyneside. I would often head off over there after the bars had closed as much of the city's criminal fraternity tended to flock there.

I finished my work scheme not long before I moved to Fawdon and decided to return to burgling and robbery with a former inmate and friend from Gill Street Hostel. Night after night we would roam around nearby estates looking for rich pickings and during this period I was making a lot of money. The summer of 1983 was a warm one, so we were out nearly every night. One song from that time sticks in my mind; it was UB 40's 'Red, Red Wine'. For some reason it always reminds me of those days and a tragic event that took place around that time.

I had a friend called Johnnie. Johnnie was part of a team that drank in the Waterloo who we referred to as the 'Wild Bunch' mainly because they were into heavy graft—robbery, tie-ups, that sort of thing—a real gang of desperados. Johnnie and myself went out on the drink one day and decided to head off to Gosforth High Street. We got so drunk that we kicked off in every bar on the High Street, fighting with the locals, doormen, and anyone who got in our way. Eventually we finished off in my local bar, the Kings Court at Kingston Park. As we staggered off to my flat at closing time, I decided to go burgling and Johnnie went to visit some girls who lived opposite me. While I was away, some friends of mine turned up looking for me. Not finding me at my house, they knocked at the girls' house to see if I was there. Unfortunately they were in possession of a stolen motorbike, a Honda 500cc and Johnnie decided to have a go on the motorbike. He roared off in a drunken state lost control and hit a telegraph pole at high speed; he ended up in a coma and was dead two days later.

I was shocked by the news when I returned from a successful night's burgling. I was lucky not to be nicked carrying a load of knocked off gear into the flats, as there were coppers all over the place due to the accident. It might have looked just a little bit suspect three men carrying assorted electrical goods into the flats at three in the morning! Luckily we just missed them.

After Johnnie's death I went on a bender, I spent the entire week afterwards on the drink and the dope. It was not a good time to be around me, I was seventeen years old and totally crazy, the violence was getting way out of hand. I was on self-destruct and even my own friends were sparring wide of me after I put a gun to a friend's head.

I fell out with the main villain on the estate after I threatened his brother with an axe, he didn't take kindly to this and threats were exchanged. At this point I went to find the guy's house with an automatic pistol in my pocket. Someone informed the police of what was going on, and fearing a blood bath, they took him into protective custody. The police were desperate to find me, there was a real panic going out across the airwaves on the police radios:

"David John Falcus, wanted for questioning about several incidents in the Gosforth area, do not approach, he is armed and dangerous, repeat do not approach, contact control room."

I was eventually arrested after an armed siege a few streets away.

I remember looking up the barrel of the arresting officer's gun and thinking 'I'm dead any minute.' The cop was shaking and seemed more afraid than I did. Luckily I had already disposed of the gun so the charges were meagre, but as luck would have it after 'spinning' my house the Police found quite an 'Aladdin's cave' of stolen property.

The local Constabulary had me and wrote off a backlog of unsolved burglaries, much to their delight. So once again I stood in the dock at Newcastle Crown Court. I had a bit of a sweat on as the judge began his summing up:

"David John Falcus, you are a menace to society and I would not be doing my duty if I were not to send you for a custodial sentence. On the first count of burglary I sentence you to prison for twelve months, on the second count of burglary you will go to prison for twelve months, on the third count of burglary you will go to prison for twelve months, on the fourth count of burglary you will go to prison for twelve months and on the fifth and sixth counts of burglary you will also go to prison for twelve months......" on and on it went.

I began to count the number of years in my head and looked across at my barrister who also had a worried expression on his face.

Eventually the judge finished his sentencing. I stood with my mouth wide open as I waited to hear the sum total of my imminent incarceration.

"....however these sentences are to run concurrently," finished the judge.

"How long?" I mouthed to my barrister.

"Twelve months" he mouthed back.

I breathed a huge sigh of relief.

"Take him away, officer"

I waved to my friends and family as I was escorted from the courtroom and down to the cells.

Once more, I was back in the arms of Her Majesty, only this time for a very generous twelve months.

7
Within these Walls

When I entered the Y.P wing of Durham Jail, after a period of remand at Low Newton, I was informed that I had contracted scabies from one of my sleeping partners. 'Charming' I thought, it was humiliating and very uncomfortable as the MO painted me with a four inch paint brush, slapping the solution all over me. He paid particular attention to the anal and genital areas and I began to suspect he was bent. He was obviously enjoying himself, slapping it on just as if he was whitewashing the garden fence; to make matters worse he whistled while he worked!

This was my first incarceration in a 'grown up' prison; I had been in borstals and youth custody centres, but Durham was a real prison. Situated in the beautiful "Old Durham Town", it had held such notorious crooks as the Krays, the Great Train Robbers, Moors murderers and was the scene of John McVicar's escape made famous in the film 'McVicar'. The place had been built in Victorian times and was stinking from top to bottom, with cockroaches running all over the place. I was on a wing with other young prisoners from all over the region. This most definitely was not like the television series 'Porridge'—there was very little to laugh about here. It was cramped with three to a cell, no toilets, just 'chamber pots.' Every morning we would have to go through the degrading ritual of 'slopping out'; the stench was terrible, enough to make you puke.

Luckily I knew one or two people on the other wings and was able to secure myself a steady supply of tobacco, which at the time was the currency of the nick, these days it's drugs. So I had myself 'sorted'. I was sharing a cell with a couple of lads from my birthplace, Carlisle. One of the lads spent most of his time crying, I must admit at the time I had very little sympathy for him.

'If you can't do the time, don't do the crime.'

I would spend my time reading in my cell, I have always enjoyed reading and the days passed quickly. Occasionally I would have a fight, I remember fighting with a bloke from Eston near Middlesbrough called Lee Duffy. I remember walking out my pad (cell) and him flying through the air at me, the Screws (prison officers) were quickly on the scene as we rolled about on the landing. Years later I was to read of his murder, shot dead on the streets of Middlesbrough by a rival drug dealer. Anyway the outcome was that he got sent to the block and I was shipped out to Castington, a youth custody centre near Morpeth in Northumberland, just before Christmas 1983.

Strangely enough, the time I spent in Castington was quite productive apart from the odd run-in with the Screws. I even attended education classes. I found it easier to study in the nick than I had at school, and gained an 'O level' in English literature! The education teacher asked me if I wanted to enrol at college on my release but I declined the offer, looking back now I wonder what would have happened in my life had I said yes. But at that time I had no intention of giving up my life of crime, far from it, I was already planning my next jobs as the countdown to my release continued. I was also meeting people who could help further my criminal career. I met young lads from the West End of Newcastle who were into armed robbery and I would work with them years later in the drug scene.

From a criminal point of view my incarceration was productive as all the time I was making new contacts with serious people.

I was released in March 1984 and arrived back in

Newcastle just before opening time at the Waterloo. After a quick haircut, I made my way to my favourite watering hole where George, the gay barman, was just opening the doors. I was soon joined by a number of friends and acquaintances who shoved drinks in my direction. I had nowhere to stay; my flat was gone with all my possessions. My ex-bird Sue landed, she wanted to have me back, but I wasn't having any of it but I eventually caved in and went back to her house that night, after all it had been a while since I'd been with a woman.

I stayed with Sue for a few days while I got myself together, then one day whilst shopping in the city I bumped into Julie again, the girl with whom I'd previously lived. She was by herself and had no current relationship with anyone; I met her a few times and we agreed to give our relationship another go. We moved into Cranbrook Road, Scotswood, in the west end of the city in April 84. Julie's mother lived at the other end of the street and her sisters Christine and Brenda who were married to two brothers, Charlie and Jimmy also lived not too far away. For a while I was part of this close-knit family. Cranbrook Road was a street where there was always something going on and was full of 'colourful characters.' During the year or so that we lived there, there were at least three murders in the street and one suicide. Half a dozen notorious prostitutes lived in the street as well and regularly I would be out chasing their punters for parking outside our house.

One hot summer's night I was lying in bed reading, Julie was sitting by the bedroom window, when suddenly she said;

"Davey, come and look at this, quick."

"What?" I answered, lost in my book."

"Quick" she urged me.

I jumped out of bed and went over to the window to see what the fuss was about. My attention was suddenly drawn to the old man who lived opposite, who was standing totally naked on his front door step with a bucket in his hand. Then he tipped the contents of the bucket over himself and collapsed on the ground screaming. We later learned that it was acid in the bucket, the whole episode was bizarre but it was typical of the kind of thing that happened there. Half of the residents of the street were mentally ill and the place was rampant with crime this gave Scotswood one of the worst reputations in the city. All this was happening in a place which John Wesley founder of the Methodist Church labelled 'Paradise!'

I would spend all my time with Charlie and Jimmy both grafting and drinking, they were a real couple of characters. So Charlie and Jimmy took me under their wing; they were notorious in the city as villains, but also very well respected by the criminal fraternity. They led me astray in a big way, but I wasn't bothered, this was what I'd been looking for, I loved the time I spent with these guys, we had a lot of good frisk.

Around this time I became an alcoholic—every penny I earned was going on drink. During the day I would be working collecting scrap metal with Jimmy and at night I would be grafting with Charlie, the rest of the time was spent in the bar. It got to the stage where I would do anything to get money for drink; I even resorted to stealing from my parents. I simply could not help myself; the drink and dope had such a hold on me that I could not get through the day without them. All that mattered was feeding my habits, it was like life or death, and nothing else concerned me except making sure I had a steady supply of these commodities. After the stealing from my parents incident, my Dad refused to let me near the house and we had no contact for years, he totally disowned me. I wanted nothing more to do with him either, Julie and her family were the only family I had in those days and they were precious to me.

My life continued in the same pattern and for a while Julie and I were quite happy, but at eighteen I didn't feel that I was ready to settle down. In June 1984 Julie found that she was pregnant with my daughter Kelly, I was delighted at the news but all the same I just wasn't ready to settle down.

My drinking sessions began to cause problems that often ended in violent arguments and fighting. Julie was no mug and on more than one occasion I had to dodge as she wielded a knife at me!

Night after night was spent hanging around bars and nightclubs trying to fill the aching void in me, I felt at times as though there was a large piece missing from me and nothing would fill it. I was going from woman to woman like I was searching for the Holy Grail or something; nothing or no one would satisfy. I would drink myself into a stupor and at times my behaviour was totally irrational. I would consume huge amounts of drink and drugs, mainly speed, acid or dope and occasionally cocaine.

Once in a while I would break with tradition and have a drink somewhere other than the city centre and would head off over to Jesmond to the Royal Archer to see my pals Eric and Bob, the "Dynamic Duo" and Scotch Alec Beveridge. I spent many a happy hour in the company of this mob. Eric and Bob were a good laugh and down to earth lovable rogues, but Alec was totally different.

'Scotch Alec' was a paranoid schizophrenic and probably the most violent man I have ever met. Alec was also related to the Tams family and was Jimmy and Charlie's step-brother. He had a reputation for being a 'Hit Man,' and someone who enjoyed violence. When I first met Alec he was on the run from Glasgow after stabbing six members of a Glasgow crime family at a party. He was like something from the middle ages! He sometimes fought with steak knives taped to his hands; the knives were fixed to his hands so that he wouldn't drop them whilst hacking into someone! As I came to know Alec I suddenly realised why the Romans built Hadrian's Wall—to keep the likes of Alec out!

Wherever Alec went violence seemed to follow. It was a known fact that he'd walked away from at least two murder trials on technicalities, even his ex-wife was currently languishing in a top security mental hospital after stabbing a man to death!!

For most of his life Alec had lived in a trailer on various campsites around the country and was known to all the top villains from London to Glasgow, who employed his services from time to time if they had a problem. Alec was like a character from Guy Ritchie's film 'Snatch'. He was a real 'Pikey' or 'Traveller.' Alec really took a shine to me and for over a year I grafted with him, the problem was, the more time I spent with him the more like him I became. The levels of violence in my own life increased but it wasn't like before, it was darker and more sinister, I was becoming rage personified.

A typical day would begin with drinking Vodka early in the morning, then, when we'd had enough to drink, we'd all pile into the van and head off looking for a suitable target to burgle. This would normally be a big house in one or other of the posh suburbs. Once a suitable residence was found—crash! In we'd charge and start stripping the place. Then we'd go off to a 'fence' (someone who buys stolen goods) unload the gear and with the money we'd head off to the bar and drink ourselves into a stupor. Every day became like this, it was sheer madness, it was like being stuck on a magic roundabout and being unable to get off. I wasn't eating anything; all that mattered was drink, drink and more drink.

I realised that life could not carry on this way forever and decided that I'd better break free from Alec's influence before I went totally insane. There were voices in my head raging at me to stab and cut people with the cut-throat razors I was carrying. I believe that some of the demons in Alec were trying to jump on me and I already had enough of my own!

Eventually I got the break I was looking for, a tie up had gone wrong and Alec left Newcastle and took off down to Bolton. It was the last time I saw him, years later he would write to me from Barlinnie prison in Glasgow after the law finally caught up with him. He died from cancer not long after his release but my association with him had a lasting effect on me, I was never the same. Any scruples that I'd once had were long gone, I was now game for anything.

After Alec left for Bolton I headed off down to Scarborough and was put up by our friends the McGovern family and other villains from Glasgow who were hiding out there, it was a welcome break after the months of graft with Alec.

8
The Monk

Prior to this, in January 1985, Julie had given birth to my daughter Kelly. At six weeks old she was found to have pneumonia and was admitted to Newcastle General Hospital. Julie got in touch with me and we had a couple of days by her bedside—it was touch and go and we nearly lost her. For the first time in years I sat and prayed and asked God to make her better and not let her die. Reconciliation with Julie was out of the question but in His mercy God healed Kelly.

A few weeks after returning from Scarborough I was once again in the custody of Her Majesty after a fight with several policemen outside a Chinese takeaway in Westerhope. There were warrants out for my arrest for a number of offences, and an eagle eyed copper had spotted me at the counter as he drove past. He radioed for assistance and whilst I was waiting for my food a mob of them gathered, hiding in the doorways of the shops that lay either side of the takeaway. As I walked out eating my supper, they rushed me and after a scuffle I was arrested.

Once again I was back in the familiar surroundings of Newburn Police station. Pearson the old desk sergeant gloated as I was dragged into the charge room.

"Well, well, well look who it is! Public enemy number one!" he sarcastically stated.

"The last I heard of you, you were on the rampage with a gun up at Gosforth. Who've you been shooting at now?"

"Nobody, nothing, I've done nowt, now get my ******* brief down here" (brief—solicitor)

"He tried pulling these on us" said one of the arresting officers and threw my two cut-throat razors, still in their pouches, onto the charge desk. Pearson picked them up to examine them. They were two cut-throat razors that were taped in the open position and the ends chunked to get a better rip at skin. They were taped to stop them closing when striking with them, a tip I had learnt from Alec.

"Oh did he now."

"And what are these for then mister?" he continued in his sarcastic manner.

"For shaving with" I answered.

"Shaving? Are you taking the piss out of me?"

"No I use them for shaving" I said to him.

Then to my utter amazement he just chucked them in my property bag and carried on logging my various items in before sealing the bag. I was then put in a cell for a few hours and then 'ghosted' off to Market Street police station with adjoining magistrate's court in the middle of the night. I was now used to the formality of going from police cells to court and then to remand in prison. For some reason the next day to my surprise the magistrate bailed me to St Christopher's bail hostel instead of remanding me, although I had to sign twice daily at the West End police station and was on a 10pm curfew.

At intervals during my life I would encounter Christians and at St Christopher's another one came into my life and this had prophetic consequences. During my stay I came into contact with a member of staff called Michael, he was a former monk who had been at the hostel for only a month when I arrived. Because I was on a curfew I would spend my nights chatting to Michael.

I found that I liked him immediately, which was strange for me, but there was an element of holiness about him and I found that I could not tell him lies.

He was an older man in his late fifties with a real softness in his voice although his piercing blue eyes could look straight through you. Michael seemed to know all about me—it was really weird, but I found myself trusting him and opening up to him.

He was a really nice guy and I got away with murder on occasions, like when I would smuggle girls into the hostel to spend the night, which was totally against the rules and could see me thrown out or sent back to custody. He always seemed to know and would give me a sort of wry smile with an "I know what you've been up to" look.

One particular morning Michael banged on my door early, I had a girl with me and her dog was lying on the floor! The staff knew that this girl was visiting me and sometimes brought the dog. Then the dog started whimpering as Michael banged on the door, Michael obviously twigged what was going on and started saying;

"C'mon David time to get up, you know you're not supposed to have dogs staying!!"

Then one day a really strange thing happened, I was in the kitchen arguing with Liz, the cook, and Michael walked in and said:

"David you shouldn't argue with Liz, one day she'll be your landlady!"

Then he turned and walked out leaving me totally perplexed. I often look back now and wonder if this man was an angel. He left the hostel not long after I did, but it was his gentleness that impacted me. (Liz did become my landlady in 1995, just as Michael prophesied back then! In fact it was her house in which the Lord Jesus appeared to me but more about this later.)

After a stay in the hostel I got a bedsit in Benwell and even though I'd recently been put on probation for two years it was business as usual! Like a dog returning to its vomit so was my return to my immoral lifestyle, thieving, robbing, drinking and drugs—my life had all the attributes of a never-ending cartoon. Like Wiley Coyote in the

Roadrunner cartoons I went from one disaster to another.

It wasn't long before I found myself in custody again, this time I was arrested for aggravated burglary and criminal damage after an incident at a house in Killingworth. It all started whilst I was in Tiffany's Nightclub in Newcastle with some friends, when a guy called 'Scotch George' approached me for help.

George stemmed from Glasgow. I had known him for a few years, I knew he was a guy who often got into scrapes, I also knew that he carried a knife and wasn't afraid to use it.

It turned out that he was having problems with his local neighbourhood gangster and needed a bit of support. We were all drunk and had been out all day and really should have ignored him but after the club we all piled into taxis and headed off to Killingworth and that's where it all goes a bit hazy!

Two hours later I found myself being arrested and taken to Forest Hall Police Station accused of jumping through a glass front door with a machete in my hand and threatening to chop up the guy who had caused my pal the grief.

I was later released due to lack of evidence, as nobody seemed able to identify me or actually put me at the scene and I had no recollection of the incident.

Relationships came and went. I lived with a girl called Carol Anne for a while but once again I couldn't settle and found it difficult to love and trust women. I also began to dabble in pornography, buying thousands of hard and soft-core magazines at a cheap rate and selling them on.

The police raided my house in the early hours after a party claiming to be looking for someone who was wanted, I suspect this was just a ruse to have a poke about. There were various bodies lying on the floor in different states of undress as I showed them round the house.

"What's in the cupboard?" the copper asked pointing at a large walk-in style cupboard.

"Nowt, just magazines" I answered.

"Let's have a look then" the copper continued.

I nearly fainted when I opened the cupboard door and found the light on, and there, sitting on a pile of dirty magazines, was a naked man wearing only red rubber gloves!

He was reading a dirty magazine and had a big smile on his face—the copper's expression was priceless as the man smiled and said "Good Morning."

9
The Profession of Violence

I moved into Cruddas Park flats in July 1986. Situated on the famous Scotswood Road, the flats are a hideous piece of architecture typical of the tower blocks that you'll find in most cities—dirty, part empty and rampant with crime of every sort. It seemed that every type of social misfit was herded into these flats, however it was to become 'home' for a while. I had gathered round me a gang of thieves who were into everything and we ruled our little area by fear. People did not grass on us, if they did then they reaped the repercussions.

After a while I came to the attention of the local Godfather and drug baron, a man whom I shall call Geordie, who decided that my talents could be best put to use in his 'firm'. I had known Geordie since he introduced me to dope in my days in the Waterloo and I knew all the families respected him and that he worked with them. Geordie taught me the in's and out's of the emerging drug scene and the vast profits of dealing. I served my apprenticeship with him and was used effectively as an enforcer, joining and working together with other 'rising talents' from the various families. I began to like my work and was on the rise. If you've seen 'Big Chris' the character played by ex footballer Vinnie Jones in Guy Ritchie's film 'Lock, Stock, And Two Smoking Barrels' then that is the kind of job I was doing!!

Geordie was a flamboyant character and was quite cultured for a West End gangster. His flat was filled with luxurious furnishings and art treasures more befitting of a 'stately home' than a two bedroomed flat in the crime-ridden West End. In fact years later he was portrayed in The Evening Chronicle as the Mr Big for heroin on Tyneside. It was quite amusing as I saw him before his trial, he told me they were trying to find out what he had accumulated through his dealings in heroin. He told me that after they had raided the flat they brought in an 'antiques assessor' to estimate the value of his home.

"So, what's the damage then George? How much do they reckon?" I asked.

"Well to start with Davey, they've got the sitting room down to eighty grand!!!"

George had a great love of Chinese food, which he passed on to me; he was a great cook and would make a variety of exotic dishes (something which I enjoy doing still, but I'm no Jamie Oliver!). George was twenty years older than me but we had a good relationship and I learned a great deal from him.

Most of the top villains in the area called at Geordie's house for one thing or another, but mainly they came for a curry, a game of cards and drugs of one sort or another. Through Geordie I met gangsters from all over, as he was well connected and well respected. I was 19 or 20 at the time and was the perfect student, making sure people paid up with the threat of violence which could mean anything from hanging someone from an eighth floor window by their ankles to receiving a good beating or worse!

Most of the Christmas that year was spent in and out of the West End Police Station. I was arrested on Christmas Eve, Christmas Day night and again the day before New Year's Eve, the whole period was filled with drug related violence. I was arrested and accused of aggravated burglary, grievous bodily harm, and a section 18 malicious wounding. It was alleged that I had chased a rival through the flats at Cruddas Park and assaulted him with an axe.

I was arrested questioned and then released due to lack of evidence. Then the following night it was alleged that I kicked in the bloke's front door and chased him through his house, from which he escaped by jumping off his balcony. I was then accused of turning my attentions on his Alsatian dog, punching it and knocking it out, infuriated that I could not catch his owner.

Five days later I was arrested again after a scuffle with a number of Police officers in my flat. Once again I was accused of attacking the same man, the man did not want to press charges and the Police warned me to stay away. By now I was notorious and constantly found myself under surveillance; it seemed I could not stop attracting attention to myself.

It was around this time a sort of relationship developed with a sixteen year old girl called Frances. At the time she was in the care of the local authority and occasionally she would stay with me in my flat, which was just across the road from the home where she lived. Once again a serious relationship was out of the question as for some time I had been seeing a woman from Gosforth called Rachel (name changed). Rachel was a very attractive girl who was very much in love with me and wanted me to marry her—the full bit. After a few months of to-ing and fro-ing I decided against moving in with her and tried to end the relationship. Once again someone had tried to get close to me and I had pushed them away, I think it was because of my insecurity and belief that I would be hurt again.

Then things became quite bizarre, it was like the Michael Douglas movie "Fatal Attraction." Rachel would blackmail girls into coming to town to try and pick me up and lure me back to her house. It was sad, she had become obsessed with me and I had no intention of being tied down.

After a while Frances moved into my flat but I continued to take girls back there, which looking back wasn't very nice, but there you have it. When I wasn't with Geordie my days were spent lolling round the house smoking dope and watching porno movies. As I said my house was under surveillance, the Police were watching from a flat in the block of flats opposite mine, every now and then I'd stand at the window giving them the two-fingered salute just to let them know that I knew they were there.

Most nights I'd go to Geordie's around six o'clock then we'd head off to the Waterloo or the Black Bull on Westgate Road. Geordie preferred to sit and play cards or dominos so I would stay with him for a while and then I'd slope off up the other end of the town. I preferred the top of the town because it was lively and there were more people my age in the "Fun Pubs" whereas the Waterloo was full of villains who were mainly older, so it was a welcome break. True to form I fell in with a gang of football hooligans led by the notorious 'Mad Mac' from Benwell. I got on well with him and still have a soft spot for him. Along with Mac came Ginger Dougie, Rama, Scotch Robbie, Jimmy Charge Sheet, Kav, Chrissie and a whole host of others.

This mob lived for drink and Newcastle United. Night after night we'd be brawling in all the bars round the Grainger Market and the trendy up and coming Bigg Market. We'd meet in the Lowther or the Rose and Crown and then do the circuit—Butlers, Clock, Tavern, Fish Bar, Blackett, Cordwainers, Cafe Royal, Lennons, then down to the Bigg Market, Half Moon, City Vaults, Ricks, Maceys, Presidents, Robinsons, Masters, Pig and Whistle and Balmbras by which time we would be mortal drunk and would be fighting all and sundry.

John sat and shared his story with us over a pint in a pub in Newcastle, which funnily enough was the same pub that sixties Gangster film "Get Carter" had been filmed in. I remember being impacted by the man Noel Proctor called "The Gentle Giant."

A lot of men claim to be Christians as an attempt to get out of jail early, but not Big John. He was very sincere and was genuinely "Born Again" also it was years afterwards before he was eventually freed. Big John was recently promoted to Glory and has gone home to be with the Lord, but I will never forget that night with him or the impact of his story. I have his testimony on audio tape and sometimes give it to villains looking to find the Lord as an encouragement. John was a genuine gangster and hardman but he would be the first to tell you it's a mug's game, he is in my prayers.

By now the Drug Squad had had enough of our antics and decided that we were ripe for picking and organised a raid against us one Friday night in February 1987 to search for heroin and other narcotics. It was around six o'clock, a guy called Snowy who had a history of drug offences had recently joined Geordie and myself and the spotlight was on us. The result was that they raided Geordie's and two other houses, which luckily were not being used. They left my house alone, which was just as well as there was a mountain of the stuff there. I unfortunately walked into the raid with five hundred quid's worth of Heroin in my pocket and was promptly arrested. I was gutted; Geordie also got nicked with a small amount.

So once again I was back in familiar surroundings. Whilst locked up in the West end Police station, a couple of Drug Squad officers offered me a deal to become an informer which I declined, unlike some who are now being exposed.

They are all at it from top to bottom, 'honour among thieves' is just an old wive's tale that went out with 'Dixon of Dock Green.'

"Do you fancy doing a deal Davey?" one DI asked me.

"Just give us a little help and we'll do the same for you" he continued. "We can make it easy for you, turn a blind eye if you give us the right information, we know that you know everybody and are trusted, they'd never know!!

"Go and **** yourself" I replied.

"Do you really think I would become one of your bumboys?" I snarled, "Just lock me up, I'll do the time"

After a short period on remand I was out again and I called to see Geordie and Snowy. Someone told us who had grassed on us, and it was suggested that I should 'blast' him. One night Snowy and myself decided to visit the 'The Happy Chappie'. Fortunately for him the street where he lived was full of police. On the very day we decided to call on him, it appeared that he had fell foul of the law himself and the police were looking for him.

A month or so later I was up for my trial at Newcastle Crown Court, I knew I was going to prison, but for how long?—that was the question.

I pleaded guilty to possession, but not guilty to intent to supply.

My trial didn't last very long and the jury quickly came back with their decision.

I was found guilty of possession of heroin, but not guilty of intent to supply, which was the heavier charge, after I convinced the jury that I had not known the heroin was in my pocket and I was only doing a favour for someone. I had also been nicked for handling stolen night storage heaters, so once again I stood in the dock of Newcastle Crown Court and waited for sentencing. I just want to say that standing in the dock is a horrible, nerve-racking experience, knowing that your future is in someone else's hands. All types of silly thoughts go through your head while the Judge is summing up, like 'has the Judge had a good day?' 'Has his wife given him stick?' The outcome is always the same, you stand there with sweaty palms and what do you do? You stand and pray to a God to whom you've given little thought, expecting him to move and speak to the Judge when if you'd done it God's way in the beginning you would not be in the mess that you are! It's crazy, God can give you so much more.

So on September 24th, 1987 I was sentenced to just nine months imprisonment, I couldn't believe it and almost did a jig in the dock—I'd been expecting at least three years.

10
Hitting the Bottom

Last thing I remember I was running for the door
I had to find the passage back to the place I was
    before
"Relax" said the Nightman we are programmed
    to receive
You can check out anytime you like but you can
    never leave"

> Hotel California—The Eagles,
> WB Music Corp 1976 Long Run Music.

I felt as though I was on the magic roundabout and couldn't get off as I pulled into the now familiar surroundings of Durham prison. My life seemed to be a never-ending merry-go-round of drink, drugs violence and prison without prospects or hope. The prison officers look at you with a kind of smug 'Knew you'd be back' look on their faces, the same old faces on reception and on the wings. I was an "Old Lag" at twenty-one and knew most of the population within the walls. I knew all the procedures by now—after going through the showers we pick our kit up, consisting of clothes, bed pack, cup, knife, fork, spoon, mug (all plastic), comb and razor (without blade) then after a visit to the medical officer and the welfare you get a tray of food and are sent off to your "Peter" (cell) then it's you and the bricks and your thoughts.

Some people have a silly notion that prison is easy and comfortable let me assure you that this is not the case. I want to stress that prison is a place of anger, violence, fear and despair and that is why the suicide rate in prison among teenagers is so high.

These silly youngsters who think they're "Hardmen" come into prison thinking it's a holiday camp, find that it's not, and get themselves into debt with the tobacco and drug barons. Once this occurs their lives are made unbearable in a variety of ways ranging from a beating or stabbing to rape. Many youngsters find it so unbearable that hanging themselves or slashing their wrists seems a better option, the suicide rate amongst the young prisoners rises each year, it is heartbreaking.

Most of my sentence was spent in a drug-fuelled haze, Snowy was on the remand wing and sent tobacco and stuff over to me. Scotch Robbie was on a five stretch for the attempted murder of a policeman and we spent our days idling the time away. Frances visited me on a couple of occasions, her pregnancy was coming to an end and the baby was due any day, I obviously would not be around at the birth. Then in the second week of October I was informed that I was to be shipped out to Haverigg prison at Millom in the wilds of Cumbria. I'd heard that it was a bad nick to go to as it was full of smack heads (heroin addicts) and as I was serving time for heroin possession then it seemed the logical place to send me.

I, however, had different views and decided to petition the Home Office, they reviewed my case but said that I had to go to Haverigg, so off I went.

Haverigg was a former R.A.F base near Millom on the Cumbrian coast; the convicts sleep in billets that once housed pilots and aircrew. Since becoming a prison it had built up a reputation as a violent prison, even the screws walked round in threes. I arrived before the riots there and was greeted with the sight of a man running across the yard being chased by a posse of screws, the man being chased had a pillowcase over his head with eyeholes in it, like a Ku Klux Klan member or a terrorist. I wondered what his misdemeanour had been as he disappeared behind a row of billets.

I was glad to see my pal Tommy Tams on the food servery as we went for our food; he gave me the run down on the place and who was in.

"Davey the place is a ******* nut house" he said, "All the Geordie lads are sticking together, you need to be tooled up in here!" (carry a weapon.)

The most common weapons were either a metal bed leg or a PP9 battery in a sock, serious injuries or deaths were common in Haverigg and the local police were never away from the place. It was good to see some familiar faces in there, as there was safety in numbers. The bath houses were shared between a number of billets and were found at the end of the lines, they were not places to hang around in. During the day my job was as cleaner in the mailbag and tank nets shop, I could sew mailbags to boost my wages. Another way I boosted what I was earning was my involvement in the rackets.

A couple of days after arriving in Haverigg I was summoned by the welfare officer and given the news that I was now the father of a baby boy, I was over the moon, the news was a great relief to me as I had been worried. A few weeks later Frances brought him to see me, he was like a little mouse and we called him David. After the visit I went on a real downer as it was just before Christmas. Prison started to hit home, I should have been at home with my son and daughter at Christmas and I began to realise what a selfish individual I had been. Christmas is a desperate time in prison, it is the silly season, and inmates were hitting the fence like flies, unable to do their 'porridge' people tried to escape.

My depression got worse as the days went by; it was as though a black cloud had descended on me. In prison you have a lot of time to think and I came to the conclusion that my life was a total mess and that I'd be better off out of it. For the first time in my life I seriously considered suicide.

It was round about Christmas Eve, and I sat in the bath reviewing my life, it was going from one scene to another. I felt a voice saying to me that I deserved to die for all the liberties I had taken with people and I agreed with it. I then started to contemplate which method I would use to achieve the desired result. Hanging was the most popular option of prison suicide, closely followed by the slashing of the wrists; I couldn't make my mind up and decided to sleep on it.

I got out the bath, dressed myself, and walked over to the hall to fill my homemade flask with tea; it was about eight o'clock and everyone was on association. I didn't speak to anyone, I was at the end of my tether, I had hit the bottom. It was as though I was trapped in my life of crime like a magical roundabout that you can never get off, like the song 'Hotel California' says, "You can check out any time you like but you can never leave."

I went back to my billet; I had my supper followed by a smoke and once again began to think about things. As I contemplated, I found myself slipping into a dream, it was unlike any dream I'd had before. Suddenly I was no longer in prison, I was back in Newcastle in the Cordwainers pub, I had a beautiful woman on my arm, then I was upstairs in the flat above the pub with the woman, then I was on a Caribbean Island—it was so real I could taste it, it was an amazing dream and I didn't want it to end it was so beautiful.

Then I awoke, I was back to the misery of prison, but the dream stayed with me and would not go away. I know now that it was God showing me that I had a future.

11
Partying in 'Gotham City'

Christmas came and went without me doing myself any mortal injury and I began to feel better as my release date crept closer. I felt in good spirits, a few friends from my past came to Haverigg and we all got on like a house on fire. The violence continued to reign in the prison with incidents of serious injury; there was nearly a riot as one young lad died after being refused medical treatment, late one night. They found him dead from a heart attack after complaining of chest pains. It was bizarre as the lad had participated in a 'bagging up' ceremony earlier on in the evening and seemed okay.

A 'bagging up' ceremony is reserved for someone who is getting released or has done some misdemeanour. It entails tying people up in their mattress cover, which is like a sack and hanging them from the billet rafters, so they are left there swinging about like a giant punchbag, then everyone gets stuck in. It is only meant as frisk, but can't be nice for those in the bag, luckily I never went through this bizarre ceremony, as there weren't too many people willing to try and bag me up!

On the night before my release there were about ten of us crammed into my room, we had three marijuana joints on the go and the place smelt like a Turkish bazaar.

"What you gonna do when you get out Davey?" Scotty asked as he passed me a joint.

"I dunno Scotty, but I know where I'll be tomorrow night."

"Where's that then"?

"I'll be in the Bigg Market stoned out of my box, with

some dirty brass, thinking about you lot stuck in here with your dirty mags!"

"....Shh, what's that?" he said craning his neck to listen.

Suddenly we heard the sound of boots running through the corridor of my billet, it was the screws trying to catch us at it, suddenly there was panic there were joints flying everywhere as people tried to get rid of what they were smoking. Suddenly the door flew open and screws started to pile into the room;

"Right what's going on here?" said Burrows the screw leading the charge as he pulled out a hanky to blow his nose.

"Nothing's going on in here, we're just talking."

Then the Senior Officer walked in and smiled at me with a knowing look and said;

"Okay Mr Burrows I'll deal with this, the lads are just having a little leaving party.".

Tyson wasn't a bad old bird he knew what was going on and he gave me that parting look as if to say "I know what you're up to but I'll let it go this time" so luckily no one got nicked, that's all I would have needed on my last night.

I hardly slept that night, it's always the same the night before you get out of prison, the excitement hits you. There is a special feeling you get as you put on your own clothes discarding the prison issue rubbish—you get your identity back, you cease to be just a number and become a person again. The rush that hit me as we drove out of the prison gates was awesome; I punched the air with a triumphant "Yes!" Tyson the old screw was on his way in as we went out the gates he nodded his head and gave me a wry smile, a 'You'll be back' look.

A friend gave me a lift home to Newcastle and I got home just after nine in the morning. Rex, my German Shepherd dog had been sitting at the door waiting for me, it was weird, but he knew that I was coming home.

I spent the first couple of days with Frances and the bairn before going round to see Geordie, I then went to the town, got paralytic drunk and picked this little blonde girl up and headed back to my flat in Cruddas Park. The next few months were spent in a repetitive haze, I began working on the door at the Blackett public house as a bouncer and each night I was going home with different women.

Newcastle is a tough city as portrayed in the film 'Get Carter'. I grew up around the streets and pubs where the film was made. Newcastle is a party city and is ranked as one of the top cities for a night out in Europe. Newcastle is also a city notorious for violence; it is not as bad now as it was before they had the close circuit TV on every street corner and the Pubwatch scheme. The London 'mob' would always refer to Newcastle as 'Gotham City' or 'Little Chicago'.

During my days on the doors in Newcastle I have been in hundreds of fights, some reminiscent of the old bar room brawls of the Wild West. I have actually been in fights where the entire bar is fighting. I loved it of course, I think it was the excitement; it gets the adrenalin flowing, and there were some nights when I would go berserk.

I think that after my recent incarceration in Haverigg I'd mellowed out a bit. Sometimes I would see my pal Viv Graham and have a drink with him. By now he was handling door security at most of the pubs and clubs in the city, but in reality people were using him and he knew it. He was a country lad with a big heart who hated bullies and all they represented, he would sort problems out with his fists, never resorting to guns or knives, he stood up to the drug gangs and the gangsters but it was eventually to cost him his life. Viv used to say to me "Aye one day they'll get me." Those words were to ring true on New

Year's Eve 1993-94 when he was shot dead outside a pub in Wallsend; his killers have yet to be caught.

Newcastle was a violent city to begin with, with its hard drinking image but in the mid-late eighties the violence took a new turn as the rave scene hit Newcastle. Suddenly there was a new drug on the scene that everyone was raving about—Ecstacy or 'E' as it's more commonly known.

The West end mob, which I was connected with, had discovered ecstacy tablets at trips to 'The Hacienda' nightclub in Manchester, where the rave scene had more or less begun. Phrases like 'Sorted' and 'Mad for it' became part of the English language and there was a sort of semi return to the sixties—'turn on, tune in, drop out'.

LSD was back in the top twenty as everyone's favourite recreation drug. Suddenly 'Strawberries', Microdot' and 'Batman and Robin' tabs were everywhere with people tripping out all over the place. But the 'E' was awesome, those first little 'Lovedove' pills were unbeatable and never to be repeated, at the time they were commanding £25 per tablet on the street. The newspapers called them 'The Designer Drug,' the feeling can only be described as bliss on those first few occasions, after that it's all downhill.

The first rave in Newcastle was in an old steel works under Byker Bridge, the location of a rave was always kept secret until the last minute for fear the Police would close it down, which they did on many occasions. Once you were inside then, "wow" you'd be transported to a different place with the music and the drugs. People who had never danced before would suddenly find themselves dancing all night, sweat pouring off them in a totally false atmosphere of love and well-being.

I remember it well, I'd drop an 'E' and it would usually take about twenty minutes to start kicking in. My brain would swim in the toxins and my body would jerk to the sound of the beat as 'the rush' from the drugs coursed through my veins, transporting me to another place. Then I'd walk around with a big daft grin like a 'Cheshire cat' on my face, dancing to the beat—I would be totally out of it.

I remember just wanting to dance all night, which was not like me, I couldn't dance to save my life.

In those early raves everyone was beautiful and loving each other, but there was also the feeling of suppressed violence. Suddenly, all the crime families were jumping on the bandwagon as they realised the enormous sums of money that were to be made from the sale of illegal drugs. All of a sudden post office robbery became a thing of the past as all the major firms moved in. A cartel was set up. Faces began appearing from London, Liverpool, Glasgow and Manchester as the Geordie Mafia opened negotiations over the steady supply of 'happy' pills. The clubs were divided up between the different firms, each firm given their own area of operation. Newcastle was now a closed shop; it was 'sorted.' Firms who did not belong to the Cartel were chased at gunpoint from the city.

Violence started to creep into some of the raves as former armed robbers mingled with the beautiful people, rave was here to stay but the 'golden era' was over.

I constantly needed to be on something or other, it got to the stage where I could not get out of bed without having a joint or something. I'd been out of jail for a couple of months and it looked as though it was business as usual when something stopped me dead in my tracks.

I walked into the Cordwainers public house and there behind the counter was the girl I had seen in my dream whilst in prison. I could not believe it when I was told that scouse Mick had sold the pub and that she was now running it, the plot thickened!

12
The Girl and the Pub

The girl's name was Kathy, I learned from Michelle, one of the bar staff who lived near me in Cruddas Park. The bar had recently been taken over by a leisure company and she was being trained as the manageress. Kathy was blonde, in her early thirties and was very attractive; she also had a good nature.

For weeks I observed her at a distance and rarely spoke to her, just exchanging pleasantries. Day after day was now spent in this place and I began to feel like part of the furnishings. As the weeks went past I found myself talking a great deal to her and sharing quite a lot of personal things, which was not like me at all. I spent most of the time moaning on about my personal circumstances, at the time I was still living with Frances, but was looking for a change. As I got to know Kath, I saw that she was very intelligent and not the blonde bimbo that I had pegged her to be! I found that we had quite a few things in common, not least that she had grown up a few miles from our family home.

She was divorced and had a daughter from her previous marriage, Lorraine, who was ten at the time. After a few weeks I eventually asked Kath out, which she accepted and for a while that's all it was, we'd go out and enjoy ourselves. After a while, as things became more serious, I decided I could no longer go on living with Frances and decided to move out, I did not want to hurt her feelings but I felt I had to go. I moved in with Kath round about September 1988, at the time we were living above the Cordwainers pub in Nelson Street, Newcastle.

From day one Kath tried to rehabilitate me and to please

her, I put a block on nearly all my criminal activities. I realised that I was being given a chance to get out of the life that I had led before. I helped out in the bar in a number of ways and Kath began to teach me about the pub trade. I became quite domesticated for a while and was quite happy, however on occasions the violence would flare up in the occasional bar fight. On one occasion I was arrested after fighting with several men outside the bar who had set their cheek up to Kath. Four of them were on the floor and I was stamping on the head of the fifth when the Police turned up. I think the Police felt I was using more than "reasonable force" and decided to lift me.

Once again I found myself counting bricks in the cells of the local Police station. Luckily for me the charges were reduced to public order offences after the lads refused to press charges against me. I tried to please Kath and realised that she was the first woman I'd really respected since my Mam or Gran. I started to open up to her about things in my life but I never really felt she understood fully. She knew from my reputation that I'd had a violent past, but when I tried explaining myself I think she found it difficult to accept and didn't really want to know.

I admired the fact that she took me at face value and couldn't care less about all the negatives that people were saying about me and for a while I carried on working on the doors as well as helping Kath out in the pub. The Cordwainers, or Corks as it is now known, had a reputation as a bar where you'd always find a fight on a Friday or Saturday night. I have lost count of the number of fights I personally had in the place. I have been involved in some fights in the Cordwainers where the whole bar is fighting and vanloads of coppers have sat outside, afraid to come in. I have actually battered people in sight of police officers and they've then thrown them into the back of the van. Police officers used to have a lot of tolerance for doormen simply because the doormen were breaking up fights that the 'law' didn't want to get involved in.

It was quite amusing at times, if you had a sick sense of humour like I did. As I said, I'd batter people then throw them to the law, who'd catch them and give them a bed for the night. There was nothing malicious in it and the same people would be back for another night's fighting the following week, such was the mentality. Most of the doormen got on with each other and would back each other up if there was trouble at one or other of the bars. Most of the lads were villains of one degree or another, this was before the licensing of doormen, which was started in 1993 to crack down on 'rogue doormen'.

Some of the lads were dealing in small amounts of drugs, which boosted their wages and also paid for their own consumption of illegal narcotics. As the eighties drew to a close and the rave scene exploded, I would bump into more and more doormen in these raves, as they experienced the delights of ecstacy pills. Most of these lads were taking steroids and were body builders. They took steroids to inflate their muscles, which in turn inflated their egos and made them violent. Most doormen have the IQ of a banana and their drug taking only made them worse.

The Drug Barons would use rogue doormen to sell drugs to the punters. You can buy drugs in almost any pub in Newcastle now but at the time, in 1988-89, there were only a couple of places in the city centre—yes you've guessed it—the good old 'Waterloo' and a bar called the Market Tavern round the corner from the Cordwainers.

I would regularly frequent these bars or 'chemists' as they are better known, to obtain my ecstacy tablets or 'acid' (LSD), 'whizz' (amphetamines) or 'charlie' (cocaine). I had a good life with Kath and definitely loved her or at least thought I did, but there was still an aching void in me which I tried to fill with drugs. I was certainly a person who liked partying; the trouble was that I didn't know when to stop. I was the boy who couldn't say "No"!!

Drug dealing at these establishments was blatant, one bloke who I'll call Paddy (name changed) used to stand on the entrance of the 'Tavern' dishing out drugs like sweets in full view. People would be greeted with a big gap-toothed smile as they came to buy their 'wares,' money would exchange hands in the middle of the busy street! It was utter madness. Even after the 'law' raided the place and people were arrested, business would carry on as if there was nothing amiss. The Police regularly took over one or other of the local buildings in an attempt to keep the whole thing under surveillance.

My own criminal activities were rather limited and were definitely watered down from what they had been. I tried a number of ventures to supplement my now decreased income, including building and roofing work, but every so often I'd lapse back into my old ways. On one occasion, bold as brass, I walked up to a copper and asked him to stop the traffic whilst we pulled our van out of a yard. The trouble was that the van was packed to the ceiling with stolen lead! The copper obliged, held up his hand and stopped a queue of traffic, waving us out with a cheery wave, which we returned in kind, waving and smiling back!

My life was definitely improving, though at times I was my own worst enemy. I would start arguments with Kath over the slightest thing, I think that it stemmed from my own insecurities—when you've been damaged as often as I have then you just expect the worst to happen. I found it difficult to accept that I was happy, this may sound strange but I was so used to things going wrong that I just took it as the natural course.

My mood swings made it difficult for anyone to get close

to me so I was murder to live with. From a young age I had built a shell around myself to stop me from getting hurt, I had closed myself off from loving and caring about people. The people who I loved always died and left me, now there was a woman who I had real feelings for, but I was terrified inside that she would reject me if I opened up to her properly. I was frightened that something would happen to spoil things and that I'd be hurt all over again. I suppose I had an in-built defence mechanism that would activate itself to stop people getting too close to me.

Poor Kath! All she wanted was a quiet life, and then suddenly she had me with all my problems and hang-ups to deal with. I suppose that one of the problems was that I never really knew how to relate in a relationship. One of my difficulties was that as I was so insecure, I was very possessive and I think that Kath found that a bit much. Trust was another area that I struggled with as I was so paranoid, and we'd have loads of arguments because of my ridiculous accusations, but for all that we still got on. It was around this time that we came into contact with the 'paranormal'. It was a well-known fact that the bar was 'haunted', the correct term for this really is 'plagued with mischievous spirits or demons.' However, many of the bar staff had incidents of one sort or another and at times it was scary. On occasions we would be sitting in the flat upstairs and the doors would fly open by themselves. Also the TV would change channels by itself and the lights would flash on and off. But it was in the cellar where most things occurred, like the hosepipe would turn itself off. Once I was in the cellar by myself and an old coin came out of nowhere and bounced off my head! On another occasion I was in the toilets after we'd closed the bar, I felt a tap on the shoulder as I stood at the urinals, I assumed it was Kath as there was no one else in the place; I turned just to see a white flash go out the door! I nearly had heart failure!

We started to travel and on my 22nd birthday we visited Majorca, which was a welcome break from the utter madness of Tyneside. It was a lovely holiday, nice and quiet away from the clubs and bars. We spent the days sunbathing and the nights dining out around the island, it was my first holiday in a long while, so I made the most of it.

On returning from holiday we decided that we'd had such a nice time that we'd go away again, so a few weeks later we took off again, this time for Florida. I'd always had a secret ambition to visit Disney World (don't let it get around, it would completely destroy all my 'Street Cred'). Ever since I was a nipper, it was always somewhere I'd dreamed about going to, so we booked a 'fly-drive' and off we went, accompanied by our friend Gail who ran the florists in the Grainger Market, opposite where we lived. Apart from the odd argument the holiday was great, visiting the Disney complexes as well as Sea world and Wet and Wild.

It was great, it was like being a kid again and I went on all the rides at Disney World. I loved the virtual reality rides in the Epcot centre; they were fantastic. After a week or so in Orlando, we drove down to the beautiful Gulf coast visiting Tampa Bay and staying in St Petersburg. We arrived in St Petersburg in the middle of a heat wave; I fell asleep on the beach getting well and truly roasted. I nearly died from dehydration, and just managed to fall into a shower in the nick of time. I was bedridden, with blisters all over my body and an American lady suggested that I put sliced potato over the blisters to heal and draw out any fluid, it worked! A couple of days later I was up and about.

The beach at St Petersburg is one of the nicest beaches

I've seen with miles and miles of sun-kissed sand. It was also used as a location in the gangster film 'Once upon a time in America'. I saw the big pink hotel that they filmed some of the scenes in. I also had a surprise in another hotel as in the bar, on the wall, they had a huge mural of the Byker Wall housing estate in Newcastle and the favourite tipple in the bar was Newcastle Brown Ale! Home from home! One of the highlights of the trip was a visit to Busch gardens and a tour of the Budweiser brewery, I sat in the hospitality room sampling all the freshly brewed drink and, as usual, made a pig of myself.

On returning to England, I was back out on the drink when I wasn't working on the doors. One night Kath and myself were drinking in the Bigg Market and we bumped into my old pal Viv Graham, who was with his friend Rob and some of the West end mob who I knew. We had a couple of drinks with them in Macey's Bar and as I chatted with my pal Stephen, I gleaned that they were going to Hobo's nightclub, as Viv was going to have a fight with one of the doormen there because they wanted control of the club.

Stephen asked me if I wanted to go, but I declined and went home with Kath, which was just as well, as they all got nicked. A very much-publicised trial followed and they were exposed as the men who controlled Newcastle and Gateshead. While they were on remand my old pal Snowy came to see me and told me that Stephen and company wanted us to show solidarity and for the doormen in the city to go on strike for a night in protest at their incarceration.

They wanted a show of strength, to let the new area commander, Superintendent Brassneck (name changed), know who was boss. So it was arranged that on a busy Saturday night, all the doormen would go on strike in support, the result would be chaos all over the city. The

Police got wind of it and drafted in officers from all over the place to cope with it. A handful of doormen decided they were going to boycott it and not support us; most of these were attacked by off duty doormen who were all out on the drink patrolling the city. One doorman who refused to strike and went to work was attacked and thrown through the windscreen of a moving car!

The outcome of it all was futile, Viv, Rob, Stephen and company went off to jail for three years or so because the police had the whole Hobo's episode on video, it had been filmed on the clubs close circuit T.V. After Viv's murder the BBC made a programme about him, they showed the video from that night at Hobo's on British TV. It showed Viv beating up a doorman using tremendous force. I was lucky that I had gone home with Kath when I did, otherwise I would have been away with them as well.

We moved to London in November 1989, Kath had accepted a well-paid job by a leisure company, which entailed running a pub just off Piccadilly Circus, in London's West End. We moved into a nice flat in 'up market' Notting Hill, in a street called Arundel Gardens, which is situated between Ladbroke Grove and Portobello Road. The area was very 'well to do' and a lot of celebrities lived in the area—Princes William and Harry went to school down the road from where we lived. I remember standing one morning on the corner of our street waiting for a taxi and a car came hurtling down our road. I was amazed to see that the driver was Diana, Princess of Wales. She saw the look of surprise on my face and started laughing, and then with a cheery wave and a lovely smile, she took off.

Notting Hill is a colourful place and I enjoyed living there. There is a multi-cultural feel about the area, with people from all walks of life living there. I enjoyed rooting around the market on Portobello Road on Saturday mornings, listening to people trying to haggle with the stallholders. While we were in London we did a lot of sightseeing when we weren't working. Notting Hill is also notorious as a drug area and the infamous 'Café' on Ladbroke Grove is known all over London.

As Christmas approached, I started to do a bit of bouncing on the doors, I just suppose I wanted to keep my hand in, and the extra money was a bonus. I remember working on a pub door in the Northwood area over the Christmas period and it wasn't too long before I was in the thick of it, fighting with this mountain of a man who didn't like Geordies. I tried to reason with him but he just wasn't having any of it and fancied his chances, attacking me. I remember catching him straight on the jaw and then it was lights out for him. He didn't get up for a while and when he did, he didn't know what day of the week it was. This happened on New Year's Eve, what a way to see in the 'Nineties.'

I met a few guys who were part of London's notorious crime families and got on well with them, we had a few mutual friends and showed each other respect. At first it was okay, but after a while I hated being away from Newcastle and at times I was a real pain in the backside. At times our relationship became very strained and at one point Kath left me and went to stay at her parents for a week as I was becoming increasingly difficult to live with. I felt alone and vulnerable in London, and was racked with insecurities and paranoia and I realised that my behaviour at times had been unacceptable.

The week that Kath was away was one of the most difficult of my life; it caused me to take a real look at myself and to ask myself some serious questions. I realised that my attitude had to change. On Kath's return, things improved for a while but at times I was unsure of Kath's commitment to our relationship. I was becoming unhappy in London, and yearned to return home to Tyneside. I was fed up with the place and started travelling to Newcastle at weekends, where I would get totally blitzed out of my mind on a cocktail of drugs and alcohol. I would be fighting and venting out my anger and frustration.

However, things improved towards the summer and we had some nice days out taking in the sights of London. We visited the various parks and Kew Gardens. We ate out at the best of restaurants including Michael Caine's 'Langan's Brasserie', we had days out rowing on the Serpentine and feeding the squirrels in Hyde Park. Some people may have seen the recent Hugh Grant film 'Notting Hill'. There is a scene in which he and co-star Julia Roberts are cavorting in the communal garden—it was the communal garden behind our flat, it is lovely and peaceful.

The Bar was quite an upmarket affair and would occasionally be frequented by celebrities and one night we had a party with members of the 'Eastenders' cast.

I had a visit from my pal Brian, who was the manager of the 'Lowther' pub in Newcastle. He and his pals were in London for the cricket and Brian phoned me from the Masons Arms in Covent Garden, which was being run by John and Christine, who had previously worked with Brian at the Lowther in Newcastle. Brian introduced me to John and Christine and we all got on like a house on fire, then Brian and I got mortal drunk and staggered off to Chinatown for a meal during which I fell asleep with my face in my food!

I began to frequent the Masons when I wasn't working and enjoyed getting plastered with John who also drank like a fish! A pleasant intervention was the Notting Hill Carnival. Our street was on part of the route and so we watched most of it from our sitting room window before venturing out and soaking in the atmosphere. It was very loud and colourful and once again another excuse for a drink!

The four of us got on well and started to go out for meals together. A friendship began to develop, which I badly needed as I was limited in my friendships in London. I knew a few 'heavy' characters in London's underworld but didn't spend much time with them and began getting to know John. Incidentally, one of my pals was jailed after a massive drugs bust in which millions of pounds worth of cocaine was seized.

Christine and John suggested that we go on holiday together and we chose the Dominican Republic, in the Caribbean. So in September 1990, we flew out to the Dominican Republic for two weeks holiday.

A rush of warm air hit me in the face as the plane doors opened at Puerto Plata airport, it looked idyllic as I walked down the steps of the plane and across the red hot tarmac of the runway, with the sun blazing hot. We then had an hour's drive to our resort in Playa Dorada. The resort was very beautiful, and the walk from the hotel to the beach was like walking through Paradise. It was a new resort and hadn't yet become commercialised at that time. I must say that the holiday came at exactly the right time; we really enjoyed ourselves and made the most of it. I had a go at all the water sports. I was hopeless at windsurfing and kept falling off the board, though I loved the jet skiing, but what I enjoyed most was scuba diving. The waters in the Caribbean are among the best in the world, they are crystal clear. I remember walking along the seabed forty feet down and being amazed at how clear it was. It was a wonderful sensation to walk along the seabed at that depth, I felt as though I was walking on a different planet.

We spent the nights sampling the local cuisine around the island; the restaurants were fantastic and the food absolutely beautiful. I spent a great deal of time eating the local lobster, which were superb and quaffing bottles of champagne. I suppose the whole holiday was just an orgy of over-indulgence but we enjoyed it anyway, both Kath and myself thought the place very beautiful and well worth a return visit.

On returning to London, we learned that the bar was being sold and that the new owners had their own plans for the place, Kath and myself talked things over and decided to return to Newcastle. I made a couple of phone calls home and within twenty four hours Kath was on a train from Kings Cross on her way to Newcastle to look at our new home in up-market Jesmond.

13
Bricks, Bricks and more Bricks

We returned from London in October 1990. I was glad to be back home, I felt that the London episode had been a farce at times, although it had been a bit of a learning curve. However, there was one thing I would miss about London and that was the weather! You sharp notice the difference an extra couple of degrees can make.

Our home in Jesmond was pleasant enough and for a while I curbed my criminal activities and did some honest graft for a change, this time I set up a building business with one of my drinking buddies from the old 'Waterloo' Bobby 'the bag' Byron.

I quite enjoyed it for a while, acting as a work agent, getting the work whilst Bob and others did most of the real graft. For a while the work flowed and Kath got a job in a shop in Gateshead, but inevitably after a while the drinking and drugging started again. I began to slope off to nightclubs, and the violence returned as I met old acquaintances.

The building work went a bit haywire to say the least, Bob was taking Prozac for his nerves and I was turning up for work with a marijuana joint in my hand! One customer whom we were working for arrived home to find his house stinking of dope; I was fast asleep on his bed with a half smoked joint on the side of the bed. He was not impressed in the slightest, especially when Richy the labourer popped out from under the kitchen floor with a pile of empty beer cans!

It might be a bit of an understatement to say that an air of 'the old wild west' hung around our jobs. The truth is there were more 'Cowboys' on our jobs than there were at 'The Alamo!!' 'Auf Wiedersehen Pet' did not have a look in! Some of the guys had actually worked with Jimmy Nail in the past on jobs, I wondered if this was where they'd got the idea from!

On one job I had to drag Bob from the Shieldfield Social Club to do an estimate, which was lethal as he was mortal drunk.

I don't know to this day how we got that job, as Bob was constantly slurring his words and sliding down the wall. There was one memorable moment, when the customer asked Bob to check the central heating boiler. His vision was so impaired by the alcohol that he staggered over to the fridge opened the door and spent several moments staring into it, then he slammed the door shut saying;

"Aye, the boiler's all right!" The woman just looked at me shaking her head but she still asked us back to do the work on her house!

Some of the jobs were just ridiculous and after a short while I began to lose interest, Bob was complaining because he was doing most of the work and I was loafing around, constantly taking the mick. One evening, at the local, I bumped into an old friend—Fred 'the head' Miller (surname changed), who was running an amusing scam with video boxes and bricks in which punters would buy the box thinking it was a new video or whatever; the bricks made up the weight in the boxes. Fred was a Gangster one of the 'Old School' who knew the Krays, Richardsons and Frankie Frasers of this world.

Fred had got out of serious crime and was doing this 'harmless' scam. It was a play on people's greed and many did fall for it. This has already been made public knowledge in a book by Steve Richards, so I'm not talking out of school. Freddie invited me onboard for a while and I thought the whole thing was hilarious, everyone knew we were at it. Freddy believed he was doing a public service in teaching people a lesson about not buying stolen property!!

When I was ten years old the Lord had told me he'd shield me and protect me, I was still far from becoming a Christian, but he was true to his word. There are a couple of incidents that happened around this time that I am at a loss to explain. Throughout my life I've been shot at, stabbed, hit with axes, glassed, hit with iron bars and been in the hundreds of bar fights—yet I've never once had a broken bone!

The first incident was a car crash in Gateshead where my brakes failed and I hit the back of a bus at fifty miles an hour. The car was a 'write off'—the crash had been so severe on impact that the gearbox ended up in the boot—yet Ginger Dougie and myself got out without a scratch. It was really weird, just before the impact with the bus I felt everything go into slow motion, I believe God put his hand on the car and saved us.

The second time was on a country road up near the village of Alston where Freddie and myself had been doing a bit graft. The road was very narrow, a single-track road with only enough room for one vehicle and the rain was absolutely pouring down. I remember flying round a corner at around 80 mph and suddenly, coming towards us, I saw a coach. I had two choices—I either went over the side of the cliff and down into a ravine or I was crushed into the cliffs on the other side. I only had seconds to react and once again I remember everything going into slow motion. I looked at Freddie and said; "We're dead"

I banged on the brakes the car went into a skid and for a split second it looked as though the bus was going to plough over the top of us but then a really bizarre thing happened—it seemed as though the car shrunk! I could not comprehend what was happening, I just remember looking up at the bus wheels, amazed that we weren't being crushed!

Afterwards I sat shaking, not believing what had taken place. Freddie said: "Davey, we've just had a religious experience there!" I was completely gobsmacked, once again my life had been spared.

It was around this time that an offer to get back into the pub trade came along when we were offered the Blackett Arms on Nelson Street, in Newcastle city centre, opposite the Cordwainers pub, where I had first met and lived with Kath. I had already worked there in the past looking after the door there.

The bar backed on to the nearby Grainger market with most of the clientele being market traders and barrow boys. It was a lively bar with a disco upstairs and a bar/lounge downstairs.

One of the reasons I was being offered the bar, was because a certain gang had been frequenting the place and causing a lot of trouble. There were several incidents in which doormen had their legs broken and the manager had a gun put to his face. The breweries knew that I had a reputation in the city and that if they put me in the bar then the trouble would stop, also that Kath was a damned good manageress.

What an offer! Most people would have run a mile, but I knew all the parties involved in the trouble, so I said I'd think about it. I went home and talked to Kath about the offer, she was all for it and wanted to jump at it. I was a little bit cagier because I knew that if I took the bar, I'd become involved in the drug scene and rackets again. It was inevitable.

Kath kept on about what an opportunity it was, I eventually caved in and agreed to go and take a look at the place. We picked a busy Saturday night and when we arrived at about nine o'clock, the place was in absolute chaos. The two doormen had taken off and were drinking elsewhere; the barmaid in the lounge was plastered, as was the barman in the bar. We decided to try our luck upstairs where there was a type of semi-rave in full swing. Then a boy who looked no older than twelve sauntered past with a joint in his mouth, the young girl behind the bar was giving drinks away to her friends and then to round off the night, the police raided the place! It was a dump; it was dirty and badly needed a lick of paint. The seats were all slashed, the ashtrays overflowing and the khazis (toilets) defied belief, yet we still took the place on. We must have badly needed our heads seeing to!

14
Out of the Frying Pan into the Fire

The first couple of months at the Blackett passed fairly quietly, we spent most of the time weeding out the bar staff who were on the take and getting the stocks back in order—this was Kath's department. My job was sorting out any bother that came, which I did; in fact the Blackett was transformed in that respect. During the three years in which we had the place, there were only three fights. I was involved in all three. The fact was, I did have a reputation for violence and people did not want to fight me, at the time I would not have thought twice about using a machete or a gun. I was also very handy, but it was mainly my back up that people were terrified of.

During my life I had worked with nearly all the top villains in the area including the 'cartel' who controlled the area. I was trusted for my integrity, as someone who never grassed, and in my younger days I had been "game for anything." My closest friends were the top villains in the area.

I set out my stall in the Blackett, and got rid of the young gang who had been causing the problems. Out went the under age drinkers and the dodgy bar staff. We then began to entice our old bar staff from the old Cordwainers (now Corks wine bar) to come and join us. One by one they trooped over the road as Kath disposed of the inherited bunch. The breweries coughed up and tidied up the place giving it a revamp and new decor.

After a while things picked up and the bar began to make a tidy profit, we were happy, the breweries were well happy, in fact everyone was happy—even the Police were happy, but then disaster struck. The Blackett was situated just around the corner from the infamous 'Market Tavern', which I mentioned earlier. As I have said, the place was a haunt for drug dealers, shoplifters and the criminal fraternity in general, a bit like the old 'Waterloo'. I knew everyone in there and regularly called in for a drink with the lads, more often than not to buy knocked off gear or drugs. If I was in trouble or needed a hand I could call on these guys for help and that's where my trouble began.

Because I knew all these blokes, (many of whom I grew up and went to school with) they would pop round to see me and have a drink. Pretty soon word got round that I was at the Blackett and it wasn't long before 90% of the Geordie Mafia were drinking in the place. It's nice to have pals to call on, but to have them there all day is something else, then to make matters worse the police raided the 'Tavern' and it was closed for about three months or so.

When this happened, there was a mass exodus round to us and we became the centre of attention for the next three years or so. From a financial point of view we were sound, and I was making a fortune, as I was accused of being involved in just about every type of racket possible, from drugs to porn. But at times the bar was a headache, and we were starting to come under the constant attention of the local constabulary.

We played 'head games' with the law for quite a while, they tried to stop us putting on our discos upstairs in 'Jumpers' (which were more like raves), because we didn't have a dance license. For a while van loads of coppers would drive past, then they would suddenly stop, dive out and run up the stairs to try and catch the punters dancing! We pretty soon got wise to this tactic and sorted out a signalling system that would have the whole bar on standby while the vans were in the vicinity. Jimmy the DJ, always had a smoochy record on hand that would bring the dancing to a screeching halt if needs be, usually it was Bryan Adam's song "Everything I do, I do it for you." from the film 'Robin Hood, Prince of Thieves.'

It was hilarious at times, the whole place was jumping one minute and then all of a sudden the lights were on and that slow record was mumbling away. The coppers were totally dumfounded and started to send in undercover cops, who we could always spot a mile away, but even then we had the timing off to a 't' so there was nothing they could do, we were too fast.

The place began to gain notoriety and people from all over came to visit. Some of my friends who worked closely with Charlie Kray, the Kray twins' brother, would visit me from time to time. Most of the day would be spent drinking, snorting cocaine and discussing 'business'.

"Davey why don't you come and join our firm, there will always be a place for you?" they would ask me, but I would refuse as I was loyal to our crew.

My drug taking was getting out of hand around this time and I started going to raves again. My behaviour at times was totally unacceptable and I was drinking far too much as well. The drinking would start early in the morning with the draymen and finish after the nightclubs at around three in the morning.

The money continued to roll in; I bought myself a Porsche and spent many happy hours driving like a maniac. Then Kath fell pregnant, it was completely unexpected and because of Kath's age at the time (she was 37) she was given routine blood tests. The results showed that there could be a problem with Downs Syndrome or Spina Bifida. I remember being very happy about the fact that we were expecting a child, but oblivious to the rest, I think it simply passed me by. I remember Kath telling me, but I suppose I just believed everything to be okay.

Then out of the blue I decided to take on a shop in

Sandyford, an upmarket area of the city. It was one of those chemist-type bargain shops selling toiletries and proprietary medicines, I decided to call it 'Essentials'. As you imagine the whole thing was a farce from start to finish.

I had all and sundry working in the shop, from the local barmaid to the dustman. It was one of those madcap schemes that I used to have, there was no way I could spend the time in the shop that was required to build it up and turn it into a successful business, I had too many other 'commitments'.

I found it really boring and spent most of the day getting stoned with the local road sweeper in the back of the shop. The shop was opposite the fish shop, next to the council yard and the road sweeper would park his trolley at the back out of sight of his supervisor, then we'd spend the day having 'buckets' (smoking marijuana through a cut up plastic bottle). As we were smoking the stuff all day I had to keep the shop smelling right for the customers and so I went through boxes and boxes of air freshener sprays. After a while the locals would come in to the shop with a 'knowing' look on their faces. Most of them thought it was all a hoot and were used to finding me lying stoned out of my box with a cloud of smoke rising from behind the counter!

"Just leave the money on the top" I'd shout.

One of my friends who was a top drug dealer in the city, popped round and we decided to mix a bag full of cocaine with some dentist's novocaine. So into the blender it went but we had so much stuffed in, that the blender exploded! We nearly went up in a blue flash! There was cocaine everywhere, all over the back of the shop; I was covered in it! My face was white with powder! It was like a slapstick sketch from an old 'Carry On' film. The whole thing became an utter farce as we tried to scrape it up

97

from the floor, the road sweeper had tried to snort some of it and was lying in a heap. Then just as we were tidying it all up the shop bell rang and a voice shouted "Can I have a packet of Strepsils, please?"

I looked round the curtain and was horrified to discover a policeman standing by the counter.

"I'll be with you in just a second" I replied as I frantically tried to remove the remains of the powder from my face, then warning the road sweeper to keep quiet I went out to deal with his request!

It seemed there was more going on in the back of the shop than in the front and at times things became quite bizarre, I remember one day mixing a mountain of one powder or another with a shovel just as if I was mixing cement! But the shop began to attract attention as the criminal fraternity began arriving, I had people turning up who were on the run from prison and burglars looking to offload some of their stolen swag. The police began to take a healthy interest in the shop so I decided that it could no longer carry on and after three or four months I had my closing down sale.

Kath felt that we needed a break, so we booked a holiday to Nassau in the Bahamas. It was somewhere I'd always wanted to go since seeing it in a James Bond film. We flew out in August 1992 leaving the bar in the capable hands of 'Mad Maggie'. The flight to the Bahamas took a little longer than expected as we were delayed at Bangor, Maine in the USA where we refuelled. 'Airforce One', the President of the United States' private plane was there and we just caught sight of it taking off—it was enormous.

We flew down the east coast of America over New York and Washington D.C. The scenery from the plane window was breathtaking as we approached the Bahamas, the waters were beautiful and there were miles of golden sun kissed beaches. As we approached Nassau there was a bit of an electric storm, but there was no indication of the storm that was to come a fortnight later. The storm soon passed, we landed and the sun came out in its splendour as we came out of the airport terminal.

We were then taxied to our hotel, which was beside the harbour, to check in. We went the long way round the Island and the bus driver gave us bits of info about the island and who lived where.

I saw 'Largo's' house from the Bond movie 'Thunderball' and other familiar sights.

We spent our days on the beach on Paradise Island next to the casino, which is the biggest outside Las Vegas, and was later to be our shelter in what became known as the worst hurricane in history, Hurricane Andrew. As usual I spent the time snorkelling the reefs around the Island marvelling at the array of fish in the clear blue waters. Some of the sights were absolutely breathtaking as I swam with the Giant Stingrays, Bass, Barracuda and a whole host of wonderfully coloured species. It had its exciting moments when I was diving for shells and a Moray eel nearly took my hand off, also a bull shark glided past me just offshore.

It was a great time and for a while we seemed to forget the turbulent life we had back home. We visited the idyllic 'Robinson Crusoe's' Island, which has been used so many times on TV commercials as the perfect Paradise Island; it was beautiful. We spent some time in the casino playing the machines and tables. We also dined there and took in one of the Las Vegas-style shows. All in all we had a great time, but on the day before we were due to fly home a hurricane warning was given on the local radio and television. We assumed that our flight home would be brought forward and expected to hear from the reps, but there was nothing forthcoming so we waited until the next day.

The following morning saw a number of concerned British holidaymakers trying to find out the re-arranged travel plans, and locate the reps.

As the day wore on panic started to set in as the hurricane drew closer and still there was no news. One girl from London was going mad trying to contact the reps and tried to get hold of our holiday company in London. The truth was, the staff from the company had deserted us and were holed up on a different island!

We couldn't believe it, they had deserted twenty-four holidaymakers and their children. Our hotel was nearly all glass and would obviously be a safety hazard, it quickly became evident we could not stay where we were. The manager of the hotel took the brunt of our anger now as the winds started to build.

The trees outside were bending in the wind as it approached three o'clock in the afternoon, the time we were due to fly home, but the reality was that our plane was still grounded at Miami airport as the Bahamas had become a no-fly zone. Someone suggested we go to the casino on nearby Paradise Island; it was one of the most stable and sturdy buildings in the Bahamas and was reputed to be hurricane proof, the problem was getting us all there. Outside the police were closing the roads, the harbour bridge to Paradise Island had already been closed and we were becoming desperate as time was beginning to run out.

The winds were climbing now as the eye of the hurricane approached the islands; people were becoming frantic and were screaming at the hotel manager to do something. Then our prayers were answered as a small bus pulled up at the doors of the hotel just in the nick of time, we almost hijacked the thing. We asked the driver to take us to the casino and he reluctantly agreed. We all piled into the little bus and set off down the road, the wind howling and rain lashing against the bus. The police were reluctant at first to let us go over the bridge as the winds were now so strong, they eventually caved in and allowed us to try after someone said; "You'll have to shoot us to stop us going over that bridge."

Progress was slow as we crossed over the harbour bridge because of the strength of the winds. As we reached the centre of the bridge I could see boats being tossed all over in the rough sea, which was rising over the harbour walls. The palm trees were bending right back as we approached the casino; we got in just in time as they were closing the hurricane doors. The relief on peoples' faces was evident as we reached our unusual sanctuary; it had been a somewhat traumatic journey.

The casino staff were first rate and allocated us one of the banqueting suites, ferrying beds in for us. An hour or so later and the eye of the hurricane, the centre of it, was over us. I remember watching the mass devastation that was happening right before my eyes; it was one of the most frightening moments of my life as I watched the awesome devastating power of nature ripping its way through the landscape in front of me. Huge trees were being uprooted, cars were flying through the air, and at times the huge building was shaken to its very roots. Water started to pour in through the roof on the upper floors as we searched for our accommodation. The only way I can describe what was happening outside is to say that all hell was let loose. As midnight approached, the winds began to die down slightly as the hurricane turned its attentions towards the United States and by four in the morning it was safe to venture outside.

The sight that greeted our eyes can simply be described as carnage; I have never in all my born days seen a sight like it. I really believe that once again that God had stepped in and sent that bus when he did. When we returned to our hotel we found that people had been killed close to the hotel, which had been badly hit. One huge tree outside our room had been uprooted and was now lying in the hotel swimming pool along with a boat that had been blown over the wall.

The following day we were taken to the airport where new reps tried to explain away their fellow workers sudden departure. People were furious; we had been left for dead. I can honestly say that if those other reps had been at the airport, they would have received serious injury. There were trees and debris all over the airport, only the runway was clear. I made a mental note to thank God as the plane took off and headed home to England.

15
Into Insanity

We arrived home a little bit shell-shocked by the experience in the Caribbean; I was still foaming at the holiday company and phoned the local newspaper, which sent out a reporter to record my complaints. It was probably just as well that we returned home when we did, the stocks at the bar were well down, Mags and her family had obviously been having one long party whilst we'd been away. She should have gone the distance really, but she had a long service contract and was quite reliable as far as bar staff went.

As Kath's pregnancy advanced it seemed increasingly obvious that at some point she'd have to go on maternity leave. The breweries didn't really want to bring a relief manager into a hostile situation at the Blackett, so we all agreed that it would be best if I carried on in charge. Kath began showing me the manager's job, and our friend Michelle joined us from Corks as assistant manageress. Michelle is very experienced and efficient which helped solve a multitude of problems, she is also honest, which is a rare commodity in the bar trade. So everyone was happy apart from Maggie who sulked for a while, feeling that she'd been passed over and that she should have been given the job.

During this period we moved to a bigger flat, just off Chillingham Road in the Heaton area. My son David had come to live with us so we needed the extra space especially with a baby on the way. Kath appeared very distant at times; she seemed totally preoccupied about the baby. Then we received an invitation to a wedding from our friend Gail, who had a flower stall in the Grainger

Market. The wedding was to be held at St Gabriel's church on Heaton Road, not far from where we lived, it was also the church where Kath had been christened and her parents had been married in.

I remember the service was very nice; it was years since I had been inside a church. When we came out, I noticed that Kath was crying. I thought that it was because women often cry at weddings, so like a typical male I nudged her and said "Pull yourself together, stop embarrassing me!"

The truth was that she'd been so worried that the baby would be born damaged, that she'd sat in church and for the first time poured her heart out to God asking for help. She promised to take the baby back to be christened; all this was entirely unknown to me until after I was saved. Anyway in true fashion, so typical of me, I'd only been in the reception for ten minutes before I headed off to the toilet for a line of cocaine and spent the rest of the day getting off my head.

It was early one morning a few days later that I was awoken by the sound of car doors opening and shutting. I looked at the clock—it wasn't long after seven o'clock. My heart started to beat faster as I strained to hear what the voices outside were saying. At the time I had a sixth sense for this type of thing, and at that moment my senses were screaming 'Police'.

I jumped out of bed and looked out of the window. Outside were a number of plainclothes officers who I recognised as being attached to Regional Crime Squad.

"Oh ****" my mind did a quick mental survey of the house—did I have anything incriminating anywhere?

"No" I thought; then I caught sight of a couple of wraps of cocaine on my bedside table. I quickly grabbed them and ran downstairs to the door, just as the police were knocking. I was only wearing my dressing gown and a pair of boxer shorts.

"Morning Davey, you're up bright and early this morning, I'm Detective Inspector…. we've got a warrant to search your house" said the first copper who was casually dressed and looked to be in his late forties or early fifties.

"What you looking for?" I asked.

"Guns," he answered.

"Guns?" I queried looking puzzled and dazed.

"Look Davey, I know your form and I know you've been out drinking with Ashie, so I've got a warrant to search your home as he has been involved in an incident."

"You'd better come in" I said and immediately there were twenty of them all over the house.

I think that this was Kath's first real indication that all was not well. I had been as discreet as possible about my drug taking; she knew I drank like a fish but had no idea I was a junkie as well. I had kept things pretty well hidden up to this point, but she must have had her suspicions.

After a couple of hours they gave up searching and left, which was a relief to me as I had been standing with three wraps of cocaine squeezed between the cheeks of my backside, terrified that they'd fall out of my boxer shorts. Clenching my cheeks together for that length of time had been a strain!

It was part and parcel of the life I lead as a notorious villain who had other notorious villains as friends. Every so often I could expect to have my drum (house) spinned by the law. I was constantly under surveillance. Everywhere I went they had me marked, my Porsche was one of the most watched cars in Newcastle.

One North East villain who constantly monitored police activity over the airwaves on his scanner would phone me to mark my card. He could tell me accurately where I'd been. It became a game of cat and mouse, always living on a knife-edge. I suppose that was part of the excitement, pitting my wits against the system, but in the end the system always won.

The result was that I was living in a state of pure paranoia all the time, everyone was a potential 'grass' and I trusted no one, which is a terrible state to be in. The bar was gaining serious notoriety and the police were never away from the place. I used to legitimately go to the Pubwatch meetings and hear how they were combating the drugs and violence! This rankled the Superintendent who considered me to be one of the main instigators in the city! He knew I was part of the main 'crew', one of the 'Firm.' He let me know that he knew, at times it was bizarre and I got the stick for it.

Everything that we tried to do in the bar met with his disapproval and if we had to apply for anything you could bet that it would be refused, he had a personal dislike for us, but it was mutual at the time. For a while I had strippers on upstairs in 'Jumpers' on a Saturday afternoon, which went down pretty well with the punters. Kath was not amused as the 'Dirty Old Mac' brigade filled the place from one o'clock in the afternoon; she promptly refused to come upstairs whilst the strippers were there.

Then someone from the strippers' agency suggested we put on a couple of 'Private Blue Shows' where, for a few quid, some of the girls would have sex with the audience. We decided to make it an all-ticket affair. We sold a hundred tickets, at a tenner a shot strictly to our pals only. The evening came and went, the place was packed, the whole thing secret.

Someone tipped off the Superintendent at Market Street, who sent a message saying that he'd shut the place down if we put on another one. I just think he was upset that he didn't get a ticket!

At the time I was part of the West End Firm headed by three brothers, one was doing sixteen years in jail for armed robbery. The other two were the main 'target criminals' in the city, Stephen & Michael. The police hated them and weren't slow to let people know. "If you mix with them expect us to come down on you like a ton of bricks" one policeman said to me.

At their trial for extortion, they claimed to run the drug scene in Newcastle and it was in all the newspapers, so once again I'm not speaking out of school. The truth was that people were terrified of them, as they had reputations for extreme violence, shootings, stabbings and worse.

Being part of the 'Firm' basically gave me license to do whatever I wanted in Newcastle and everyone knew I was part of that firm. Nobody wanted to fall out with me let alone them, not even my old pal Viv Graham who by now was a household name on Tyneside as a sort of genial Mr Fixit, who would sort anyone out if the price was right. Viv, who had been jailed with Stephen for the attack at Hobos, no longer had any dealings with the 'Firm', deciding to paddle his own boat.

He made a very good living from the clubs that employed him to look after their security, but rumour had it that he was a heavy gambler and would often lose fortunes. The clubs paid for him to keep the drug dealers out, which brought him into conflict with just about every gang in Newcastle.

I continued to get along okay with him, and from time to time we would have a drink together. I remember being out with him one night when he went berserk in the Tuxedo Junction nightclub because some bloke kept winding him up. The man, who was from a known family, was a bit drunk and kept insulting Viv who gave him chance after chance. Eventually Viv snapped and 'bang' the bloke was on the carpet. As he staggered to get up, Viv ran over to him and 'bang,' once again he keeled over. A minute or so later the bloke was helped to his feet; by this time Viv was chatting to me. He looked at the man trying to get up again and said to me;

"Hang on a minute Davey" and then ran over to the bloke and banged him again.

By now the man's face was unrecognisable, and was just a red mass. He was lying totally spark out on the carpet. Viv then shouted for water to be thrown over him. The bloke tried to get up, and was just getting to his feet when... you've guessed it—'bang.'

By now I was beginning to worry that Viv was going to kill him, then I happened to notice two coppers peering through the club doors watching what was going on.

They saw me looking at them and they spun around as if they hadn't seen a thing, and proceeded to walk away as quickly as possible; they obviously did not want to interfere with what was going on.

A crowd had now formed in the foyer and were watching the performance. Viv was jumping about looking for someone else to hit and the man's friends were next in the firing line. I decided that enough was enough, and took my life in my hands getting in between Viv and the bloke's mates.

I managed to persuade him to leave them by saying the law was on its way and there were coppers outside, luckily for those blokes he saw reason.

Meanwhile things were getting out of hand up in the West End as young up-and-coming thugs began to challenge the old guard. Gang warfare was rife between the various families and almost every night of the week there were running gun battles and drive-by shootings. I knew all the parties involved and took a neutral position.

It is not within the scope of this book to name names, or dwell on the violence or crimes that I have personally committed, or that others have committed. Suffice to say, I have done a lot of things of which I am not proud and there are obviously many things that I am unable to write about. I have many friends who are still in bondage to crime and I still have a certain amount of respect for some of my former colleagues and pray for them daily. I can honestly say that no person has ever been sent to jail because of me. The purpose of this book is to show them that there is a way out, even for the worst in society and I would like to take this opportunity to warn people of the dangers of living this sort of lifestyle. I have been lucky to get out, through the grace of God.

I have seen many of my friends go to the grave early, dying from drug overdoses and gang warfare, and over the next few months I was to witness the deaths of more friends and associates. One of my pals died from a heart attack in bed after snorting large amounts of cocaine. Another friend put a gun in his own mouth and killed himself after being tormented to death by voices in his head raging at him to kill himself. Yet another called Ray was shot dead after becoming involved in someone else's argument.

It seemed for a while that all I seemed to do was go to funerals. As I sat in church, it gave me time to think about my own mortality, and for probably the first time in years I actually stopped to think about what I was doing.

In February 1993, my daughter Victoria was born; she was like a ray of sunshine in my dark turbulent world. I was over the moon at my little bundle of joy and thanks to my Lord, she was born perfect, no Spina bifida or other problems, what a relief.

Kath kept her promise to the Lord, and she was baptised at St Gabriel's, the church that Gail had married in. The service was lovely and we spent a fortune on a celebration afterwards, sipping gallons of the best champagne. It was a really nice day for us all, as by now I was back on good terms with my adoptive Dad and Mam. All the family turned out for the party, and for the first time in ten years I spoke to my Gran who was now in her nineties. It was a brief return to normality for a few hours, but seeing my Gran again had an effect on me, she was such a kind, loving, decent person that I was ashamed of what I was, and from that day something in me began to change, for the first time in a long while I began to hate the life I was leading and the monster I'd become.

I was becoming so desperately unhappy that I went on drink and drug benders to try to hide the pain, I was so empty inside. Kath and I began rowing, and at times I would become violent, shouting and bawling. The truth was, I was becoming less able to control myself and at times was demonically possessed. There are times when Kath said that my eyes would burn bright red and she could see pure evil in my face.

I was on self-destruct, I was taking enough drugs to kill an elephant and I did overdose a couple of times in the Venue, an all-night dance club in Spennymoor, County Durham, which Viv looked after. One night I took about fifteen Ecstacy tablets, six grammes of whiz (speed) and snorted a quarter ounce of coke! I collapsed in a heap in the corner of the Venue, I was lucky to wake up, many people who OD don't. The life I was leading was sending me crazy; I was quite insane at times, as were the people around me.

The drug taking and dealing in the bar was way out of control, and on occasions the bar was raided, but no one was nicked, which was a miracle in itself as nearly every punter in the place was either buying or selling something. My life at times was just like that of Henry Hill, the main character in the film 'Goodfellas!'.

The Bar was becoming like the old Waterloo, which had long since been closed and many of the old faces from there were now resident in the Blackett. It seemed as though we had a magnet on the roof that attracted villains. At times it seemed as if every gangster, armed robber, psycho and thief frequented the place.

On the nights when there was no all-night dancing, we'd have lock-ins in the bar or at other bars in the West End and Cowgate area of the city, but after a while this too lost its appeal and I longed to leave the life I was living. The lock-ins were cocaine fuelled affairs and were often frequented by many professional footballers and it was common knowledge that one former England manager would turn up at three in the morning to drag his players out!!

Throughout my life I came into contact with many famous people, most of them had drink and drug problems. Many of the stars came seeking drugs from the Firm. It seemed everyone had an emptiness in them, no matter how much money they had or how famous they were. I met TV stars, film people, pop stars, England players and world champion boxers who all told the same story. Money, fame and material possessions do not necessarily bring happiness as we saw in the case of two famous women who died in the same week. It is possible to live in a palace and the gutter at the same time, it is also possible to live both in the gutter and in a palace. Princess Diana was a classic case of someone who had the world at her feet—money, power, success and yet she was a desperately unhappy person. Mother Theresa of Calcutta died the same week as Diana. She lived and worked in the slums of Calcutta but spiritually she was living in a palace. When you have God at the centre of your life and the Holy Spirit dwelling within you, it does not matter what your circumstances are or the environment around you, you can live in a state of absolute contentment. Mother Theresa had nothing, yet had everything, whereas Princess Diana had everything and yet nothing. Only a life in Christ can bring true fulfilment. Diana did many great works which brought blessing to many people, I only wish she had known Christ the way I do, then she would have been more at peace with herself. Her story is tragic but is a prime example of how beauty, fame and riches are but a fleeting thing which bring no lasting happiness or contentment.

Just before Christmas 1993 we moved house again, this time to a new estate not far from South Gosforth. The Christmas period was pretty quiet at the bar, myself and Ginger Dougie, my right hand man, spent most of it blitzed. Then on New Year's Eve we had our yearly water pistol fight with Freddie, Geoff and the other doormen from Corks. We had decided to close the bar at seven o'clock and have a private party for the staff and our friends. It was about 8 or 9pm when Craig and Amanda arrived from The Scrogg public house in Walker, and told us that my pal Viv Graham had been shot on Wallsend High Street and was in hospital. We were shocked at the news and the following day we heard that he had died from his injuries.

16
The Point of No Return

Things seemed to change in the city after Viv's death, I suppose it was because he seemed larger than life that nobody believed it could happen to him. People who had been under his protection were now living in a state of fear, worrying about the reprisals for using his services. His mini empire was in effect, up for grabs. It wasn't too long before reports began to filter back to us that many of the bars under his protection had received visits from one cowboy or another looking to cash in. The BBC screened a kind of tribute programme, which included many publicans who had employed his services. It was pathetic to see these grown men cowering at the thought of what might happen to their precious businesses. Then a local police superintendent was wheeled on who also praised what Viv was doing. It was unbelievable—the Police were praising a man who had cabbaged at least one person and was rumoured to be dealing in drugs! If the police had done their job in protecting the public, then the publicans would not have to go to criminals for protection. It was bizarre, it was as if the police were endorsing what he had been doing. Viv was my pal, I had respect for him, but he was no angel and his death should serve as an example to young people not to follow his example as it may cost you your life.

The 'Firm' moved in and began dividing up the various clubs. The doormen at the clubs were powerless to do anything about it, for fear of being shot. We took over the majority of the bars and clubs, nobody could stop us, party time really began now! The Firm asked me to look after most of them and it was my job to see that other people didn't trespass on our turf—which included all of the city centre as well as other places around the region, at times this meant dishing out extreme violence.

For a while it was like being a movie star; at last I had the power, money and success I'd always craved. All my life I'd wanted and dreamed of being in this position and for a short time I had fulfilled that ambition. I could easily see how people get caught up in this power craze thing. Once you get into this position your ego runs mad with you and you just naturally start acting like Al Pacino in the movie 'Scarface', the cocaine helps to fuel this. Everybody wants to be your friend, women are falling over themselves to jump into your pants—'everybody wants a piece of the action'.

After a while the glitter started to go and the whole thing began to lose its appeal to me.

Nobody seemed to know who actually shot Viv but rumours were flying that it was one or other of the 'Firms'. It seemed that everyone had their own theory as to who and why. The Police questioned a number of people about it, including us, but no one was ever charged with it, Michael was interviewed about three times but nothing ever came of it.

The clubs in the city really nose dived now, as respectability became a thing of the past. The people who Viv kept out of the clubs were now calling the shots and giving the orders. Everyone was jumping on the bandwagon, trying to earn an extra few quid, everyone from the managers of the club to the doorstaff, from the bar staff to the bottle washers—they all had their hands out, turning a blind eye to what was going on.

It was around this time that I was arrested for a robbery at a building society in the city centre opposite the main police station. The area manager from the breweries arrived just in time to see me being carted off by the

Robbery Squad. The police had no evidence against me and had acted on a telephone tip-off by some 'lowlife' looking to cause me some grief. At the time I was in the company of a film crew who were using the Blackett for scenes in a movie. The Police released me without charge but it was quite embarrassing.

The breweries finally gave in to our requests to move from the Blackett and we were offered 'The Raby' on Shields Road, just outside the city centre. It was like a ton weight being lifted from our shoulders, although I was to carry on with the door security at the Blackett for a while. The police in Byker weren't exactly thrilled at the prospect of having me on their patch and when Kath went to see the Superintendant at Clifford Street police station about the license, she was told that if I had anything to do with the bar then they would oppose the license. Kath assured them that I was still at the Blackett and would not be involved with it.

I continued on a course of self-destruction as my drug taking spiralled out of control and I would have blackouts at times, not knowing what I was doing. My behaviour was bordering on the bizarre. One example of this was when I was in a nightclub and was standing at the bar talking to the club manager. I suddenly got the urge to go to the toilet, but because I was so inebriated, I just whipped it out there and then. I began urinating against the bar counter whilst the manager stood in amazement, not believing what was happening, carrying on my conversation as though nothing was amiss. I staggered off again, apparently muttering: "The club's a khazi anyway!"

Because of my position on the 'Firm' I was expected to keep some sort of order in the clubs we were involved in and at times I'd patrol the clubs just looking for someone to hit. People would spar wide of me, as often I was on a short fuse. I longed to leave the life I was leading but felt totally trapped and didn't really know what else to do. I felt as though I was on the 'Magical Mystery Tour' and couldn't get off the bus. The paranoia became worse, and for a while I really was mentally sick, the never-ending nights of clubbing and lock-ins began to take their toll on me, I was heading towards a breakdown. I realised that I couldn't continue on this road and I needed help, I was mentally, spiritually and emotionally drained.

I was losing a grip on reality and becoming unstable. I was sometimes frightened of myself, not knowing what I would do next. Things were coming to a head—I went berserk one night in the 'Ritzy' having six fights in the space of an hour—I was off it. On leaving the club I punched a bloke who tried to get in a taxi before me, this was right in front of a vanload of coppers who totally ignored my antics and nicked my pal Ginger Dougie.

They refused to arrest me and carted Ginger Dougie off instead, so I ran round to the police station and started shouting and bawling. Once again they refused to arrest me, instead they took it out on Dougie keeping him locked up for the full weekend.

People in the 'Firm' could see all was not well with me and on more than one occasion Stephen came and asked me what was going on. I was constantly warned to stay away from the all night raves as I was treading on toes all over the place and attracting a lot of attention to myself, also I was becoming a liability.

My behaviour got so bad that the Police had a special meeting about me, enough was enough and they decided to bar me from every nightclub in the city, threatening to take away the license of any club that allowed me in.

The police continued to raid my home on a regular basis always searching for drugs and weapons, but I never kept anything in the house. One copper came across my scrapbook whilst searching the house and quipped:

"Aye Davey, we'll be seeing this in paperback in a few years time!!" How right he was!

Then Stephen appeared in the 'Sunday Times' along with Paddy C in an article entitled 'Crime UK Ltd' in which it had a map of Britain and the various leading villains in each major city, once again the spotlight was on. It was time to get out, my home life was a mess and my relationship with Kath was rapidly going out of the window. I became totally paranoid through all the drugs I had taken, I trusted no one, they were all grasses. On one of my last visits to the clubs I felt a voice say to me: "Life doesn't have to be this way Davey, it's not too late to come back."

I went home from the club early that night, my daughter Victoria was crying upstairs; she was only about eighteen months old. I went upstairs and picked her up, she really clung to me and for the first time I realised how much she needed me. She was sobbing her little heart out and something snapped inside me, it was the straw that broke the camel's back. I knew I had to make the break, it was now or never and I knew that it would cost me everything but I didn't care, I had to take the risk. I talked to Kath, I told her that I'd had enough and my days as a villain were over and that I needed to come off the drugs I was taking. I was desperate to sort myself out, especially when Kath announced that she was pregnant again.

We talked things over deciding to give up the pub, try our chances elsewhere and make a total break of it. We decided to move house, giving up our nice home for something less grand. We packed what we could carry and left the rest including sun beds, furniture and a Mercedes. We rented a small house on the other side of the city for a few months but we couldn't really settle as the next-door neighbour turned out to be a known drug dealer! I couldn't believe my luck; it was going from bad to worse.

Here I was for the first time in my life trying to do the decent thing and then this—was there no escape from this life?

After a few days of living there I realised my next-door neighbour was under police surveillance. I became completely paranoid, believing that I was caught up in some cosmic conspiracy. I was smoking dope from morning to night in an effort to try and break the hold of the hard drugs. I was living in a state of siege, I was not sleeping well at all and when I did manage to fall asleep, I was constantly being tormented by nightmares. It got to the stage where I was frightened to go to sleep. I started to become aware that there was a real spiritual dimension and that there was more to life than meets the eye.

I began to hear voices that shouted at me to kill myself; I was on my way to hell and probably deserved it. I desperately needed help but I knew I couldn't talk to anyone about what I was experiencing, because they would think I was barking mad. I remembered how other people had told me how they'd heard voices, but I'd dismissed it thinking that couldn't be right, but now that it was happening to me I knew how real it was.

For weeks I climbed the walls as I came off the hard drugs. Anyone who has gone through the process knows the hell I went through those weeks. The withdrawal pains were bad and my nights were spent lying in rivers of sweat, being tortured by thoughts of the past. I knew I had to hang on and that there was no going back. I had stomach cramps and at times I felt as though my insides were being ripped out.

I became aware now that there was a real fight going on for my soul and I was being bombarded from hell on all sides. I knew I had to be strong and to weather the storm otherwise I would go under. I desperately needed peace in my life and I started to search.

17
The Quest for Peace

As the weeks went by, I felt the need for hard drugs leave me and I was winning by sheer determination. I knew that I'd never take Ecstacy or Cocaine or Speed or Tamazepan or Heroin again, I could not face the withdrawals again. I clung to the dope as if it was my lifeline, but I knew that eventually it would have to go as well.

Kath was less optimistic saying: "You'll never be able to get off that" which was not particularly helpful, but I was determined to beat it.

Over the next few months, our relationship started to improve as Kath saw the sincerity in what I was doing. We occasionally had the odd row but they were few and far between.

I still had a drink problem but I managed to keep out of the bars and clubs, which was very difficult after spending a lifetime in them. The temptation to return to my old life was always there, but I kept on fighting it believing there was a way out, I just had to find it. Every now and then I'd hear a voice of encouragement amongst the cacophony of voices that were raging in my head, someone was telling me to hang in there.

For a while I had to have a stock of alcohol in the house, along with my dope and I clung to these for security, I knew I could only try and deal with one thing at a time. I went to the doctor's and told him that I was trying to break the habits. He encouraged me to continue and gave me some tablets to help me.

I began to look for things to do with my time as I had a lot of it on my hands. I tried my hand at golf for a while, but I wasn't particularly good at it and lost loads of balls.

During my time in prison I had enjoyed drawing and always had a drawing book on the go, so for a while I would spend my time drawing, but then I discovered a love for painting. I began by doing pictures of 'Fireman Sam' and other cartoon figures for the walls in Victoria's bedroom and after a while it progressed to landscapes and buildings. Then I found that I quite liked painting trees, I had never realised before how many different kinds there were, to me a tree was a tree, but as my interest in painting developed so did my interest in nature and the world around me.

It was all good therapy for me, a great escape from my dark turbulent world, and as I studied things it began to dawn on me that all this had not come out of a big bang. Order did not come out of chaos; the world wasn't created out of some universal cataclysmic disaster. Nature is ordered and perfect, my mind started to ask the question "Who had created it all? Was God real?" My spiritual search began in earnest.

I knew that a lot of eastern religions claimed to be filled with peace and contentment, so I decided to check them out. One of the learning channels on satellite TV was dedicated to this kind of stuff and I watched programme after programme on the Holy men of India. I was amazed at their claims of mystical healing powers and of the ascetic life that they led. I was totally fascinated by their life of self-denial, spending much time praying and fasting. They seemed to have so much peace in their lives, with big smiles on their faces and bright shiny eyes. I wondered if they were on the 'gear' and were dropping Acid or something but there was nothing visible. The whole idea of meditation started to appeal to me; little did I know the devil was out to deceive me.

I became totally infatuated with the whole subject of the afterlife as I searched my way through a whole web of deception in my quest for peace. I began reading books on Buddhism and Spiritism and at the time most of their theories seemed plausible, simply because I didn't know the truth. They all claimed that they were right and many of them had a belief in reincarnation. I watched fascinated, as they 'supposedly' cast demons out of people, the whole thing looked quite bizarre.

Many of the Indian Holy men believe they have lived many times before and that each life is a natural progression towards spiritual perfection. They believe that each time you're here you learn and perfect yourself more, with the goal being a mystical Nirvana. Many of these men devote the final third of their lives to their own spiritual search. This is in direct opposition to what the Bible teaches— that we live once then die and pass either to heaven or hell where we spend eternity but at the time I didn't know this. I suppose I had a dim view of Christianity as I didn't know any real Christians, I knew one or two people who professed to being Christians but in reality were anything but! I didn't know what real Christianity was.

In the midst of all this Kath gave birth to my son John, in March of 1995, which brought great joy to me. We were so blessed, it was like I was being given a second chance at fatherhood because I'd made such a mess of things up to this point.

I continued my campaign against alcoholism and reduced my daily intake over a number of weeks, but I was never able to completely shake free from it. One night I went to pick some marijuana up from an acquaintance who lived nearby and on the way home I stopped at the off licence to pick some drink up. When I returned to the car I sat and rolled a joint thinking:

"I'll have this before I go home."

I lit the joint and took a couple of draws, all of a sudden a voice spoke very loudly to me.

"You ********, I'll get you, why don't you kill yourself?"

I sat bolt upright at the sound of the hideous demonic voice as it boomed at me. Terrified, I jumped out of the car and threw away the joint, I was in a total panic, and it was at this point I knew that demonic forces really possessed me. For a moment I stood shaking by the side of the road as the voice continued to make vile threats against me. Then after ten minutes or so things quietened down again and I was able to return to the car. My mind was in a terrible state as I drove home; I'd heard voices before, but not like this.

I knew I needed exorcism, but I didn't know anyone who could do it, I was panic stricken. Then a couple of days later I got a lucky break. I was on the phone talking to my pal Bob Byron who I'd done some building work with, and he told me that he had been doing some work for an old Indian bloke called Baba who was apparently some sort of mystical healer.

"Does he do exorcisms?" I asked excitedly.

"I'm not sure, why?" asked Bob.

I then proceeded to give him the whole tale about what had been going on. Bob promised to get in contact with Baba and find out if he would see me. The following evening Bob phoned me and told me that he had spoken to Baba who agreed to see me later in the week. I felt a surge of hope as I put down the phone believing that I had a way out. All week I waited in anticipation, my mind was awhirl with different possibilities.

On the Friday evening I went to Baba's home in Jesmond. Bob was already there waiting outside for me when I arrived.

"Are you all right?" Bob asked.

"Aye, let's get it over with" I answered not knowing what

I was letting myself in for. Bob rang the bell and after a few moments a young Indian girl answered the door.

"We've come to see Baba, he's expecting us" Bob said. She smiled politely and invited us in, leading us through the house to the kitchen, where the old man was waiting. Bob introduced me and we shook hands, then got straight down to business.

Baba looked to be in his late sixties, a small man in stature, he was dressed in pyjama-style clothes and sat and listened attentively as I poured out my whole sorry tale. Occasionally he would ask questions that he already seemed to know the answers to. After I'd finished talking he said:

"David you've come to a point in your life where you must leave the past behind, you must repent and do no more wrong, I can help you, but you must make your peace with God."

Then he started quoting bits from the Bible to me. I was quite amazed as I thought he was a Hindu or something. He went on to tell me that because of the life I had led and the drugs I had taken, I had opened the doors to demonic forces and that they were trying to destroy me. He told me he could help and asked me to go back the following Tuesday.

When Tuesday came I was there bang on time, this time he took me upstairs into his temple. I didn't know if I was doing right or not, and at all times was cautious, but I was desperate for peace. We removed our shoes and sat on the floor with crossed legs. He lit a couple of sticks of incense and sat chanting a mantra of some description while in my head I prayed to God, asking for his protection.

I don't know what happened, but I went home that night and slept peacefully for the first time in years. I continued to go to his house for a few months and during this time he encouraged me to meditate. He also talked about spirit guides and how everyone has a guide. The Bible calls these 'familiar spirits' and tells us to keep away like the plague—but more on that later.

However, at the time I was naive, and Baba started to prepare me to meet my 'guides.' I started to discipline myself, spending many days and hours sat in front of a candle staring at it. I read books on transcendental meditation, spiritism, new age and occult—after a while I even got myself a crystal ball. I was gullible and naive, and I took it all in like a rubbish bin. I believed all the nonsense about Atlantis, ley lines and the pyramids. I read books by false prophets, sleeping prophets and lying prophets. I read books about this dimension, that dimension, this heaven and that heaven. I began to believe all the rubbish about re-incarnation, but at the same time I felt uneasy in my spirit.

For all my mistakes, there was never a time when I worshipped any other God. I fumbled around Buddhism and Hinduism, but I never worshipped their idols. I suppose I believed somehow and in some way that Jesus was God, but Baba considered him to be a prophet. I was being deceived however, and was quite looking forward to meeting my 'spirit guides'.

When you practise this sort of stuff the devil will make sure you get a response to encourage you, the deeper you go the harder it is to get out. Be warned, the cemeteries and nut houses are full of people who messed around with the occult and paranormal. The devil will perform lying signs and wonders, he will give you the ability to do things, but the price is too heavy—eternity in hell.

So I practised meditation in an attempt to open the mystical 'third eye' which allows you to see into the spirit realm. After a while I achieved this and saw into different realms. After months of training and practise I was also able to practise astral projection or soul travel, the ability to leave your body. This may sound quite mad and unbelievable but I assure you it takes place within the confines of witches covens and spiritist churches. It is extremely dangerous and an abomination to God.

I remember listening to the testimony of former queen of black witches, Doreen Irvine, who is now also a Christian minister. She talks more in depth about this sort of stuff, and tells how it is widely practised. I would recommend Mrs Irvine's book 'Witchcraft to Christ' as an invaluable source of information in this area. I have members of my own church who were involved in spiritism and the occult and who also practised this and made their testimonies public knowledge. We met Doreen Irvine in August 2001 and made a video with her as she shared her testimony with us and we use it as a powerful evangelistic tool, she is a very witty and charming lady who is a real trophy of Grace.

After a while I would hear spirits speaking to me, I used to feel them touching my head. On my visits to Baba I would ask him loads of questions as he monitored my progress, but still I felt an unease, a fear in my spirit as the months passed by. I had an even worse feeling about the house we were living in and told Kath we had to move, she reluctantly agreed.

So the house hunting started again and we decided that it would be better to move out of Newcastle altogether. Occasionally I would hear the demonic voice threatening me, mostly when I'd had a drink or a joint, though by now I was reducing my intake of both of these substances. I still had quite a way to go and wasn't out of the woods yet. The nightmares continued, as did the paranoia. Despite all my prayer and meditation, I still had no real peace although after my trips to Baba's I'd have the odd night's sleep, but I wasn't cured.

The search for a house stepped up after the police nicked

the next-door neighbour. For a while we viewed different houses in the Durham area but nothing was suitable or felt right. Every night we scoured the local papers to see what was available, and then Kath came across an advert for a house in Killingworth, on the outskirts of Newcastle. We discussed the possibility of a move to Killingworth and decided to go and have a look at the properties available.

So we cut the various adverts out and made arrangements to view the properties. At the first house we went to see, the estate agent failed to turn up and the house really looked too small. After we'd waited a while Kath suggested we view another property in Killingworth that had been advertised even though we didn't have an appointment. It wasn't too far to the other house, which was near the lake. I stayed in the car whilst Kath went and knocked on the door. There was no answer so she went to look round the back, a few minutes later she came back and waved to tell me there was someone in. I got out of the car and walked over to the house, I could hear someone fumbling with keys. When the door opened and I saw who lived there I nearly fell through the floor, it was Liz, the cook from St Christopher's bail hostel—the one who Michael the monk had prophesied would be my landlady all those years ago!

I don't think she recognised me, at the time I had a beard and full head of hair and tried to look as inconspicuous as possible. The house was exactly what we were looking for and we went away pondering what to do. I shared with Kath about me knowing Liz and then another thing happened, Liz phoned us saying: "Look, I really feel that you should…" So that was it, we decided that Killingworth was our next port of call and made arrangements to move as it felt so right. I decided to celebrate and headed off to get some dope and a few cans, then it happened again!

The demon shouted at me to kill myself as I gave a lift

to a couple of friends. This time I felt my leg freeze and my foot lock on the accelerator of the Porsche, I began to panic as we hurtled around the country roads. The demonic laughter got louder and louder as the speed increased, I could not move my leg at all, it was frozen solid. I decided to risk everything by taking evasive action and pulling on the handbrake of the car, which was not the best thing to do at nearly one hundred miles an hour! I pulled on the brake as hard as possible and spun the steering wheel as we rounded a bend. The car went into a spin and we ended up spinning completely off the road and onto a grass verge, then the car stopped with a bump.

Three of us clambered out of the car on all fours, shaking, lucky to be alive; once again I had been spared.

18

My Eyes have seen the Glory of the Lord

"As he journeyed he came near to Damascus, suddenly a light from Heaven shone around him."

Acts 9:3 (NKJV)

For some strange reason the house in Killingworth seemed almost like a sanctuary, there was a peace about the place that I had not experienced in a long time. The neighbours were very friendly, but my natural instincts caused me to be paranoid and to wonder which house the police would be observing me from, such was the state of my mind. The unrelenting nightmares continued, to the point that I was terrified to go to sleep, voices raged at me to kill myself and sweat would pour from me. One night I dreamt that I was wrestling with someone, it was so real that I lashed out and caught Kath on the side of the face by accident, luckily she groaned and went back to sleep!

The truth was that I was wrestling with myself. For a year or so life had been an unbearable nightmare, I was racked with remorse for the life I'd led. I was living in a state of siege, a paranoid, nightmare world with Satan raging at me to kill myself. I was climbing the walls trying to get off the dope; it had been my friend, my lifeline, and the antidote to the hard drugs. For months now I had depended on it to help me off the cocaine and all the other garbage I was taking. I knew that it could not go on for much longer; I was having 'whities' all the time (panic attacks) and I was still drinking heavily.

The voices seemed louder when I was on the drink or dope—they had to go. Kath's claims of "You will never be able to give that up" were continually ringing in my ears. Thoughts of school came flooding back—"You're a loser", then my Dad saying "You'll never make anything of yourself."

My mind had become like a movie theatre or a television screen, the walls were closing in on me, as my life seemed to shoot by going from one event to another. Desperation was setting in, my heart was racing ninety to the dozen and I was about to crack, the strain was getting too much. Suddenly my attention was drawn to our bedroom table, on it was an old battered King James Bible. Liz and Barry had left a couple of books behind and this was one of them. Something was drawing me to this book. I got off the bed where I had been lying, went across the room and picked it up. As I flicked through the pages, I stopped at Psalm 23:

The Lord is my shepherd I shall not want
He makes me to lie down in green pastures
He leads me beside the still waters
He restores my soul
He leads me in the paths of righteousness
For His name's sake

(Psalm 23: 1-3) NKJV

Fleeting memories of Sunday school began to come into my thoughts; they were hazy—something about Jesus. It was as though there was a mental block, but it was beginning to break into my mind. It started as a trickle as memories of Gran and St John's came into mind, there was something about Jesus too but I couldn't quite remember what it was. Pictures of Robert Powell in the TV series 'Jesus of Nazareth' flooded into my mind as I continued to leaf through the well-worn pages of the old Bible. Various verses seemed to spring out at me and it was becoming apparent that I badly needed to get to Jesus if he were there.

A million thoughts were now racing through my mind 'How would I reach Jesus?' 'Was he really there?' 'Could he stop these attacks on me?'

'Was he really God?' 'Would he really care about me?' 'Perhaps I was already in hell and God had sent me here, didn't I deserve this endless mental torture?' I had hit the bottom, nowhere left to go, Jesus was my last chance. It was August 16th 1995, it was 1.30 in the afternoon, I was totally broken as I fell on my knees and began to pray and pray and pray.

My prayers were clumsy—it was over twenty years since I had really prayed as a child, perhaps I was saying the wrong ones? I began to meditate, as had been my practise, but that wasn't getting me anywhere, then as the afternoon drew on, Psalm 23 came back into my mind. I began to meditate on that, but once again my emotions started to run high. I could no longer concentrate on it and I became despondent as the time approached three o' clock. Little did I know I was three minutes away from having every question I ever wanted to know answered in a flash.

Completely exhausted, both mentally and physically, I got up off my knees and collapsed on my bed, I had no more prayers left, I was totally at the end of myself. Gazing up at the ceiling, the sun pouring in the window, I said:

"Jesus if you are really there and you are God, if you come now and help me, then I am yours."

I had no sooner said these words than I became aware of a light beginning to flow through the bedroom ceiling. It reminded me of a light I had seen in the film 'Ghost', it was slow moving, very gentle, almost like snowflakes.

It began to roll over my body and a feeling of well-being began to take hold of me. I had taken every drug possible, but this was something else. As the feeling increased, so did the light until it became brighter than the sun outside, I was in a state of what I can only describe as bliss. The more the light rolled over me the more the feeling of absolute heaven increased. Wave after wave of it came, it was as if I were swimming in this light, my attention was then drawn to the ceiling.

The ceiling seemed to have vanished and I was looking up a kind of tunnel, at the end of the tunnel I could see a river of pure light with a waterfall. In front of the waterfall was a rock, and standing next to this rock was a man holding the staff of a shepherd, it was Jesus! I was in a state of absolute bliss, but the sight was both awesome and terrifying. For a moment I was completely paralysed by the sight, then He spoke in an audible voice:

"Son, your sins are forgiven, go now and sin no more," and then:

"Go now Saul of Tarsus, call yourself Paul" the Lord's voice boomed. Smith Wigglesworth once said whilst standing next to Niagara Falls that the voice of God was like the sound of many waters—I know what he meant.

I felt a release now, it was as though a ton weight was being lifted from my shoulders, a visible blackness was lifting off me, all the demonic bitterness and hatred that I had carried since I was a small child was leaving me. At this moment a twenty-year alcohol addiction and a fifteen-year drug addiction were broken instantly! My mind was awhirl as I struggled to comprehend what was happening, I later discovered that this was the light that the Apostle Paul had seen on the road to Damascus.

It is really impossible to describe the whirlpool of thoughts that were engulfing my mind as I lay and looked up at the glorious spectacle of the resurrected Christ

Jesus, I suddenly felt the fear of God enter my life and broke down in tears.

I jumped up from the bed as the room returned to normal and tried to get my head straight, I was now in a state of shock, unable to speak, this was no dream or hallucination—this was real, God was real and he had forgiven me! Forgiven? Me? After everything that I had done! A piece of scum like me! I felt an urge to write to people who I'd hurt asking for forgiveness and apologising for my behaviour. I felt a new lightness in my spirit and felt as high as a kite; I wanted to tell people that I had seen Jesus. I wanted to tell people that Jesus was alive! A million thoughts and possibilities raced through my mind, 'Would people think I was mad?' So, what if they did, I couldn't care less—I knew the truth.

I learned later that this was what Jesus was talking about in the Gospel of John (3:3) when he was talking to Nicodemus the Pharisee about being born again. The minute I had cried out to Jesus and asked for His help and repented of my sins, my prayers were heard. I was accepted and forgiven, everything I had done in my life was being washed away—I had a second chance, a fresh start, I was Born Again.

> *"I tell you no man can see heaven unless he is born again."*
>
> John 3:3 NKJ

It was awesome, I couldn't get the image of Jesus out of my mind, radiant and magnificent, shining in all His glory, no wonder the Israelites had to cover the face of Moses after he had been on the mountain of God.

I went downstairs where Kath was buzzing about in the kitchen. I wanted to tell her but I couldn't, the words simply would not come out. I paced about back and forth between the living room and kitchen, each time wanting to speak out about my recently received salvation but the words would simply not come.

"Kath, I err..." I would start.

"I've, err..." I tried again.

Kath would look at me, puzzled, she knew I was going to say something, but each time I bottled out of it and walked away leaving her totally perplexed.

Eventually I gave up altogether and went back upstairs to see if I could find the Lord again, but as hard as I tried in prayer it just wasn't happening again.

A couple of days later I eventually shared my good news with her, I'm sure she thought that I was barking mad but I didn't mind. Another bonus was that a couple of weeks prior to this Kath had been out walking one sunny afternoon and had felt drawn to wander into the local church, the ecumenical 'Church of the Holy Family.'

The local parish priest, Michael Malleson was holding the weekly lunch club for the pensioners. He made Kath feel welcome and made her a cup of coffee as he listened to her. Kath realised she needed the Lord and made a commitment and started attending Holy Family Church every Sunday and Tuesday for the communion. The Lord our God is awesome and the adventure was just beginning! It was 16th August 1995, David John Falcus, previously known as Davey Tams, was a 'Born Again Christian'—who would have believed it?!!

19
In His Presence

For days at a time I would sit in my bedroom and read the Bible. It was a joy to learn and meditate on the scriptures; they now seemed alive to me, whereas before I might as well have been reading Chinese—it was as though there was a block on me reading the Bible. I know now that the demons that were in me had refused to let me anywhere near a Bible! But this time things were different and I delighted to read it, the book was never out of my hands. As I meditated on the word each day, I would feel the presence of God in the room. Those first few months of my conversion were awesome, the Lord allowed me some really wonderful spiritual experiences and there were times when the Lord would come and take me out of body and show me things. I have had some really wonderful experiences with Jesus, which are really private, as he came and spent time with me.

The Lord was busy restoring my capacity to love and I really did start to love people, it was a blessed time and I began to view things in a completely different way.

One of the down sides was that I found it difficult to accept my forgiveness. One of the reasons for this was that now I was a Christian, the satanic attacks really took off. When you become a Christian you are enlisted into the army of the Lord and the real battle begins. I was now a real threat to Satan because of the knowledge that I possessed. Satan and his demons were now going to try and discourage me from following Jesus, he wanted to stop me learning of the great power available to me as a Christian.

As I read my Bible I began to learn that there was

awesome power available if I knew how to tap into it, the problem was that I didn't as I didn't belong to a church and I didn't know any Christians who moved in real power. The first few months were trial and error as God allowed me to explore and I realised the foolishness of practising astral projection and transcendental meditation after one out of body experience in which I found myself face to face with a demon! It had a grotesque face, high cheekbones and where the eyes should have been there was a yellow light—it gave me a real shock as I almost bumped into it! I quickly returned to my body and never practised it again.

The fact of the matter was that I was looking for Jesus, but in all the wrong places. I believe I have been forgiven and believe the Lord allowed me to do it to show me the reality, it really was a terrifying experience and I repented of it. I will warn people to keep away from these occultist activities as they can be fatal and it will definitely lead to demonisation of one degree or another.

I also began to have my doubts about my relationship with Baba Ghai. I knew that he was helping me the only way he knew how, but he was a Hindu and I was a Christian and I knew that the two faiths were incompatible. Never once did he try to convert me to Hinduism, though for a time before my conversion I saw him as a guru type figure who helped me in a variety of ways. My visits to his home in Jesmond became less frequent as my faith in Jesus as my Lord and Saviour grew; now I meditated on the Laws of God.

I want to teach people here about meditation and the dangers of it and say that any meditation that causes people to empty their minds is dangerous because it means that their guard is down and the brain is susceptible to suggestion. The con is to get people to concentrate on a flower or something, harmless you may think—don't believe a word of it! If you go down this path you will find yourself becoming more and more open to the devil's lies and deceit. Natural curiosity sets in and the devil will always make sure that you have an experience of some sort, like a spider with a fly he entices people into a web of deceit and all the time he is looking to control the person and ultimately destroy them. Don't sit and stare at candles, it won't bring you the peace you crave—take it from someone who knows and has experienced it as I have. The only safe way to meditate is on the Word of God; the Psalms are marvellous to meditate on. I really found a lot of joy in doing this as well as receiving a blessing from God. As I meditated on the Psalms I was beginning to form a great love for the Lord. I felt that some of the Psalms spoke right into my situation especially Psalm 116. I loved to meditate on it, reading the word was feeding my spirit.

I learned that King David had written the majority of the Psalms and I read about God's great love for David and vice versa; how David would dance around all night singing God's praises. I began to see that our Father in Heaven is full of love and that he rejoices in us, his children.

This really blew my mind, the fact that God not only forgave me my sins but that he really loved me as well, and better still that he wanted a personal relationship with me as his pride and joy! It was all too much to take in. It took me a long time to forgive myself for things I had done. Every day I had Satan reminding me of my past, he had me on a guilt trip and I thought it was God, so after a while I wasn't experiencing the victory and at times I felt bound up and a slave to my emotions. I knew all was not well, but whom could I talk to?

For a while now Kath had worshipped up at Holy Family Church. Every Sunday morning off she'd go, kids in tow and after a while I started to get curious, so I went and had a look. The people seemed very welcoming and warm and nobody really knew or cared who I was. They knew I was Kath's fiancé but nothing else—especially not the fact that I had seen God, and I wasn't ready to share that with them yet, so I went along on odd occasions just to see how the land lay.

Church was totally alien to me, it was a new experience, definitely not what I was used to. It was a world away from the sweaty bars and nightclubs that had been my home for nearly fifteen years and at times my mind would slip back briefly. Satan would say "C'mon, you don't belong here, why don't you come back to graft?" For a fleeting moment I would consider it, then the memories would come flooding back. With a shudder I would decline the offer.

On the work front Kath was still officially on sick leave and her maternity leave period was coming to an end. We were still on the books at Scottish and Newcastle Breweries but we knew we could not go back to run any more bars. In any case we felt that the Breweries would drag their feet at re-appointing us to another bar after the fiascos at other places. We also knew the objections that Northumbria Police would raise and that we had more chance of a bar on the Moon than we did anywhere in the North of England. So we gambled that the Breweries would offer Kath a chance of voluntary redundancy, and if not we were going to quit anyway. So we rolled the dice and 'hey presto' the Breweries decided to cough up a few quid and they were 'Sorry to see us go.' Like hell they were! You could hear the sighs of relief from Gallowgate to Edinburgh, saving everyone embarrassment!

So S&N paid up and for a while we were content and happy. One of the reasons we didn't go back was that we believed, or rather I believed, that God wanted us to do something for him. I felt a still small voice from within say:

"Don't worry I will look after you."

I had been off drink and drugs for almost six months by the time Christmas arrived. For the first time in years I really enjoyed spending Christmas with my family—and for the first time in years I spent it sober. I was also getting to know my children, I wasn't the foul-mouthed, arrogant ogre that I had once been.

Thanks to the Lord my children would grow up differently now. No longer was the house in a state of siege with everyone living on a knife edge, God was changing me and dealing with areas in my life. I could still become angry but it was nothing like the uncontrollable rage that had possessed me before. God was also dealing with the nightmares that I was having. I remember some nights clinging to my Bible, as demons would taunt me in my dreams. I didn't know it at the time but I had authority in Christ Jesus to rise up against this and put a stop to it. I would like to say to people that if you suffer from fear and are having nightmares, then take authority over your sleep and give it to the Lord to sort out, he will—try it.

Every night I would pray and read my Bible and as the months went by I felt stronger.

March came around, I had now been saved for eight months and I felt the Lord telling me to go to Church regularly. I began attending the Holy Family Church, which enraged Satan to the point that on the fourth week I went he promptly had it burned down! I was starting to believe that Satan was afraid of me going to church because of the testimony that I could give.

I was also feeling that I should be sharing my testimony with someone other than my wife and family, so I decided to go and see the new vicar at the church.

I really wasn't sure if he was ready to hear my story, but

Mike Laybourne's eyes nearly fell out of his head as I told him what had happened to me, one sunny Wednesday afternoon in the office of his house in Killingworth. I told him the full story, my background, my conversion, the lot. I explained that I was finding it difficult accepting my forgiveness and that I felt that God was reminding me of my past.

This proved to be incorrect, as Mike assured me that Jesus had forgiven me my sins one hundred percent, and the matter was now closed. I learned that when Jesus had hung on the cross for those six hours he had taken into himself the sin of every person who has ever lived and that he had paid the price for you and me. I learned that Satan had a claim to every single person who did not have Jesus as his or her Lord and Saviour. I realised that it was also a legal thing and that now I did not have to stand trial when I died for the things I had done. Jesus had actually stood in the dock and took the rap for me! It was awesome, now every thing that I had done or would do, had been forgiven! Case dismissed! Hallelujah, it was awesome. Praise the Lord!

> *"But God demonstrates his own Love towards us, in that while we were still sinners, Christ died for us."*
>
> Romans 5:8 NKJ

Armed with this new information I realised that my whole life could now be totally revolutionized. I also realised that there was far more to Christianity than the local church was teaching and that the answer was to get as close to Jesus as possible. It was Satan who was constantly reminding me of the wrongs of my past, not God! God had given me a fresh start and wanted to teach me his ways not keep me dwelling on the past.

The more I read about Jesus, the more my love and respect was growing for him, I had wrongly thought that Christianity was a sissy thing, I began to see the real Jesus emerging. As I read about the steps leading up to the crucifixion, I was horrified and ashamed to be human. I had seen and fought with some so-called 'hardmen' but let me assure you, Jesus Christ was the hardest, but most loving and caring person ever to grace this earth. Jesus was subjected to the most terrifying, vicious and cowardly attack that I have ever heard of. To summarise I have taken the 'highlights' from Isaiah 53 and also the four Gospels.

After Jesus' arrest he was:

* Whipped 39 times by a Roman scourge.
* A whole Garrison of soldiers, stripped him, mocked, spat on him and battered him beyond human recognition!. (Isaiah 53 says he was marred more than any man.)
* A crown of inch long spiky thorns was pushed into his head.
* forced to carry his own heavy cross for nearly a mile.
* had ten inch spikes driven through his hands and feet.
* left battered and bruised to die naked on a cross from suffocation of the lungs or a broken heart.
* then they pierced his side with a lance.

Isaiah 53 says 'He opened not his mouth but was led like a lamb to the slaughter.' I tell you, when I read about this, when I realised what Jesus suffered for me, it blew my mind, mighty and all-powerful King Jesus came down from Heaven to reconcile man to God the Father and rescue us from the devil's bondage and eternal damnation.

Jesus could quite easily have exercised his Godly powers as he did at the transfiguration and come down from the cross and destroyed the devil. But Jesus had to fulfil all the

300 or so scriptures that preceded his coming and he also knew that he had to suffer at the hands of men, God the Father required this. Jesus became far more than any hero to me, he had become my Lord, my Saviour, and my friend; he was a real Champion.

I felt responsible for the fire at the church and felt certain that Satan had sent someone to burn it down because I was going there. The church was out of action for a few months and we met in an old people's home while the restoration work was carried out. I phoned the vicar to see if I could help in any way. During this period I felt the Lord telling me to get baptised, so one day I approached the vicar about this.

"Were you christened as a baby?" Mike asked

"Yes, I was christened January first, nineteen sixty-seven" I answered—I had my certificate in my drawer at home.

"I'm sorry, I'm not allowed to baptise you," he said

"Why on earth not" I asked "The Bible says repent and be baptised?"

"The Anglican church believes in infant baptism, it's more than my job's worth to baptise you twice." I could not believe it, I felt sure the Lord had told me to be baptised and the Bible seemed pretty clear about it, but this was just one of a whole set of 'religious' rules and regulations that I would come across over the next few months. I realised that 'religion' was a tool created by the devil to keep believers in bondage!

I saw that what happened on Sunday morning was nothing to do with what I was reading about in the Bible or what I had experienced. I sensed that a lot of people were just going through the motions and that most of them were heavily in bondage. This was not the freedom and liberty that I had found in Jesus, there was very little joy at all in the regimented services. I became suspicious, as I could not feel the Lord's presence at many of the services. The people were nice enough; most of them had been there twenty odd years and seemed proud of it! But the fact was, there was no power, no anointing, nothing. I thought, "Lord, there's got to be more than this!"

There I was, having super spiritual out of body experiences and everything, and then this. A typical service was forty five minutes to an hour long, a couple of old hymns, the Rite A communion, which was belted through, word for word straight from the book, with little or no feeling. Even the prayers came out of the book, with no chance or time for the Lord to do anything at all. Then after a quick cuppa everyone would leg it off home till the following week's instalment! It was totally insane.

We moved into our newly refurbished church in September 1996, I was becoming increasingly despondent and began to see it in very critical terms. Nobody seemed interested in getting the gospel out at all, the fact that the country was going down the pan and that society was crying out for help seemed to have passed everyone by.

I enrolled for painting classes at night school, I loved my painting and was becoming quite good. I was not your typical art student—a twenty stone, ex-gangster with shaved hair, covered in tattoos! Most of the other students were retired professionals but I got on well with them, I think they saw me as a bit of an oddity! Goodness knows what the police, who still had me under surveillance, were thinking! I think they eventually realised that God really had changed me for the better. I painted two six feet by four foot paintings which hung in Holy Family Church till it was demolished in 2005.

My life had turned 180 degrees; I was appointed to the position of Church Warden and was also on the parish council! The whole thing was entirely laughable. 'Dear, oh dear, what would my old pals think of that; the

Marx brothers could not have wrote a funnier script!'! I thought.

Kath had gone from being a licensee to a Sunday school teacher! Her 'O'level in RE had finally come into use for something!

I continued to meditate on the things of God and found that I would be filled spiritually to a greater degree in my bedroom than I would in the church. I started to get a bit bored with church life and so I turned to God in prayer.

During Christmas 1996-97 the Holy Spirit told me to go to a place called the Sunderland Christian Centre, I didn't know where it was so I went to see the vicar.

"Do you know where the Sunderland Christian Centre is"? I asked.

"Oh there's been funny things going on there" he replied "How do you know about that place?" he asked looking perplexed.

"The Holy Spirit told me to go—will you take me?" I asked.

He stared at the wall for a moment considering my request, after a moment or so he said:

"Yes we'll go on Friday, I'll pick you up at six we need to get there early!"

"Great" I said as excitement rose in my stomach. "What next?" I thought!

20
Hannah's Promise

On a sunny Friday evening in February 1997, Mike the vicar and his wife June arrived at our home to take me to the service. The vicar enlightened me about the 'funny goings-on' at the Sunderland Christian Centre. As we drove to the centre he shared about people rolling on the floor, laughing uncontrollably and such like. So I didn't know quite what to expect but was excited at the prospect. The church was run by Pastors Ken and Lois Gott in Hendon; a dodgy, run down area of Sunderland. It was plagued by high unemployment and a high crime rate.

We arrived early in order to get a seat. 'The Renewal', as the vicar called it, had begun at the Sunderland church in 1994, with God pouring out his Holy Spirit in great measure after the Gott's had visited The Airport Church in Toronto, Canada and other areas of Renewal bringing a touch of the anointing back to Sunderland.

It was awesome, I had never seen anything like it, people queuing an hour before a church service! It was like going to a pop concert or something, the atmosphere was very highly charged.

As we pulled up at the door of the church I saw a face I recognised on the door of the church, his name was Jim, he was a club bouncer from Sunderland. I was puzzled at what he was doing working on the door of a church!

"Are they expecting trouble?" I asked the vicar.

"What?" he answered looking confused.

"They've got bouncers on the door" I said.

Jim looked totally puzzled at the sight of me coming up the path that led to the church, he looked a bit worried for a minute as he looked around to see who was with me.

"What you doing here?" I asked "Are you working here?"

"Err, no Davey, I'm a Christian" Jim said "I go to Church here."

"You what??" I exclaimed, surprised at Jim's revelation.

"Honestly Jim?" I continued.

"Yeah" he said

"What about him?" I asked pointing to another familiar face, also a bouncer.

"He's a Christian too!" Jim said.

"Honestly?" I said stunned, Jim laughed at the shock on my face.

"So, what're you doing here Davey?"

"I'm a Christian Jim," I answered a bit nervously.

Now he was totally shocked, I could see it on his face.

"Honestly?" he asked "Why, what happened?"

"I'd had enough Jim, I was going mad with all the drugs, I just had to get out, I was sick of all the violence, my head was in bits, what about you?"

"Same with me, I had enough and needed to get out of it, I've been coming here for ages now, I love it" he said "I go to sleep at night now."

"Yeah me too, see you later Jim," I said shaking his hand, amazed that he too had given his life to God.

As I went inside the building, which had recently been built, the first thing I noticed was the stage with drums and amplifiers. The building itself was nice and comfortable, more like a concert room in a club than a church, this as you can guess, was my first excursion into a Pentecostal church. The church soon filled up, there were about a thousand or so people in the place. The praise band came on stage and took us through a few vineyard numbers, which I really enjoyed. As I sang along, I became aware of an awesome presence filling the place. For the first time in a church, I really knew that God was there—I could feel him all over me. I began to feel light again like the day I had seen Jesus, it was happening again. Once again I was feeling the joy of the Lord washing through my whole body and spirit, I could hardly stand up the air was so thick with the presence of God.

I realised that this was what I had needed, a touch of the Glory of God. All around me people were passing out under the presence of God, I quickly realised that as I praised God, I filled up spiritually, it was better than cocaine or ecstacy tablets or whatever other drugs I'd had. Let me say this, there is nothing and I mean nothing, which can compare with the blessings of God, everything else fades into insignificance.

The main speaker that evening was a Greek Cypriot evangelist called J. John, a short stocky man in his early forties, he was very funny and I enjoyed what he had to say. J. John radiated a very powerful presence of God, he was very direct and easy to understand, but I was soon to get a shock! All of a sudden he stopped preaching and said:

"I've got a word here for someone."

Everyone held their breath.

"The Lord says you've been very foolish, setting your sights on the things of the world—Porsche's, money, nightclubs…"

"Oh no, he's talking about me" I nudged the vicar.

I just had to sit and take it, the Holy Ghost spotlight was on me.

"God will use you powerfully in this nation and others" he continued.

After John had finished his word the Lord spoke to me and said:

"Ask him to pray for you."

I joined the lines of people who were waiting for prayer after the service, I didn't know what to expect as I waited for him to get to me. People were falling down as he laid hands on them, then it was my turn:

"I baptise you with fire in the name of the Father, the Son and the Holy Spirit" and then whoosh I was gone as the fire of the Lord shot through me, once again I found myself in bliss. As I lay on the floor wave after wave engulfed me as I was baptised in the Holy Spirit (Acts 2, Acts 19) the experience can only be described as awesome. My whole body was on fire but the feeling was beautiful, I was literally being plugged in to God's Holy Spirit, this was the missing piece that I had been searching for all my life, from this moment on my Christianity changed forever. Things were to become powerful and dynamic as I was plugged into God—the power source, Jesus said; "I am the vine you are the branches." I now felt a part of the vine and felt complete; it was a beautiful moment!

As I lay basking in the Glory of the Lord, I saw a picture of my Gran on her knees praying for me—suddenly I realised that her prayers had contributed greatly to my salvation.

I realised that night in the Sunderland Christian Centre that I had found my vocation in life, and that things would never be the same again. As I watched J. John and the Gotts on stage I knew that one day I would be doing just that, I wanted everything like now! But I knew I had to learn God's ways.

I also wanted to see my Gran and let her know that I'd found Jesus, so I went to see my Dad who told me Gran, who was now aged 94, was in an old people's home and that she hadn't had a lucid conversation with any one for a long time.

"I'll take you but don't expect too much" he told me

So a week or so later he took me up to the home, Dye

House which was situated in the hills of Northumbria.

Gran recognised me straight away, she looked really old and frail, she gave me a lovely smile.

"Come on let's sit down," she said grasping my hand.

We sat talking for a while, and then I told her:

"Gran I've met Jesus and I'm going to church."

"What?" she said looking startled and surprised "Honestly?"

"Yes Gran I've been going to church regularly for some time now, my life's changed!"

There was a look of sheer joy and excitement on her face, tears started to fill her eyes

"Well Hallelujah, I'll give thanks to God in my prayers tonight!" she exclaimed excitedly her countenance became radiant.

"I've waited such a long time for this!" she said.

It was as though a cloud had lifted off her, all the years of praying for me had finally paid off, now she was rejoicing. For a while she sat holding my hand catching up on the news. She was still rejoicing as we left. The following Wednesday the priest from Gran's church, St John's, called to see her. He said all the time he was there Gran was just singing praises to God. A week or two later Gran went home to be with Jesus, it was as though the Lord had kept her hanging on there long after everyone else in the family had passed on, to see the fruit of her prayers. Hannah's job was over—mission accomplished.

I was devastated on hearing she had passed away but I knew she was with the Lord and that I will see her again in Glory.

I continued to go to Sunderland on the Friday nights, getting right into the Praise and Worship, when the ministry time began I was jumping over seats and running to get hands laid on me. I would spend hours on the church floor, totally out of it, I was drunk on the power of the

Holy Spirit just like the disciples on the day of Pentecost, it was absolute bliss.

It wasn't long before the vicar took me to the leaders days at the centre, these were awesome as well, and on one or two occasions I was knocked off my seat by invisible waves. On one of these days Ken Gott prayed for me and I shot up in the air about six feet, a bolt of power hit me straight in the stomach and it seemed that after that I was totally on fire! It was as if I had an inferno blazing away in my stomach.

When I wasn't at these meetings my time would be spent reading the Bible and praying. I bought some praise tapes and I learned to fill myself with the Holy Spirit at home by singing praises to God. I realised after reading Isaiah 61, that there is a spirit called Heaviness that attacks unsuspecting believers, leaving them feeling heavy and oppressed! The verse carries on to tell us how to deal with it, by singing praises to the Lord! The Bible says the Lord inhabits the praises of his people! I quickly realised that I could have the blessing of the Lord in my own home by singing along to praise and worship tapes. This was really refreshing and exciting, to know that I did not have to be in church to experience the presence and anointing of God.

I would like to encourage readers at this point, if you are experiencing heaviness or depression, to break out of the shell Satan is trying to put on you. I would encourage you to sing praises to God, no matter how bad your situation may seem at the moment, it will change; tests and trials come to us all, but it lasts only a season. The Apostle Paul tells us that these things are just passing away. I was really encouraged when I read about Paul and Silas in prison, when the chips were down they sang praises to God and 'Hey presto' the prison shook and the doors to the prison burst open. Paul knew that the key to the matter rested in the hands of the Lord and how he responded!

So many days I've felt a heaviness and oppression even before I've got out of bed, but I've put the praise tapes on and got into the glory of God. The decision is yours you can live in the darkness of depression or come over into the light and Glory of God, when you get full of light, darkness leaves, clouds of depression disappear—try it!

I continued to go to Sunderland every Friday night and felt that I was becoming stronger spiritually as well as mentally and emotionally. I was beginning to get a new sort of confidence again, I was finding that I was becoming stronger in the areas of temptation and was able to say no to things I'd struggled with in the past.

One area that I had problems with in the past was pornography. I had a large collection of video tapes filled with everything a perverted and twisted mind could come up with. I had the lot, except kiddie porn, which really infuriated me, but I had everything else. I knew that it was no longer right for me to watch this filth and binned the lot. Next the magazines went, each time I threw stuff out I felt a little more light come into the house.

One night my son John woke up crying, he was about two at the time, it was around 4.30am and still dark outside. Kath got out of bed to go and see to him and I decided to start praying. All of a sudden the whole bedroom lit up with the presence of the Holy Spirit!! It was an awesome experience; I was really blessed and was deep in prayer as Kath tiptoed back into the room. She noticed the light in the room and thought that I'd switched the light on, I can remember laughing as she fumbled about half asleep looking for the light switch!! Eventually she realised what was going on and crept out again!

21
The Promise of Transformation

As my faith continued to grow, I began to go to Charismatic Conferences, I really enjoyed this and had hands laid on me by many distinguished preachers. I spent many a happy hour on the floor totally drunk in the Holy Spirit, but I didn't feel as though I was sharing my faith enough or doing anything significant. At a leaders' day at Sunderland, one of the prophetic people stood up and gave a message from the Lord about how the Muslims were praying five times a day and the Christian church as a whole was doing very little, or nothing at all.

One day early in May I was watching Richard Attenborough's epic film 'Gandhi' and I was amazed by this little man's life. The film had a very humbling effect on me, I was impressed with his life of self-denial and it put me in mind of Jesus. I was impressed at the way Gandhi brought civil war to a stop by threatening to fast unto death. As the film continued I felt the Holy Spirit challenging me about prayer and fasting, he brought back to my memory the leaders day at Sunderland, which I had attended. At one point during the day it had been suggested that the local churches attempt a forty-day prayer and fast. I suddenly felt a witness in my spirit that this was what the Lord was calling me to do.

After several discussions with members of the Holy Family Church it was agreed that we would all participate in this and would work out a rota. I was prepared to do the thing by myself but people were enthused so it was decided that I would do the majority of the night shifts, normally 9pm till 8 am and I would fast. So on the eighth of May 1997 at eight o'clock, I began my first shift, which was fifteen hours long. During these nights it gave me a lot of time to reflect on my past and to look to the future. I was lucky to have a future and a fresh start, so many of my friends had not had that opportunity. I reflected on some of the people I had known who had had their years cut short by tragedy. Many had died through their drug taking habits, either by taking overdoses or suicide.

I knew that Satan was behind the drug scene, and how he delights in enslaving the unsuspecting youth through curiosity. Doctors babble on about the side effects of drugs, totally unaware that the real damage is being done spiritually. Satan is playing for keeps, the real truth is if you take illegal substances into yourself over a long period of time then demonisation will take place.

Don't do it, why open yourself up to demonic attack? There is such a thing as a 'demon of addictions' he will quickly move into your life if you flirt with drugs often enough. After a few years of taking drugs you will begin to hear voices, you will become short tempered, your scruples will go out of the window—anything goes. Blackouts will start along with memory loss, and suddenly a whole host of different illnesses appear. This is all part of the devil's wearing down process, his time is short and he wants to make sure that yours is too. I shudder when I think of how violent I was whilst under the influence of Satan. Some of my friends could not handle the voices and committed suicide.

I prayed and prayed that God would intervene in this problem; I prayed many prayers for people who I knew were under the devil's influence. Altogether on the prayer watch I spent thirty-five nights in prayer, it was great to spend so much time in the Lord's presence. Although at times it seemed as though I was passing through a wilderness or a desert, I was like a pilgrim on a journey travelling through the 'Wilderness of Prayer'. I knew many great saints and apostles had travelled this path of concentrated prayer and during this time I saw the answers to many prayers, including cancer healings! Each night was different, some nights I would spend hours praising and dancing around the empty church. Every night would be different; some nights would be spent totally in prayer with worship on the hour, other times there would be great tears of repentance, then travailing prayers, other nights would be meditating on the word.

I learned to pray in the Spirit, as the apostle Paul had when he talked of a man being caught up into the third heaven. Not to be confused with praying in tongues, praying in the spirit is at a much deeper level and is so powerful. I was blessed with the gift of tongues at a later date, but this was something different altogether.

During these nights I learned of the power of praise and worship, you can have access to the Lord's presence through praise and worship.

One morning I watched the sun come up with the Lord—it was as though he had cloaked me in his love. I could feel his arms around me it was one of the best moments of my life; he told me:

"Son I will transform this region and this nation!"

He asked me to pray and intercede for the different housing estates in Newcastle and the North East in general, at that moment I knew God was going to change this nation.

The prayer watch was very tiring but it was also very educational, as I have already said, each night was different and some nights were full of revelation.

Night after night I'd learn something new, at times it was a hard slog but definitely worth it and all the time I was getting closer to Jesus. It was great—prayers were being answered by the sack full and for the first time the Lord used me in the healing ministry as people were healed of things ranging from arthritis to bowel cancer. I was just beginning to learn of the awesome power available to us in Christ Jesus. At the end of the watch I had completed 35 nights and felt totally blessed by it.

Around this time the Lord put Kath and myself under conviction about our marital status and the fact was we were living in sin. We had practically no money at this time but the Lord came to the rescue once again. People began to phone from all over suggesting different ways in which they could help; it was amazing. Kath was given a lovely wedding dress and veil, someone else provided bridesmaids dresses, someone else the photos, the car, the reception was paid for, the vicar refused money for the service and borrowed the cathedral organist who also refused payment—the list was endless, it went on and on.

So on June 21st 1997 we were married at the Church of the Holy Family, Killingworth. It was a wonderful day! I was very nervous before the ceremony, for some reason the thought of my wedding service was something that had terrified me since childhood, and on the video we had taken, my face was priceless as I sat, with my brother Steve as my best man, waiting for Kath. As Kath arrived and the organ started up I remember thinking

"Right boy this is it, over the top" as though I was in the Somme or something! Luckily the Lord came and blessed me half way through the service and put my nerves at rest. We had a lovely service and reception and then had a party back at our house that went on till all hours.

22
My Discipleship Begins

Not long after my wedding, the Lord brought two men into my life who were to help change the course of it and really encourage me in the things of God. For a while I had been feeling that most of the people around me were either playing religious games with one another or they were quite happy to have their ears tickled with watered down gospel. I was becoming despondent, as I really wanted to serve the Lord and share my faith and testimony with people. I realised that thousands of people were dying every day and were going to Hell because they had failed to accept Jesus as their saviour and I felt as though I was doing nothing to prevent it. Here I was with a brilliant testimony, having seen the Glory of God, the full package, yet was doing nothing or very little with it.

I began to pray and asked the Lord to join me with like-minded people and it wasn't too long before he responded to this.

He said to me: "Davey, I have a lot of followers and a lot of believers, but I don't have many disciples."

I replied: "Lord, I want to be a disciple."

Then one night in June 1997, the Lord encouraged me to go to an all-night prayer meeting at Bethshan church in the West End of the city, the Church pioneered by Herbert Harrison, Lois Gott's father. The meeting was being led by Mahesh Chavda, from the USA, a man moving powerfully in the Holy Spirit, a man who'd prayed and had the dead raised! I remember him praying for me, it was so powerful. I felt a real spiritual impartation and I hit the ground like a sack of potatoes!

After I got up from the floor, the Holy Spirit drew to

my attention to a man sitting directly in front of me. He looked to be in his thirties, clean-shaven, a bit shorter than me and of average build. The man seemed well into the worship, he was dressed casually in jeans and a t-shirt and I noticed a Newcastle United tattoo on his upper arm. His name was Dougie March and he was a street evangelist who preached mainly at Grey's Monument in Newcastle city centre.

Dougie was notorious in the city, a former speed (amphetamine) freak and football hooligan who had been converted to Christianity in 1986. Some people had told me about Dougie and that it would be good for me to meet him. The Holy Spirit said to me:

"Davey, go and introduce yourself to Dougie," I felt a bit reluctant not knowing what to say.

"Go on" the Holy Spirit urged me.

So eventually I went and introduced myself to Dougie and found him very open and receptive. I chatted to him and shared a bit of my testimony with him, arranged to meet him on another day and gave him my phone number.

A few days later I received a call from him and arranged to meet him in the city centre. Dougie was already at the monument when I got there, he finished his preach and we went for a cup of tea at a nearby cafe.

Dougie told me about his life. At that time he attended City Church in Newcastle, he was single, forty years old and lived in the Byker Wall. In the eleven or so years he had been a Christian he had attended a number of churches including Heaton Baptist Church who recognised the call on his life and promptly sent him off to the renowned C H Spurgeon's Bible college to train as a minister. Dougie, reserve speaker for the college, found that he was spending more and more time preaching on the streets and felt that this was where his calling was, as a street Evangelist. The college agreed and released him.

On returning to Tyneside, Dougie and his friend Paul Fenwick totally disillusioned with the 'religious system and rigmarole,' felt they were being called to start a new work. They left Heaton Baptist and started the Byker City Fellowship where they concentrated on street evangelism. After a few years of discipling a number of people, he grew tired of leadership and felt he had to sit at the feet of other more mature leaders to develop further, so he moved to another church—City Church, part of the New Frontiers group.

As I got to know Dougie over the next few months, I found a true friend. What you see is what you get, no hidden agendas. I saw that he was full of the Holy Spirit and moving powerfully in the 'Gifts' of the Spirit. He lived totally for Jesus and led a very simple and uncomplicated existence. He lived by faith and would never compromise on his faith or values—a man to be trusted (when world champion triple jumper Jonathan Edwards was seeking the Lord about whether he should jump on Sundays, one of the people he sought for advice was Dougie.)

At first going preaching on the streets of Newcastle terrified me, and for the first couple of weeks I just handed out testimony tracts while Dougie was preaching. I would often lurk around the doorways of the shops surrounding the monument, standing a good distance from Dougie. I was terrified that someone would recognise me, after all the monument is directly around the corner from where we ran the Blackett public house, what would people think!

After a few weeks I decided that this was no way for me to be carrying on and after much soul-searching I got up and preached which broke the fear stronghold in my mind. I could not have cared what anyone thought; there I was up there for the entire world to see! I felt the Holy Spirit bless me as I preached, Satan had thrown fear at me but I had overcome, never again would I be afraid to speak out my faith or testimony.

It started as a trickle, first sharing testimony at Holy Family, then again one night at City Church. Dougie began to disciple me, he gave me books and tapes to encourage me and build up my faith. I began to live the reality of real Christianity, I was completely fed up with wishy-washy religion and watered down Gospel; with Dougie I was being taught how to move in the Power of the Spirit it was exciting and dynamic, the way Jesus had meant it to be, I was literally finding life.

Around this time the Lord brought someone else into my life, it was the former parish priest, Canon David Wood. David was in his seventies, a much revered and respected man, he was well known, a very Godly man and at times a bit of an eccentric. He was a big man well over six feet and weighed at least twenty stone. He was a living legend up here; his home was open to all and sundry. He kept animals in his home as well as a constant stream of ex-drunks and addicts. He had an enormous heart to go with his enormous frame and his generosity knew no bounds.

Whilst David had been the parish priest, his parishioners would wait to see him at the bus stop. David would do his rounds on his horse and cart! He would stop at the bus stop, someone would get on, and he would listen to their problems as he trotted along the road, then they would jump off at the next stop and someone else would jump on! It was a common sight to see a pig or a calf in the back seat of David's battered old Volvo as he flew past!

'Woody' was a real character who oozed the presence of God, I loved the man dearly even though I only knew him for a short time, a year or so before he died. He was always in trouble with the hierarchy of the Anglican Church, being seen as a bit of a mischievous schoolboy because he spoke his mind. Though a loyal Anglican priest to the end,

Woody felt the Anglican church was totally inadequate in every aspect of its worship of Jesus Christ and that it did little or nothing about the country's social problems.

Another of David's qualities was that for over forty years he had been involved in the deliverance ministry, the casting out of demons, first at St Anne's in Wolverhampton then at Holy Family. David left Killingworth in 1989 after more than twenty years, to move to the less demanding parish of Mitford. None of his replacements quite measured up to the extraordinary David who was loved and respected by all in Killingworth. This proved to be a problem after he left because people would still go to him, the new vicars were passed by and a kind of jealousy arose, as David would come back and sort their problems out. The Bishop intervened and asked David to stay out of Killingworth! So David would visit me under the cover of darkness! People had told him about me, how I was on fire for Jesus and how people were being healed when I prayed. Curiosity got the better of him and I met him during the prayer watch, as he sneaked in and out of the church after midnight! We hit it off immediately, and I felt a real closeness with him. He shared his wealth of experience with me, especially in the area of deliverance and at times he ministered to me. He was like an excited, overgrown schoolboy and he would phone me daily to hear what had been going on.

Life was becoming an adventure as these two men of God poured their lives into me. No longer was I bothered about who saw me preach and I began to enjoy it as I realised that I had truly found my vocation in life. As I shared my story with the down and outs and drug addicts on the streets, I felt a real love for them. I knew many of them to be hopeless cases, but every so often one them would find the Lord. I realised also that the Lord was equipping me as I went and as I needed.

I was to become a lot more confident in my praying. One day Cindy, a lady from Holy Family, asked me to pray for her hand that had been crippled with arthritis. In the name of Jesus, I commanded the arthritis to go and it did—it was amazing. Then a lady called Irene received her sight after a brain operation had left her blind in one eye. All the while Dougie and David were teaching me the power in the Word and how to tap into it, which people like Smith Wigglesworth had known and understood. The Bible is called the living word and it is important to know what it says, but this must also be lived out, Christianity is for participators not spectators. As I mentioned earlier, the more bad habits and things I gave up, the more blessings the Lord gave me. I was hungry for more, I was never satisfied and was always pushing into God for more; I learned that this was what God wanted. I felt the Lord calling me into a season of prayer, so every Friday night I would do an all night prayer watch, I became a watchman.

> *'I have posted watchmen on your walls o*
> *Jerusalem*
> *they will never be silent day or night*
> *You who call on the Lord give yourselves no rest*
> *and give him no rest*
> *till he establishes Jerusalem*
> *and makes her the praise of the earth.'*
>
> Isaiah 62 v6-8 (NIV)

Some people thought I was mad staying up praying all night in an empty church, at times I did wonder myself, but then at other times the Lord would bless me for the sacrifice of sleep. I also used the time to get closer to the Lord and hear what he was saying into my life. I would pray and intercede for many problems and on occasions

I would be dancing all night in the empty church, full of the Holy Spirit.

I found it difficult to understand why members of the church didn't want to become involved in the all-night prayer sessions, but the fact was that although they professed to love Jesus, their hearts were far from him and it was always the same handful of people who would become involved.

In summer 1997 we went down to the Lake District for the Bible week at the Keswick convention, along with several other families from Holy Family church and nearby St Johns. We stayed on the campsite at Crossthwaite in a tent borrowed from Kath's parents, Ivy and John. It was our first family holiday since we had visited the Bahamas and we really needed it. The Lord had encouraged us to go and I asked:

"What for?"

"Rest" the answer came back.

The kids loved it in the tent, it was a real adventure for them and Keswick is a lovely place, well worth a visit. The sun shone all week and I went snorkelling in the lakes in between taking in the sessions at the convention centre. I felt really challenged during my time in Keswick and felt that I should make my own testimony tract.

So on returning from Keswick with the help of Mike the local vicar I wrote my first testimony tract, the now infamous "Gangland to Christ" tract, which the Lord has used all over the world to bring people to him. I would really encourage Christians to make your own personal testimony tracts if you don't already have one, your story is so important and a tract may help save lives without you being there. Did you know that world evangelist Billy Graham's mother was saved by a personal testimony tract and look what has been achieved through that. You never know whom you will give a tract to, so be encouraged!

Thousands of my tracts have gone out all over the world now and I have prayed that the Holy Spirit will use each and every one of them. I have heard amazing stories of people giving their lives to the Lord after reading them. Another area in which Dougie March really encouraged me was to make a personal testimony on audio tape, again these were mass reproduced and given away free of charge. Once again these are really effective tools of evangelism and we now encourage all new converts to make a tract and a tape.

Sometime in November 1997, I felt the Lord urging me to register for a conference to be held in the Oakwood Centre in Stockton. The conference was to be organised by Revival Now, and the main speaker was Lindell Cooley, the Worship leader from a church in Pensacola, Florida. The Lord urged me to register for this conference and told me to expect something to happen, that his servants were bringing a gift for me. So Dougie and I registered for the conference and I felt quite excited about what the Lord had told me. There were a few members of the Byker Fellowship living in Yarm next to the venue and Dougie arranged for us to stay with them.

A couple of days before the conference tragedy struck, when my friend David Wood was taken from us. I was devastated. Even though I'd only known him for a short while, I had a really good relationship with him. Two days before his death he had been at our house praying for me and we had talked about the possibility of his return to Killingworth—it wasn't to be. I felt as though I'd had the rug pulled from under my feet. I had learned a lot from him in a short period of time and would genuinely miss his visits and daily phone calls. David was a big man with an even bigger heart, eccentric at times, but a man with utter devotion, he was absolutely selfless—a very, very rare commodity. David Wood was a gift to the body of

Christ, he had a Father's heart for all and was loved and respected far and wide, I miss him dearly.

On the day of David's death I was booked to appear on the BBC's 'Thank God it's Thursday' radio programme, a religious affairs programme where various topics are debated by a team of panellists who represent different faiths and beliefs. I was choked with tears and was ready to cancel but I felt the Lord urging me to go on, so during the day many people came and prayed with me to give me strength. I arrived at the BBC studios in Barrack Road at quarter to seven and was met by Peter Cordell, the presenter of the show, who introduced me to the other members of the panel, which included a Methodist, an atheist, and a member of the unification church (Moonies). Then the unthinkable happened! The Holy Spirit filled me with a spirit of joy and laughter just as the show was about to go out live. I could not stop laughing as Trevor the 'Moonie' tried sharing about his faith. The poor man must have thought I was laughing at him, but the programme became so bizarre that everyone started laughing at what he was saying; it was a real gem of a show. Once again I was shown how the Lord could change circumstances in an instant, my day had turned from sadness into joy.

'Blessed are they that mourn for they shall be comforted.'

(Matthew 5:4) NKJ

The following day Dougie and myself drove down to Stockton and booked in at the conference, David's death had only enthused me further to push deeper into the things of God. I felt the Lord telling me to leave Holy Family and drawing me to Longbenton Community Church, which had recently been taken over by Ken Gott's 'Revival Now' outfit, and was being led by the very energetic and charismatic Peter Wreford, who is also the editor of 'Joy' magazine.

The conference was very good, the worship led by Lindell Cooley was fantastic, but I was still curious to see what the Lord was going to bestow on me. I had fasted for three days before the conference in preparation and I was hungry. Every time there was an altar call or an opportunity for prayer then I was first one out in the hope of receiving whatever it was the Lord had for me. At the time I was still smoking, and I remember going outside into the car park for a smoke, but when I got out there the presence of God was so strong that I was almost on my knees unable to taste the cigarette.

So the conference came and went and I was still no further forward. It wasn't till I was driving up the motorway and I burst into 'tongues' for the first time that I realised what the Lord had done! Amen. I was over the moon, the gift of tongues is very precious to me and I thank God that I have it. I believe the devil discourages the use of tongues in the organised church because it is so powerful and also because he has no idea what it is that our spirits are asking of God.

On returning home I felt that the Lord was asking me to make the move to Longbenton. I handed in the keys to the church and resigned as churchwarden, I also gave up my place on the parish council. I felt sad to be leaving Holy Family, I had spent so many hours alone in there, praying for a breakthrough. During 1997 I had completed fifty-five all-night prayer sessions, praying and fasting for the church, the region and the nation. They had been times of great joy, it was a worthwhile sacrifice, getting to spend all that time in the presence of the Lord and I believe not a minute was wasted.

I started to attend Longbenton Community Church in January 1998. The church is situated on an estate plagued with high unemployment and many other social problems so typical of nineties North Britain. The church was situated between high rise tower blocks and poor quality maisonettes (subsequently pulled down in 2002) the main focus of local attention are the various pubs scattered across the estate, drug taking is rife with children as young as nine and ten taking one illegal substance or another. The kids seem to wander about looking for mischief; their prospects are bleak indeed, as most of the people exist on government handouts.

I had not been attending long when we were informed, that a new pastor would be taking over, it was quite a surprise to discover that it was Alan Finlay, my old maths teacher from West Denton High School! Coincidence or God-incidence?

It had been more than seventeen years since I left school and he hadn't changed much. I didn't think he recognised me at first and I was definitely not the same person I had been, but we soon got on okay as I began to fit in with Longbenton. Kath followed me a few weeks later after she had handed over her Sunday school responsibilities and she began to enjoy the informal Sunday morning gatherings.

We loved it at Longbenton, the worship was less formal than at Holy Family and the people were nice, but more importantly we could feel the Lord's blessing on the meetings. I continued to help out with the lunch club at Holy Family, doing dishes and praying for the pensioners but my heart for the lost was increasing to the point where it was on my mind twenty four hours a day. I was becoming less tolerant of people who professed to love Jesus yet were doing nothing to help the lost.

My speaking engagements were beginning to increase as I shared my testimony at different venues. At the end of January I had a couple of days sharing testimony behind the walls of top security Frankland prison. As I drove in to the place I could hardly believe that it was happening, it was amazing. Here I was, ex-villain, born again Christian, preaching to the cons—only God could have organised it!

It felt really strange to be going in as a civilian. As Dougie, the Chaplain and myself made our way through the prison yard and snow began to fall, a million thoughts were going through my mind like, 'Who would I see?' 'Would the lads think I'd lost the plot?' the devil began attacking my mind with negative thoughts. Jesus could set them free from drink, drugs, violence, fear, anxiety, stress, nightmares, addictions and give them a new lease of life, a fresh start, all their sins washed away and accounted for; the devil did not want the lads to hear the 'Good News'!

The Bible says that when you personally invite Jesus to be Lord of your life, your sins are totally forgiven; he has already paid the price for them at Calvary. We had some great meetings and the lads were blessed by our visit, I had a wonderful time witnessing, most of them knew who I was and knew that they could trust me. They found it easy to relate to me as I was one of their own and they really grilled us, I was amazed at some of the questions. Some of the men I spoke to are never going to get out and they are desperate for answers. They need to know more than most that they can be forgiven, that Jesus truly loves them and wants to know them. They need to know that he is real—someone has to tell them there is light at the end of the tunnel.

I suppose it was inevitable that the newspapers would eventually find out that I'd become a Christian, this is the price of notoriety and I was notorious.

Someone tipped off the Evening Chronicle and the media in general, then the fun began, I know now how a fox feels when it's being chased.

'Meet The Godfather' the front-page headlines rang out, there it was for the entire world to see, my face plastered all over the front page. Inside they had pictures of me and other members of the 'firm'.

I was described as a 'Gangster' and a 'Hoodlum.' The newspaper went on to tell how my partners and I had ruled over the drug scene in the North by terror. It talked a bit about the 'Drug Wars' and the gunning down of my pal, Viv Graham.

I wasn't exactly thrilled at all the media attention and personally, I wanted to hide under the stairs till it was all over, but then I realised the evangelical implications of it all, it was actually better than handing out tracts. The 'Chronicle' has a readership of hundreds of thousands, so it would be hitting home all over the place. The BBC radio news team were also chasing me about for an interview and then Peter Wreford of 'Joy' magazine phoned up. Peter asked if I'd pop over to see him about an article he was doing for 'New Life' as well as 'Joy' and so it went on. I began to get a lot of media coverage. The important thing to me was that people were coming to the Lord through my story. It was amazing; every now and then a story would filter back to me about people being saved.

I began to realise how God could use my notoriety and put all my bad experiences to good use. By building up my bad reputation and putting loads of years into me, the devil had once again shot himself in the foot. He had tried to destroy me in every way you could possibly imagine: I've been shot at, stabbed, bottled, glassed, hit with axes and iron bars. I've been in car crashes where the cars were smashed to pieces, only to emerge without a scratch, I've overdosed on enough drugs to kill an elephant only to get up and walk away, I was caught in the middle of the worst hurricane in history and I nearly died from heat and exhaustion in the middle of the Sinai desert and rocket attacks in Tiberias, Israel. In the hundreds of gang fights and bar fights I was involved in I never once got a broken bone—why? The answer is that God protected me. He was my shield, just as he had promised me as a ten year old boy, even through all my sinning he was there and never left my side. Now I felt very small indeed and very humble, embarrassed to know that in my worst sinning the Lord had been there. I felt the Lord say:

"Many times I stood at the door of your life waiting to be invited in, I was jealous for your attention."

23

Baptised and Led into the Desert

Peter replied "Repent and be baptised everyone
of you, in the name of Jesus Christ for the
forgiveness of your sins."

Acts 2:38 (NIV)

I was baptised by full immersion at Somervyl Chapel, Longbenton on 19th of April 1998 along with Kath and my then thirteen-year-old daughter, Kelly. I had been saved for nearly three years. The Lord had urged me to get baptised even though I'd been christened as an infant.

The Bible tells us to repent and be baptised, some people believe that infant baptism is enough—it is not.

The Bible is very clear about this, although our parents may have us 'Christened' or 'Dedicated' we still have to make that choice as individuals at a later stage of our life. The Bible says that all have sinned and fallen short. I believe we are protected as children but at some stage there comes the age of accountability and then we need to have our sins forgiven.

The people in the church gave a rousing cheer as I came up out of the waters, I felt totally clean inside, it was an awesome experience, a real spiritual shower! The old self had been left in the waters and the new self had arisen, I felt as clean and shiny as a new pin!

I felt as though I had achieved something, it was a final two-fingered salute to the powers of darkness that had controlled my life for many years, a real severing of the umbilical chord. I was happy that my Dad and the family were there to see it.

After the baptism service we went for dinner at the home of Ian and Helen Longfield, two of the leadership team from the church.The Longfields were and still are an inspiration to us, they have been a source of strength and encouragement, we love them dearly.

After a time of fellowship with this godly couple, I drove down to Manchester with Dougie March and our friend Paul Boyer from North Shields. Paul was another like Dougie and myself who had escaped the world of crime and drugs, sadly he went home to be with the Lord after a tragic accident in 2002.

The next morning we took a bus to Manchester airport and the three of us flew out to Israel.We arrived at Ovda airport five hours later and took a bus down to the southern resort of Eilat, where we checked in to the Youth Hostel. I was knackered and needed the rest.The following day we hit the beach it was great to be on a beach in a hot climate again. I was constantly in and out of the water with my mask and snorkel, some of the best snorkelling in the world can be found off the reefs in Eilat with many different species of fish. I found that Eilat was a typical holiday resort, there isn't much in the way of biblical sites or anything and really we could have been anywhere in Europe. I suppose it was not what I was expecting with its modern malls and McDonald's etc!

We stayed in Eilat for a few days then ventured over the border into Egypt at Taba. Crossing the border was like going into a different world, the first change I noticed was the spiritual climate, you realise that God really has his hand on Israel whereas over the border it's different.

Our destination was Mount Sinai in the Sinai desert, where it is alleged Moses received the "Ten Commandments", though the Bible states that Mount Sinai is in Arabia not Egypt, and that Jabael-el Laws in Saudi Arabia is probably the real mountain.

So after passing through the border checkpoint we found a bus that would take us part of the way, to a place called Nuweiba.

Nuweiba is actually the place where God parted the seas allowing the children of Israel to cross and escape Pharaoh's army. There is a huge sand bridge under the sea at Nuweiba, it stretches a few miles from Nuweiba over to Arabia, it is incredible! The under sea sand bridge can be found on British Admiralty maps, there is a five thousand foot drop on either side of this.

Also the beach at Nuweiba is massive, well able to hold the two million or so Israelites that were escaping Pharoah's chariots, also mountains surround the place cutting off any escape route, which, is in line with the biblical description. There was nowhere for them to run as pharoah's pursuing army advanced upon them, they had no option but to go through the sea and I believe that as God stirred up the waters, congealing them, then this was what formed the huge sand bridge and allowed them to escape. An archaeological diving team led by American Ron Wyatt found some wonderfully preserved chariot wheels in the nineteen eighties on the underwater sand bridge, the remains of Pharoah's chasing army which only goes to prove the truth of the Bible and possibly the validity of the site.

The Sinai Desert is very beautiful, the scenery breathtaking, but it is also very hot, the heat there can be a killer, the temperature rises to over forty plus.

I thought that Dougie had a touch of sunstroke when he suggested that we hitchhike down to the mountain! The Sinai desert is not exactly a busy place and is hardly bustling with a steady stream of available transport. I was starting to think that Dougie had lost the plot when suddenly a taxi pulled up out of nowhere! It was a battered dusty old 7 seat Peugeot, but was a real sight for sore eyes!

After a bit of bartering and amicable negotiation with the driver we set off on our merry way.

A couple of hours later we arrived at our destination, the driver dropping us at St Katherine's monastery which is situated at the foot of Mount Sinai.

I am not the fittest person on earth and to be honest the thought of climbing a 7500ft mountain in 110 degrees of heat filled me with terror. I weighed twenty stone at the time and was sweating like a pig as we approached the bottom of the mountain. Dougie and Paul, both keen hill walkers, were relishing the challenge. I had been sunburnt on the legs pretty badly the day before and was hobbling along feeling quite despondent.

Then Dougie came up with the perfect solution to my problem—a camel! He came round the corner of the monastery with a big smile on his face, he had with him a Bedouin boy of about fourteen and the skinniest looking camel that I'd ever seen, the animal looked at me and snorted. The prospect of carrying all twenty stone of me up the mountain obviously did not appeal to the camel. What a racket it made as I got on it, everyone burst into fits of laughter, "Davey of Arabia" was definitely a sight to be seen and not forgotten.

It is a very strange feeling being on a camel, it is not one I am anxious to repeat. It was a frightening experience going up the side of a mountain on a camel; I was in tears as the camel burst into a run going up the 'Steps of Repentance'.

At three thousand feet the inevitable happened! The camel decided that it had had enough and it sat down unable to carry on any further. I was hanging over the edge of the cliff as the silly animal went to sit down and nearly had a cardiac arrest! I was shaking in terror as I jumped off it. It totally refused to go any further and that was that!

I grabbed my Rucksack and climbed the rest of the way on foot, on a number of occasions I fell flat on my face; the heat was exhausting me. The climb in the hot midday sun was proving too much for me, I wondered if I was going to make it, thoughts of home flooded into my mind, would I ever see my wife and kids again? I started to reflect on my life, at times I had been so unreasonable, I wished that I'd been a better husband and father. So now on the 'Steps of Repentance' I realised how much I loved and missed my wife and children. I began to repent of my unreasonableness promising the Lord that I would try harder on the home front. So often, especially in Christian Ministry, we get so caught up in other people's problems that if we are not careful our own families can feel neglected and suffer because of this. I constantly have to remind myself that the home is my first mission field.

Sweat poured off me and my legs ached as I struggled on up the mountain, every so often I would walk round a corner and bump into a kiosk that sold Coke it was quite bizarre, a welcome sight but not what I was expecting. I was about forty feet off the top when I bumped into Dougie and Paul, we decided not to follow our plan of sleeping on top of the mountain and decided to head back down.

By now I was exhausted and did not fancy going all the way back down, my legs were starting to stiffen up, I was not in good shape. Paul and Dougie raced off, I quickly dropped behind taking it easy as I went. As I slowly climbed down I became aware that I was being watched, every now and then I would stop and rest taking in the magnificent view of the Sinai desert which was incredibly beautiful you could see for miles, but every time I stopped I would glance back and I could see a head ducking down behind a rock. As the descent continued I became intrigued and wondered if it was a bedouin. Tiredness was catching up with me and a few hundred feet off the bottom I could go no further. I collapsed over a rock, absolutely finished, my eyes shut and stayed shut for a while.

Then I became aware of someone standing over me, lazily I opened my eyes to see who it was. A man of about forty was standing over me, he was dressed in a long green gown and had a little black hat like the ones that Greek Orthodox Priests wear on his head. The man was smiling his eyes were piercing but had a warm shiny glow about them, in fact there was a radiance about him. I suddenly thought 'I recognise that face', perhaps I was delirious, but this man looked very much like Jesus, then he spoke to me in clear English,

"Are you all right?" He asked with a look of concern.

"I think so," I gasped.

"You'll be all right" the man said "You've got two hours to get off the mountain" he added.

"Two hours?" I repeated perplexed at the man's statement.

'Why two hours?' I asked myself, 'would it get dark or something?' I wondered why the man had said this.

Then he smiled again and said "You'll be all right". And with that he was off.

Absolutely amazed I stood up and watched him skip away off down the rocks, at the bottom I could see Dougie and Paul waiting for me.

Renewed by this latest incident I started to follow after him, "Was it the Lord?" It certainly looked like him, "Was I hallucinating?"

Whoever it was, the incident gave me a new lease of life, as I had been totally finished. I staggered my way down the slope, at the bottom Dougie and Paul were waiting. A bedouin approached me to sell me something but I was not in the mood and shooed him away. I asked Dougie if he had seen the man come down the mountain but predictably both Dougie and Paul saw no one!

We then had the problem of what to do for the night as it started to get dark and we had no accommodation. Then miracle number one—out of nowhere this minibus appeared and the driver offered to take us to a nearby town where he knew of a small hotel. The man dropped us at the hotel, where (another miracle), we just caught the manager leaving to go home for the night. He booked us in and made us some supper, two hours after the meeting with the man on the mountain! Hallelujah, Praise the Lord!!

In our rooms were three beds that reminded me of the beds in 'Goldilocks and the three bears' but they were ever so comfortable. I gratefully slept like a log.

The near death experience on the mountain had broken me in many ways and I decided that I would go back to Israel. However, my legs were seized up and I couldn't walk for a couple of days.

Once I was up and about we decided to leave, however we missed the only bus to the Israeli border; by this time I was on a short fuse and at times the air was blue. We eventually got a taxi the 220 km to the border. I was relieved to get back to Israel and breathed a huge sigh of relief as we passed through the Taba crossing.

The holiday in Israel was the first time I'd been away from Kath and the kids and I had missed them all the time I was away. I was amazed at how the Lord had changed me from a snarling psycho to a family man who loved and missed his children, the lesson had been learned on that mountain when I thought I was not coming home, only then was it really driven home to me how much I loved my family and how lucky I was to have them.

I thank Jesus for every time that he has broken me; it's only when you're in that place that God can really work with you. The old mould has to be broken, and then the potter remoulds the clay.

On returning from Israel the Lord increased my Evangelistic activities giving me speaking engagements all over the place. Once again I went in to Prison, this time Holme House, Stockton. I had a great afternoon sharing with the lads and it was well received, once again they could relate to me because of my past, I even got to pray over one or two. By now I was becoming more confident in leading people to the Lord, I was also getting used to speaking and giving testimony. The crowds got bigger as my apprenticeship continued, then came a big break.

Youth for Christ, a Christian organisation, phoned me and asked if I'd speak at a youth event at Newcastle City Hall, I jumped at the chance.

I prayed and prayed leading up to the event asking the Lord what to say, I knew that this was a great opportunity to reach many youngsters and warn them of the perils of drugs and crime.

I felt the Lord telling me to challenge them about spreading the gospel and that he wanted to equip them spiritually. So on 31st May, Pentecost, I stood on stage at Newcastle City Hall addressing a crowd of over a thousand youngsters. The anointing on me was awesome; it was so thick it was a real apostolic anointing. The presence of God that was in the place when I was speaking was totally overwhelming.

Unfortunately I was limited to giving testimony otherwise we may well have had a revival on our hands. Over forty youngsters gave their lives to the Lord that night, and also many others after I threw out a challenge for the kids to pray for their local villains. The evening was a tremendous success and the Lord had really blessed everyone.

24
A Miracle in Manchester

"I shall not die but live and declare the works
of the Lord, The Lord has chastened me, but not
given me over to death."

Psalm 118 v 17&18

Amazing things were happening around me, a couple of days prior to the city hall event, I had been standing in the intensive care unit of Whittingham hospital in Manchester praying over a man who the medical profession had given up for dead. A neighbour of ours had an uncle who had been taken into hospital. Sue, the man's niece, came and asked me to pray for him as his medical condition was deteriorating and the hospital did not expect him to survive the night. Apparently he was on a kidney dialysis machine, his lungs had packed up and he was being fed oxygen. The main artery to his heart had also collapsed, things were looking grim and the hospital called in his family telling them to expect the worst!

That night I prayed for the man, whose name is Eric, and he made it through the night. The following day Sue's husband, Rob, came to the door and said to me "Davey, the Lord has said something to me, but I am not going to tell you what it is, so would you pray and ask the Lord to confirm it." So I prayed and the Lord said to me:

"Davey I want you to go to Manchester and lay hands on this man."

I relayed this to Rob who smiled and confirmed that this was what God had said to him.

We all piled into Rob's van and took off down the A1 motorway. On the way down I felt the Lord saying:

"Don't be discouraged by what you see when you arrive!"

A few hours later we arrived at the hospital and made our way to the intensive care unit. Doctors and nurses were buzzing around; there was an air of urgency about the place.

Outside one of the rooms there was a small group of people huddled together consoling one another, I guessed this was Eric's family.

"Oh no" I thought, "We're not too late, are we?"

Then I remembered what the Lord had told me. Sue went up and gave her aunt a cuddle, then introduced her to me.

"This is Davey, he's come all the way from Newcastle to pray with Eric," she said.

Sue's aunt then went on to explain how Eric's condition had become worse over the last couple of hours and that he was expected to go at any time. It looked as though I would not get a chance to pray with him and that it was all over.

I was really despondent as I sat in the corridor watching the clock tick away, the endless click, click, click of heels on the stone floor was driving me crazy. After a couple of hours Rob and I decided to get some food. We headed off to the cafeteria and, as we ate our food, discussed the possibility of being allowed in to pray with Eric.

On returning to the Ward we got our breakthrough, the Doctor said; "We can do nothing for him, you might as well have a go praying , you've got ten minutes!"

"Yes, here we go" I thought.

The scene that lay before my eyes as I entered into the unit was not one I was prepared for. There were four beds in the unit, which were occupied by people with horrific injuries, the smell of death was heavy in the air, I was praying in tongues like mad. My respect for doctors and nurses at this point was increased a hundred fold.

In the corner of the room I could see a man lying on a bed, he was jerking all over, I believe they are called the death throes, steam was rising from his body as rivers of sweat poured from him. He had an oxygen mask on his face and various tubes and drips were wired up to him. His body continued to jerk as he tried to gulp in the air— this I assumed was Eric.

"Oh no Lord, could you not have given me an easier one?" I thought.

I was alarmed at the sight but not put off as Rob and myself approached the bed. Rob spoke a few words of introduction about who we were and what we wanted to do, Eric nodded in agreement. I then proceeded to pray every warfare prayer that I could think of, "In the name of Jesus Christ of Nazareth I command every bit of sickness to leave this body" I said; "Your sins are forgiven and I loose you from all curses and covenants with darkness."

"I address and cast out every spirit of sickness and infirmity, you will loose and go right now"

"Jesus has said 'all authority in heaven and earth has been given to me, so go in my name and cast out evil spirits and heal the sick'." I also quoted scriptures like Luke 10:19: "I give you power and authority over all the enemy and nothing shall hurt you!"

After I had finished the warfare prayers I began on the prayers for healing and their scriptures:

"I command and decree healing this very hour in the name of Jesus Christ of Nazareth, I command life and health and strength to fill this body, I command every organ to be renewed, I bless every organ with health and command them to work as on the day they were created"

I finished off with Isaiah 53:

"By his wounds and stripes we are healed."

After ten minutes of furious prayer Eric's breathing became easier and the convulsions stopped so we left him, I felt a little disappointed, I had expected him to jump out of bed in a raising like Lazarus!! As I sat outside on a bench the Lord spoke to me and said:

"Watch, I am going to do a work here."

I went back in and walking down the corridor was a woman in her fifties; the Lord again spoke to me:

"Davey, do you see that woman? I want you to pray for her."

I asked Rob and Sue who the woman was and it turned out to be Eric's sister!

"Sue" I started, "the Lord wants me to pray for her, is she a believer?"

Sue looked a bit uncomfortable and said that she didn't know.

The Lord persisted with me to pray with the woman, so after a quick introduction I asked the woman whose name was Pat if she believed in Jesus or had a faith, she replied "Sort of."

"Okay" I said, "Would you like to meet him?"

I could feel the power of Jesus all over me right there in the middle of the intensive care ward. The anointing just hit me like a bolt of lightning; then I asked Pat to say the repentance prayer.

"Right" I said to Rob and Sue "get hold of her."

The next thing we knew, all four of us were on the floor under the power of the anointing!! Rob and Sue were sliding down the walls with big cheesy grins on their faces, Pat was lying in a heap and my legs were totally unable to function! I was laughing, full of the joy of the Lord!

All this was happening in the intensive care ward! Goodness knows what people were thinking as they looked at the four of us, it was amazing! Anyone who says that God has no sense of humour does not know God; after all he gave us the gift of laughter.

After the commotion had died down, Sue gave her aunt a scripture to read over Eric as she sat with him, it was Psalm 118 verses 17 and 18.

It was getting late and we had to return home, I told Pat that I believed the Lord was healing Eric, I felt an assurance in my spirit that the work had been done. This proved to be true, as the following day we received a phone call saying that Eric was in a normal ward, sitting in a chair drinking a cup of tea!! This was an absolute miracle! This is the power of the risen Lord at work. I nearly passed out when I got the news a week later that all his organs had been restored and he no longer needed a kidney transplant, our Lord is awesome! Amen.

On our return we felt that we were in a season of spiritual warfare and that the devil was not a happy chappie. We were taking a lot of ground and winning many souls to the Lord, so he attacked our prayer group with the deadly meningitis.

Within a fortnight, five people went down with it; Rob and myself rushed straight to the Royal Victoria Infirmary in Newcastle to pray over the victims. We recognised it as an attack of Satan and took authority over the disease in the name of Jesus Christ and once again prayed Isaiah 53:

"By his stripes we are healed."

It was amazing, the doctors had done all sort of tests and could find all the outward symptoms of meningitis, but Hallelujah, nothing inside!! After a week or so everyone was sent home fit and well. Once again the Lord had worked by his mighty arm in protecting his loved and anointed ones. We are lucky to have the favour of the Lord upon our lives, his word is true and he is faithful to it.

'No weapon formed against you shall prosper.'

There is awesome healing power at every believer's disposal, all you have to do is go and claim it. There are thirty-nine different categories of sickness and Jesus took a stripe on his back for every one of them. Jesus wants you to go and exercise the victory, by speaking out the word, commanding sickness to go, it is awesome try it!

25
Lakeshore

"Go into all the world and preach the gospel to every creature."

Mark 16:15

As I began to get a better grasp of the scriptures, I started to realise the freedom in Christ. Jesus was more interested in people's needs than in temples or buildings. My house meetings were more anointed than most church meetings and I realised that this was the way forward. I began to see that God wanted to be in the home, not stuck in some building where he is only visited a couple of times a week. God wants to be at the centre of our lives, helping us in our everyday problems, also he has a plan for us that we need to claim on a daily basis. He is our Father and he wants to spend time with his children at home.

I saw that God is progressive and wants us to move forward with him, his plan is for us to experience the fullness of life and as Jesus says:

'The works that I do you will do also and greater!'

John 14:12

If you look at the average Sunday service, many words spring to mind, but dynamic is not one of them. The gospel is a Gospel of power, yet rarely do you see it preached raw in a Sunday service. Christians are simply not being taught the power in the word or that God has a personal plan for them. Beloved do you know that God has a personal plan for you? Start to claim it daily in prayer it is amazing!

As the months went by at Longbenton church, I felt the Lord telling me that it was time to come out; at first I thought it was the devil and so I resisted. Then I asked a lot of prayerful people to pray and ask the Lord if this was what he wanted. "Yes" came back the answer. I felt the Lord saying to me "Davey, I need somewhere, I can send the lost and the unloved and have them cared for." I responded to that call immediately. I left Longbenton church in October 1998 and founded Lakeshore Christian Ministries, it was great, I felt a new freedom; it was as though a huge burden was lifted from me. Who would have believed that God was calling me into full-time ministry?

It meant living by faith and signing off the dole. Kath reluctantly agreed to it and off we went, supported by evangelist Dougie March and a small group of our neighbours, with Alan Finlay visiting every Tuesday morning to keep an eye on what was going on—and quite a lot was going on! Immediately after I took the step in faith, my speaking engagements increased, and once again the media came looking.

This time the "Sunday People" did a full page about me, the article was a bit "tongue in cheek" and OTT but was okay and I got a few engagements because of it.

Then I was invited to the UCB, Christian Broadcasting studios at Hanchurch, near Stoke-on-Trent. I was booked to do three shows—two live shows and one recorded one.

The programme went very well and was broadcast over Europe and Northern Ireland. Meanwhile, John Gates, chairman of the Craigavon chapter of the Businessmen's Fellowship International in Northern Ireland was driving to work. John was busy pondering who to ask to be their Christmas speaker. Several prominent speakers were going through John's mind, when suddenly yours truly comes over on the radio in John's car and the Holy Spirit shouts "That's your man!"

So John contacted UCB, who gave him my number. He rang and asked me to speak in Northern Ireland. He invited me to stay for five days and to speak at a number of events including dinner functions and school work. I told him that I would love to go.

The following day a lady called Rosemary interviewed me for a Swedish Christian newspaper "Trons-vald" and so my story went out over there, and people started to write to me; I believed that God was opening the International doors for me.

With renewed vigour I continued to get out on the streets with Dougie, and the Lord began to send people for me to disciple. I quite enjoyed preaching on the streets, and found that the Lord really anointed me when I did this; I got a lot of words of knowledge as I barked out the Gospel at Grey's monument in the centre of Newcastle.

It's out on the streets where you see the real world in all its ugliness, that's where the needy are, those who nobody loves. They're all there, all the characters—the junkies, the winos, the tramps and bag ladies.

Ralph McTell's song 'Streets of London' rings true of every city in this nation. It brings me to tears; the suffering that goes on in this nation, man's greed and self-centredness is disgusting. The rich get richer and the poor get poorer. It gets up my nose to see these charismatic, self-appointed 'Apostles' doing nothing to help the real needs. Yes, platform preaching is wonderful, but Jesus instructed us to go to the highways and the byways. That is where real men of God are moulded, and where the 'Father's heart' is developed. You can never fully understand the lost unless you have been there yourself. The real church of Jesus Christ is emerging from within the inner cities, and that's where you'll find the true apostles, coming from suffering and off drugs. They won't be schooled or educated, but neither were the first lot. Jesus said:

"It is sinners that I have come to save, not the righteous."

The end-times church will be built by everyday folk, not by a system. It will be built by the master builder himself, the Lord Jesus Christ; it will be a church of love with individuals who will walk in God's awesome miraculous power!

It was quite an unexpected surprise when Gary and Sherrin asked me to perform their wedding ceremony! I'd never performed one before but I agreed to do it much to their delight.

We agreed a date around the middle of August but we needed a venue for the event as we did not have a church building, but luckily Sherrin's mum's church kindly agreed to loan us their facilities. I would conduct the ceremony in the presence of the registrar to make it all legal.

I had known Gary for a number of years, he had been one of our regulars at the Blackett Arms in the bad old days. Gary is a large powerful man, he is a builder by trade but has also worked as a bouncer. For years all he ever thought about was work and drink, the drink often led him into brawling around the Newcastle pubs and clubs.

But now he was a Christian; he met the Lord after a nervous breakdown and like many other characters from my past I was his first port of call after becoming a Christian.

Gary and fiancee Sherrin had been attending church for seven or eight months when they decided to tie the knot.

Also another ex doorman began coming to church, his name was Eddie.

Eddie was another local lad who lived in the Dunston

area of Gateshead where he ran his own gym. He was a boxer and bodybuilder who had a history of drink and drug-related violence. He was known to a number of villains and drug barons as a hardman and they would often seek to employ his talent for violence. I had met him only once in a nightclub the night our firm tried to recruit him to be part of our 'Dream team.' But he very sensibly decided to cut us a wide berth deciding not to join our gang of pirates, preferring to paddle his own boat rather than joining the crew of 'Jolly Roger!'—one of his better decisions!

Eddie's mum was a Christian and for years she prayed for him, one day she bumped into Dougie preaching at the monument and asked him to write to Eddie who was currently languishing in Durham Jail.

So Dougie wrote to him and during this spell in prison Eddie began to consider his life, he broke down in tears sobbing like a baby and it was then that he felt the peace of the Lord and a voice say:

"Don't worry Ed, everything will be okay"

On release Eddie slipped back into his old ways and several years past before once again he hit rock bottom. He tried to commit suicide on a number of occasions, but failed each time only to wake up in hospital days later. He tried again early in 1999 and was in a coma for over a week, at the time his mother's church were praying heavily for him, but this time something had happened when he awoke, he had met with the Lord and seen Hell during his time in a coma!

Six weeks later I went to his home to meet him and his fiancee Christine, after someone from his mother's church contacted me. He had seen me in a newspaper article, he had recognised me from the past and wanted to meet me.

So I started to go regularly to the house and he began

to come to church. He decided he wanted to stay off the drink and get his life straightened out. Dougie baptised him in the North Sea whilst I was on a trip to Northern Ireland and for a while everything was okay.

I started to spend a lot of time with him, praying with him and teaching him. I would do weekly Bible studies at the house with him and some of the neighbours.

The Lord would come very powerfully into the house meetings and there were healings being done. Christine was healed of ovarian cancer and baby Georgia was healed of a couple of problems.

The months went by with the church growing and we began to have our meetings in the function room of the local pub. This was great fun, it was an unusual place to have church but the place was quickly packed out and the presence of the Lord was very heavy at times.

Many signs and wonders were taking place during the meetings in the 'Station Hotel' there was laughter everywhere and some people got covered in a golden dust or oil. But the fruit of the meetings were that people were healed by the power of God, including Eddie's mum who was on six medications for angina and other heart problems—eventually her doctor confirmed she was healed and took her off medication. We had some great nights and fantastic testimonies. One night a former blind man called John came and testified how he had been given his sight back in a church meeting—he went to see his doctor at the hospital to hand in his guide dog and the doctor refused to believe that he could see, so John pulled out his Bible and read him the story of Jesus healing blind Bartimaeus! Today John is a bus driver miracles do happen!!

Around the end of June I began to feel a pull towards the Holy Land and I felt led to ask Eddie to go with me, he said he wanted to go so I made the arrangements.

We managed to book a couple of cheap 'flight only' seats on a plane going from Gatwick to Tel Aviv, only problem was it landed in the early hours of the morning and we had no accomodation as we had decided to stay in different hostels as we travelled around.

So we set off accompanied by a copy of the 'Rough Guide to Israel'.

The five hour journey was a rough one as we had atrocious seating that was far too small for us. I was convinced that the airline had designed the seats to accommodate garden gnomes rather than human beings! It was the most uncomfortable five hours I had spent on a plane and I had it in my mind to be first at the airport on the return leg of the journey so we could get a choice of seats—preferably an exit or bulkhead seat so I could stretch out!

So I made a mental note in my mind –'Be first at the airport on the way home!'.

We arrived at Ben Gurion airport Tel Aviv at 2am, the place was in darkness but the atmosphere was still warm. After collecting our rucksacks and going through a number of security checks we left the airport and plotted our next course of action.

We decided to head off into downtown Tel Aviv to see if we could get in to a hostel for the remainder of the night, but there was 'No room at the Inn'! We wandered for hours like Mary and Joseph looking for a place to stay, but everywhere the answer was the same from the night desk, come back at twelve noon! I looked at my watch it was nearly six am and it was starting to get light.

"Okay Ed, let's hit the beach and crash out there" I decided. "We'll try and get a little bit of shut eye."

We walked a hundred yards down Gordon Street to where the beach was situated and crashed out under a sunshade.

We slept there for a few hours and then headed back to the hostel to check in.

We spent the first couple of days on the beach getting acclimatised to the hot weather. It was Ed's first time away abroad and he was enjoying it.

The beach in Tel Aviv was packed with holiday makers from many different nationalities we got a couple of sun beds to lie on, making the occasional brief excursions into the sea to cool off.

At one point during the afternoon I opened my eyes lazily, Ed was perched on the edge of his sun bed looking very thoughtful as he gazed out to sea, all of a sudden he started to laugh.

"Davey, the Lord's just spoke to me" he said with a grin on his face.

"What did he say Ed?"

"He said, 'See Ed there's more to this world than Dunston Excelsior Club!' "

I started to laugh as Ed sat and shook his head, once again it was another example of the Lord's humour.

We spent the next few days visiting the biblical sites, first we went to Jerusalem and spent the day wandering around the 'Old City' which was absolutely fascinating. We did all the usual pilgrimage sights such as Calvary, the Via Dolorosa before heading out to the Mount of Olives and the Garden of Gethsemane, where Christ spent his last hours before being arrested and taken to the cross.

There is a beautiful peace and tranquillity about the place, both Ed and myself felt the Lord's presence very close to us, for a while we sat on the benches scattered around the Garden, enjoying the sun as well as the beauty of the place.

We didn't say very much, there wasn't much to say, I think we each had our own personal thoughts as we sat contemplating, allowing our minds to take us on a journey back in time to the greatest moment in human history. I felt a lump in my throat as I thought about Jesus sat here sweating blood knowing what was about to come to him, while those whom he loved were sleeping.

The following day I got up early to go up to Tiberias next to the Sea of Galilee, Ed had decided to stay in Tel Aviv for the day and so I caught the bus by myself.

"I'll see you later" I said to him as I left for the bus station.

"I'll be back around six" I said "Don't forget it's the Sabbath and everything closes around four."

"Yeah have a good time" Ed replied rolling over and going back to sleep.

The journey up to Tiberias was nice, the sun was up and the scenery beautiful as the bus headed north passing the coast and then across inland. We headed across the Meggido plain and up through Nazareth the hill town where Jesus had lived as He was growing up. You get a fantastic view over the Meggido plain from the top of the hill in Nazareth, site of the last battle to come— 'Armageddon!"

After a couple of hours we drove down the hill into Tiberias, the view is quite spectacular as you drive down into the place, the rolling hills and peaceful sea in the background. I was struck by the beauty of it in my mind I had visions of Jesus and the Disciples wandering around or out on the boat fishing.

On arriving at the bus station I enquired about the time of the last bus as I knew everything closes in Israel from sundown Friday to sundown Saturday—the Sabbath and I didn't want to be stranded in Tiberias. I then caught another bus to Tabgha which is situated a mile and half from Capernaum the town where Jesus and the disciples lived.

I enjoyed the walk along the lakeshore and down to

Capernaum although it was blistering hot with the temperature way into the high nineties! I stopped for a while at the 'loaves and fishes' hill where it is reputed that Jesus fed the five thousand. For some reason I felt quite emotional, the place was really beautiful and I really didn't want to leave, in fact I would have quite happily stayed there full stop!

Eventually I came to the ancient town and spent a while looking round the ruins and the remains of what was once the Apostle Peter's house.

I lost all track of time and the fact that the sundown was coming had escaped my notice! I was wandering along the lane gazing across the lake when it suddenly hit me that it was now three o'clock, the last bus was coming shortly and I was now miles from the bus stop!!

"Oh no" I thought "I'm going to be stuck here and we go home tomorrow!"

For a brief moment fear started to kick in but then a miracle happened just as it had at Sinai in Egypt!

All of a sudden a taxi appeared the driver pulled alongside me and said "Get in!"

"Where do you need to go?" the driver asked me as I jumped in.

"I desperately need to get to the bus stop at Tabgha!" I explained to him. "I need to get back to Tel Aviv" I continued.

The man said nothing else as we drove the few miles back to the bus stop, I was stunned and wondered if the guy was an angel. This was certainly a 'Divine' intervention without doubt! My peace returned to me as we pulled up at the bus stop, I paid the guy and thanked him for coming to my rescue. He had no sooner pulled away when the last bus came charging round the corner! His timing had been perfect—a moment or so later and I would have missed it.

By the grace of God I managed to get back to Tiberias and onto the last bus headed for Tel Aviv. On the way back I thanked the Lord for pulling me out of yet another tricky situation.

26
Into Africa

In March my home group was privileged to receive Apostle Harry Das from Chrisco Ministries in Africa. Apostle Das brought a great blessing with him, it was a joy to sit and hear how the Lord has used him. He currently oversees hundreds of works in Africa, America, India and has works all over the world, his church group used to be part of the Assemblies of God, Pentecostal Group.

For some time I had felt that our small church needed to be accountable to a larger body, but I knew it had to be the right one. I had been asked by a number of large and well known ministries if I wanted to bring Lakeshore under their covering but each time I felt the Lord say "No". But when Apostle Das came the Lord told me to submit myself to him and learn from him.

"Davey I've called you to be an apostle you need to learn from an apostle and be commissioned by one!" the Lord told me.

So when Harry returned to visit us in September 1999 I submitted myself and the work to Apostle Das and Chrisco Fellowship of Churches. We then had an ordination service, where Apostle Das and his team ordained myself and also prayed over our five-fold ministry team commissioning us as a five-fold ministry Church. Whilst he prayed over me, it was as if heaven opened, the blessing was so strong. In the spirit I saw five big stones being hammered into the ground and the Lord said:

"These are the foundation stones of my church they can never be removed."

It was an awesome night and from that day I felt a

powerful increase in the anointing and presence of God around me.

The Potters Revival Centre was situated in the midst of the Cheviot Hills, near the town of Kelso, which is a few miles over the border into Scotland.

The house, a former hunting lodge, had been converted into a rehabilitation centre by the 'Youth With A Mission' organisation in the late nineteen sixties. Since then the building had changed hands on a number of occasion and was currently in the hands of a Mr Williams.

I was first asked to visit the place by my dear 'Brother in Christ' Patrick Hinton who at the time was a director of the 'Teen Challenge' organisation. Patrick had wanted me to visit a former drug dealer from Teeside who was residing in the centre, the lad was having a rough time and I was to go and encourage him.'

During my first visit to the centre in late September of 1999, I got talking to Mr Williams the owner, who had been in charge of the place for several years. The place was starting to get run down and he was getting on in age and really didn't have the time or inclination to invest too much more of his time or money into the place.

The valley in which the centre is situated is quite beautiful, especially in the summer time, it is also the gateway to the Pennine Way.

I sat chatting to Mr Williams for while telling him about the work we were doing on the streets and in prison. I told him the about the vision I had seen concerning the rehab farms and also that I was on the lookout for a farm type centre of my own.

I tried to encourage Chris, the lad that we'd been asked to visit, he was a drug dealer from a notorious Teeside family, but the lad didn't seem ready for the Christian life to me.

So after a full day with the lads we set off for home,

the sun was just going down as we sped along the windy country roads that meandered their way through the beautiful Northumbrian Hills. There was a sort of divine peace and tranquillity about them, the stuff that picture postcards are made of, also there were pheasants running all over the road it made quite a beautiful picture.

So we went back home and never really give the centre another thought.

My friend Dougie March was heading off on a seven-month preaching tour that was to take him through Kenya, Tanzania, Uganda, Rwanda, Burundi and the Congo with our 'Brother in Christ,' Rev Dr Peter Samuels. Dougie came to see me with his itinerary and so we decided to have a 'Sending Out Party' for him at the 'Station Hotel'.

I also decided to put the 'Transformations' video on the big screen to encourage people, which it did. Our friend Dr Robert Ward was totally bowled over by the video and, not one to miss an opportunity, went on to negotiate a franchise to sell the video!

The Christmas came with the 'Millienium' celebrations, all the fears of Y2K proved fruitless, the world's computers did not go mad leaving the globe in a state of chaos as had been predicted by the 'Doom and Gloom' brigade.

Over the Christmas period I felt the Lord encouraging me to also visit our friends in Africa, so I contacted my friend Reverend Daniel Gitau who lives in Dondori, a village outside the city of Nakuru in Western Kenya. We discussed the visit and Daniel said he would arrange a preaching itinerary for me.

"Get a flight to Nairobi and we'll meet you at the Airport, okay?"

"Right-o Daniel, I'll see what I can do" I said as we finished our conversation.

So for the next few days I tried to get a flight to Nairobi. I was quite excited about the trip and wondered if I would see Dougie and Peter on my travels, they had been away for nearly two months, I'd had a couple of letters from them saying that all was going well.

It proved to be impossible to get a flight to Nairobi and I just managed to secure a seat on a flight to Mombasa the day before I was due to fly. I tried to contact Daniel to let him know that I would be arriving in Mombasa not Nairobi but there was no answer from his phone and so I set off, planning to contact him when I reached Mombasa. The problem was that I had no accommodation in Mombasa, I knew that the 'Chrisco' ministry had churches in Mombasa but I did not know where they were or have any phone numbers, so I was out on a limb, totally reliant on God's mercy! What an exciting place to be!

I had just booked my flight when I received an unexpected phone call from Mr Williams at the Potters Revival Centre.

"Davey would you like to take over the running of the Centre with an option to buy it?" he asked. I nearly hit the floor in shock! This was totally out of the blue and for a moment I was lost for words.

"Erm…yes I'd love to." It did not take much thinking about, this was an answer to prayer.

"Okay, when can I see you?" he asked.

"I am going out to Africa tomorrow, I'll be away for a couple of weeks," I replied.

"Okay I'll ring you when you get back" he said and then the line went dead.

I stood with the phone in my hand absolutely stunned for a moment, then as the rush began to impact me I jumped up and punched the air. "Yes, thank you Lord, hallelujah." I was ecstatic as I ran round the house celebrating "Whooa, party on!!"

The following day I flew out from Manchester en route for Mombasa. We had a brief stop in Cairo to refuel. As we flew in to Cairo I looked out of the window, hoping to see the pyramids, but it was too dark. After an hour or so, we were on our way again and five hours later we landed in Mombasa. It was around eight in the morning and the sun was blazing as we taxied down the runway, I was deep in prayer asking the Lord my course of action on getting off the plane. I felt his presence around me and a deep peace came over me, I knew I was in safe hands—Africa is a dangerous place and I would not advise anyone to go out there without pre-booked accommodation. On clearing customs I walked past a number of tour reps, the Lord spoke very clearly to me—he said:

"Davey, do you see that man over there?"

He drew my attention to one particular rep, a tall coloured gentleman in his early forties. The Lord said:

"Go and tell him you need accommodation."

I walked over to him and explained my predicament. The man's name was Walter and he was very courteous and helpful. Within minutes he had arranged for me to go to a hotel called 'Le Soleil' which was just outside Mombasa, so I paid a small fee and boarded the transfer bus with the other guests. On leaving the airport I got my first glimpse of real life in Africa, which looked to be very hard. As we passed through the shanty town I saw how difficult life was for most people in Kenya and realised once again how easy we have got it in the UK compared to other parts of the world.

After an hour or so we reached the 'Le Soleil Beach Club' a nice little three star hotel complex next to the ocean.

I managed to secure an 'all inclusive' deal for thirty pounds a night, after a bit of negotiation with the manager who turned out to be a Christian. Originally the desk clerk had wanted ninety pounds per night, so it was worth the haggle. I had a couple of days just relaxing around the pool and acclimatising myself. It was very hot and I was tired from the long journey so I spent the time resting.

I heard from some of the guests that there had been an air crash at Nairobi airport with hundreds of casualties and I later realised this was why I had been unable to get a flight to Nairobi. Once again I believe my life had been spared.

After a day or two I felt the Lord urging me to contact Daniel, so I phoned his home and spoke to his wife, Fenhi who informed me that Daniel was in Nairobi and had been expecting me to arrive there. Fenhi informed me that they had been checking the passenger lists to see if I had been on the flight that had crashed, and she was very relieved to speak to me.

A day later Daniel phoned me at the hotel and told me he had spoken to the pastors in Mombasa and they would be sending someone to the hotel to see me.

I was sat in the foyer of the hotel when two men walked in and I thought I recognised one of them. My suspicions were confirmed when I heard his Geordie accent, not what I was expecting to hear in the wilds of Africa!! The man had obviously recognised me and decided to come over to speak. His name was Mark and he was a club doorman from Chester Le Street, County Durham. He said to me "Excuse me, are you from Newcastle?"

I answered "Yes, I am."

He said "I thought it was you, Davey, what are you doing here?"

"I'm out here preaching the gospel," I said.

"You are doing what??" he replied, with a look of shock on his face.

"I'm here preaching the gospel," I repeated. "Haven't you heard? I've become a Christian."

"You're joking?" he said.

"No, it's true—I've met Jesus and I've become a Christian, I now travel the world preaching."

"Honestly?" he said, with a look of bewilderment.

I could see he was having difficulty understanding what I was saying so I thought I would give him one of my testimony tracts, which I had in my briefcase.

"Here, read this" I said, handing him the booklet. "I am due to have a meeting with some pastors in a moment, so I'll see you later."

"Yeah—ok" he said as he wandered off to rejoin his friend, still studying the booklet.

"You'll not believe this…." I could hear him exclaim to his pal as he related our conversation.

Just then the pastors from Mombasa arrived and for an hour or so we sat and chatted. They invited me to speak in a couple of meetings before I was due to head off to Nakuru. They asked me how I wanted to travel to Nakuru—did I want to fly to Nairobi or take the overnight train. I think I would like to go by bus, I replied. "Are you sure?" they asked me, "the buses here are not like your buses at home!! It's a long way to Nakuru by bus and the roads are quite hazardous, are you sure you wouldn't rather go by train or fly??"

"No, I'd like to see something of the country" I replied, quite naively.

"But it's six hundred miles and a thirteen hour journey!" the Pastor exclaimed.

"That's ok," I said.

After the Pastors left I spent some time relaxing playing water volleyball in the pool and sharing my testimony with some of the other hotel guests, I remember one couple who lived near Sheffield were very interested in my story.

That night as I sat down to dinner, I decided that I was going to try the lobster. I was quite embarrassed when it came because it was so huge and all the other guests were looking at it as the waiter passed their tables!

After dinner we were treated to a show by 'Masai Warriors' in tribal dress, which I quite enjoyed. Once the show was over I decided to head back to my room and get my head down.

I had just got into bed and turned out the light when the Lord spoke to me.

"Davey go up to the 'Roof Bar'."

"The Roof Bar?" I answered "Where's that Lord?"

"Upstairs," came back the answer.

So I got ready and headed up the staircase until I came to the place. I did a quick survey of the place and spotted Mark sitting at the bar by himself, again I heard the still small voice;

"Go and witness to him."

I went over to the bar counter where he was sitting, he was staring down into his drink obviously deep in thought and didn't see me. I noticed my testimony booklet was lying open in front of him he had obviously been studying it.

"Hiya Mark how you doing?" I said.

The words brought him out of his trance like state "Oh, all right Davey."

"Where's your pal?" I asked.

"He's gone to bed for the night" he answered.

"Look Davey, this is amazing" he said, picking up the tract. "I've been reading it and I really believe it, I thought you were winding me up, but now I know it's for real!"

"I saw you in the papers back home and thought you were up to some kind of scam" he continued.

"I think most of the lads in the town think that" I answered.

"Davey, I think God's on my case" he said.

"Why do you think that Mark?" I asked knowing full well that he was right.

"Because my sister is a 'born again' Christian and she is

always preaching on to me and everywhere I go I bump into Christians, I thought I'd be safe out here in the middle of nowhere!" his eyes started to fill up with tears.

"I cannot believe that I would have bumped into you out here, you're the last person I would have expected to see!" by now tears were starting to run down his cheeks.

"Mark, I believe that Jesus loves you and yes, he is on your case," I said. "He asked me to come up here and speak to you tonight!"

"I knew it," he said.

"Mark, Jesus loves you and has a wonderful plan to change the bad things in your life, you can run, but you can't hide from God, but it's your choice, God won't take away your free will, but I promise you that if you take up God's plan for your life you will never look back, it's the most important decision you will ever make. I would not swap my life for all the money in the world, it is a fantastic life!!" I encouraged him.

I then shared my testimony with him and he went off back to his room, as he went the Lord said to me: "One day he'll come to your church."

After Mark went back to his room I spent the next hour or so sharing my testimony with Otto, a German tourist from near Munich, which was a bit of a challenge since the man couldn't speak English and I don't speak German, but he got the message!

The following day Mark and his friend left to go back to England and I spent the day sunning myself on the beautiful beach and studying my Bible.

And so on the Friday evening the Pastors packed me onto the bus and I set out on what was to become the worst journey of my life, it was like the 'Express to Hell!'

I was sat on the back seat of the bus so every time the bus went over a bump I lifted off the seat and banged my head on the roof. There are very few smooth stretches and we hit a bump every few yards on the road that is known as 'The Highway to Hell'. The road stretches some four hundred miles between Mombasa and Nairobi and most of it is like a dirt track.

The windows on the bus were open and the dust was pouring in which made matters worse. I soon managed to drink my two bottles of water and was becoming desperately thirsty as the journey continued. We had a couple of stops where I was mercifully able to buy some drinks and refreshment.

I had no rest or sleep that night, and on a couple of occasions everyone had to leave the bus whilst the driver and his assistant fixed a burst tyre. The dust was getting everywhere and I spent most of the night rubbing my eyes, which resulted in an infection in both my eyes and ears.

Mercifully the roads improved as we neared the capital city and we began to make some progress. We had a brief stop in Nairobi before setting off on the last leg of the journey to Nakuru, by now the sun was up and people all along the route were starting their day.

I was totally exhausted and bewildered as I clambered from the bus in Nakuru wishing with all my heart that I had taken the Pastors' advice and flown instead!

To add insult to injury the bus had dropped me at the wrong place, half a mile from my arranged meeting point with Daniel. It was only by sheer chance that I met Daniel, as he had gone to pick up some papers from an office next to where I was standing. I don't think I had ever been so happy to see somebody in my life!!!

"What are you doing here Davey?" he asked. 'What have you been doing?' he asked looking me up and down.

I caught sight of my appearance in a shop window I was covered in dirt from head to toe!

I then proceeded to give Daniel the full nine yards of my epic journey.

"You had better come to my home and get cleaned up, I'll get Brother Gilbert to look at your eyes" he said with a look of concern on his face.

An hour or so later I was standing under the shower at Daniel's home on the road to Dondori washing the dust from me. Fenhi and the girls were scrubbing my suitcase, which had been caked in dust.

Gilbert, the doctor from Daniel's clinic, came and looked at my eyes and ears. Both were infected so he gave me a course of antibiotics and some drops.

Afterwards I went straight to bed, I had not slept at all on the long journey and badly needed some shut-eye.

I slept on and off for almost a full day, just getting up for meals and a prayer time with Daniel's family.

The day after that was Sunday, I got up around seven o'clock feeling refreshed, the sun was already streaming in my window as I got up to pray. After my prayer time I headed off for a shower, by now members of the family were up and the house was a hive of activity. Daniel introduced me to his family, plus the other people who lived in his home, in all about fourteen people.

After breakfast we all clambered in to an assortment of different motor vehicles and headed off to Daniel's church in the small town of Dondori. The 3km drive was a pleasant one despite the number of potholes that plague the Dondori road, all along the route people were making their way to church, many of them waving to us.

This was my introduction to one of Kenya's favourite modes of public transport—'The Matatu,' Kenya's unofficial bus service. A 'Matatu' is a cross between a taxi and a minibus, it does regular routes for very little cost and is usually cram packed with people, sometimes clinging to the sides or sitting on the roof!! Riding in a Matatu is an experience not to be missed when travelling in Kenya and will certainly broaden your horizons!

It was a wonderful privilege to preach to the three hundred or so people in Daniel's church, every so often someone would come up to me, pull out a little booklet and say:

"Do you know Meester Dougie March?!"

I would laugh and say:

"Yes, I know Meester Dougie March!"

I found out that Dougie and Peter had passed through Dondori a month or two earlier and had held a small crusade in the town. They had obviously made an impact in the town as people remembered them with great fondness.

After the service we went for lunch at church members' home, where Daniel discussed the week's itinerary with me.

I was booked to do two meetings a day at two of the Chrisco churches in Nakuru and then at the end of the week I was to return to Mombasa where I would preach in one of the churches there. Daniel also informed me that I would be joined mid week by another Englishman— Pastor Walter Cartwright who lived in Dronfield near Sheffield. Walter was coming out for a month or so and would be bringing medical supplies for the clinic.

That evening we returned to Daniel's home and went into prayer, to pray for the week's events. We had a very powerful time of prayer; Fenhi Gitau is a real prayer warrior who pushes through till she gets an answer. Once she did a forty day fast seeking God for the answers to some problems, at the end of the fast she had still not received answers to her questions, so she immediately did another forty days—Fen got her answers!

The following day I rose early to seek the Lord, asking him for a word to share in the daily meetings I was doing, and each morning the Lord would give me a fresh word, fresh manna, it was wonderful.

The next three days were spent in a repetitive manner. After my prayer time we would have breakfast, then after breakfast we would head off to Nakuru where I would have my first preaching session of the day to around three hundred people. Then we would have lunch and in the afternoons I would have my second preaching session at a different Chrisco church in the Nakuru area then we would return to Daniel's home for our evening meal and another powerful prayer time.

Something happened on the Wednesday evening, which was to teach me a valuable lesson in spiritual warfare and gave me great insight into how the devil holds people in bondage. It is a lesson that I have not forgotten and it is important that we grasp how the devil attacks us if we are truly to walk in freedom.

It started when I phoned home, I was talking to Kath, giving her an update on events and asking how things were going at home. She filled me in on the current news and I asked to speak to the kids. I had a few words with Victoria and then asked to speak to John, but Kath told me he had gone to bed. Just as I was about to hang up, Kath said to me:

"Oh, by the way, Davey, will you pray for Hannah? She is in hospital with a burst appendix and her situation is critical." (Hannah is the daughter of Rob and Sue, who I went to Manchester with when Eric was miraculously healed.)

"Of course I will" I answered "when did this happen?"

"A couple of days ago" Kath answered, "but the situation is touch and go. She now has blood poisoning and the hospital can't find an antibiotic her body will tolerate, she has had an allergic reaction to every one they have tried."

"Ok, I'll get everybody here to pray. I'll phone you on Friday."

So I hung up and went back to my room, to begin praying. As I walked into the room, I heard the devil speaking to me very clearly. He said:

"How do you know it is Hannah in hospital and not your John?" I stopped dead in my tracks for a minute.

"You didn't speak to him, did you?" the voice continued.

"No, I didn't" I thought. Then he said:

"If something was wrong while you were away, Kath wouldn't tell you, would she? She wouldn't want to worry you, would she?"

No I thought, she wouldn't want to worry me. The next thing I saw, in my mind's eye, was a picture of John in hospital. Then fear began to rise up in my stomach, I started to panic and was about to go and phone Kath back when the Lord interjected very powerfully saying:

"Davey, are you going to stand for this? Take authority over this."

"What?" I said.

"Take authority over the words, the pictures and the feelings."

"How?" I asked.

"Pray and command them to leave you" the Lord replied.

So I began to pray in tongues, exercising the power of the name and blood of Jesus Christ of Nazareth. In His name I commanded the fear to leave me, which it did after a few moments. The picture disappeared from my mind and I commanded the devil to be silent in the name of Jesus Christ. Within a few minutes, I was back in a state of total peace; it had been a valuable lesson. Since then I have learnt not to trust feelings or instincts as they can be totally false. Fear is a tool which the devil uses to keep people bound up, they need to know how to take authority over their fears. Through praying in tongues for a few moments I got to the real truth. It says in Romans 8:26 that the Holy Spirit will lead us in perfect prayer in all situations so if in doubt pray in tongues! It was a reminder of how the devil can only paint dark pictures and yet another example of the power of Jesus' victory on the cross of Calvary.

The following day I was leading a meeting at the Chrisco Central Church in Nakuru and I directed the three hundred strong congregation to intercede for little Hannah. We formed a chain and for the next half hour we battled away in tongues, it was very powerful. This was Thursday lunchtime.

We fought in the spirit until we felt an assurance that God had moved and intervened in the situation. (I later learnt from Sue, on my return to the UK, that this was when Hannah's condition took a turn for the better.) And so we rejoiced and gave glory to God.

The whole episode had been an invaluable lesson to me and I was starting to trust God on a new level, however the first thing I said to Kath when I phoned on the Friday evening was:

"Where's John?!!"

I finished off my engagements in Nakuru and Daniel arranged a car to take me to Nairobi to catch my flight to Mombasa—there was no way I was going back by bus! So on Saturday evening I boarded the evening flight from Jomo Kenyatta Airport to Mombasa. The sun was setting as the plane took off; it was a beautiful spectacle. En route, I could just see the top of Mount Kilimanjaro, as the night began to draw in. There was a bit of drama as we came in to land in Mombasa; just as the plane began it's descent onto the runway, all the power went off at the airport and the plane had to land in total darkness. Myself and everyone else on the plane went into immediate prayer and the second the plane's wheels touched the ground the lights went on again, praise the Lord.

I was met at the airport by Sister Nzinga, the wife of one of the Pastors in Mombasa. She asked me if my journey into Mombasa had been better than my journey out. It was quite obvious that news of my epic bus journey was now common knowledge on the Chrisco grapevine!

The following morning I was preaching in the Sunday service at the Koblenz Hall in Mombasa. Down the street we could hear an incessant wailing coming from the loudspeaker of the local mosque, it became so bad that it began to interfere with my message and I became quite irritated by it. I decided that some drastic action was needed and once again decided to take authority, so I shouted in the direction of the open window:

"In the name of Jesus Christ of Nazareth, I command you to be silent."

Everyone waited in expectancy.

After a couple of seconds we heard a fizzing noise coming from the mosque's loudspeaker and suddenly there was silence. The church erupted into cheering; it was like Elijah's victory on Mount Carmel, once again the Lord had prevailed.

I spent the next couple of days relaxing before returning to England. The trip had been a real learning exercise, my relationship with the Lord continued to grow and now I was looking forward to the prospect of acquiring the rehabilitation centre.

27
The Rehab

"He has sent me to heal the broken hearted, to proclaim liberty to the captives and to open the prison of those who are bound."

Isaiah 61:1

After returning from Africa, I continued to preach at many venues around the North of England, sharing testimony and leading many souls to Christ. A week or so after my return I received a call from Mr Williams, the owner of the Potters Revival Centre.

"Have you had any thoughts about what I proposed before you went away?" he asked.

"Yes, I'm still interested and excited at the prospect, there is so much potential." I answered.

"Ok, are you free for a chat next week?"

"Yes," I replied, and so we set up a meeting for the following week.

After a few initial meetings with Mr Williams it was decided that we would take over the running of the centre and the charity that owned the place. He said that he wanted to retire and wanted the house to stay on in a Christian organisation, the building was in need of urgent repair but he had no money to sort it out, I said that wouldn't be a problem as we would raise money to renovate it.

So we met his trustees in February of 2000 and it was agreed that we would take over the centre. They asked us a lot of questions about what we proposed to do in the centre and questioned us as to what we would do in certain situations.

Leading up to this I had prayed, asking the Lord to show me how best to minister to the lads in the centre. The Lord had shown me that it was about discipleship and making disciples. He showed me how the disciples had been with him for three years and I knew from my own life, that change comes through time and is not an overnight occurrence. He showed me that people coming to the centre would need deliverance and healing, but also they would need to be taught how to live a Christian life. So the Lord gave me a three-stage plan, which was to span over three years, depending upon how quickly the person moved on. People are different, and have different needs, some progress more quickly than others, but the basic outline of this plan was that they would spend up to a year in the Centre. Part two was for them to go into a halfway house, which was the necessary bridge and stepping stone between rehab and resettlement in the community. Many people find life in the community too much to handle after leaving rehab and need to be gradually integrated back into society—so the halfway house is a key stage. It means that they still have most of the support at hand and aren't left to their own devices.

The Centre was in a terrible state when we took over, it was dilapidated, filthy and was more like a doss house. There was only one full-time volunteer looking after the place and only a handful of men in residence, they were left to their own devices. These men had no structure whatsoever to their day and many of them had little or no understanding of Christianity, so we set about the task of sorting the place out. The first thing we did was to lead these men to Christ and then organise a baptism service at the Centre.

There is a small Burn, which runs past the Centre and we decided to baptise the men in the water there. A few people in our fellowship had also asked for baptism, so we set a day for the service at the Centre. People from the local churches were invited and Mr Williams decided that he would introduce us as the people who were taking over the centre. The service went really well, we had a powerful time of praise and worship and then we baptised a dozen or so people. There was a wonderful presence of the Lord as the sun shone across the rolling hills.

We gradually started integrating our team into the daily running of the Centre, which was really run down.

Our first task was to deal with the septic tank, which was overflowing and urgently needed emptying after its contents began to spill out around the back of the house. It was becoming a hygiene risk.

Next, we began to get some structure into the men's day. Our day began at seven o'clock with 'morning glory' prayer time, followed by breakfast at eight thirty. After breakfast we would go through UCB's 'Word for Today' booklet and then our Bible study, which would finish around eleven thirty, then the men were given an hour's free time before lunch.

In the afternoon we began to create work for the men to do. In addition to the basic household chores, we encouraged them to help tidy up the property—involving them in decorating, gardening and furniture restoration. We prepared a personal plan for each of the men in the house, reviewing each case separately.

We got to know the men and their personal problems, and through the power of prayer, the Lord showed us how to minister to each of them individually. During the work period we would often call them individually to sit down and we would talk them through their problems. They began to respond and trust us, as we showed them the love of Jesus Christ, they could see that it wasn't just words with us, but acts of love.

Tea was at 5.00pm and then they were free until 7.30 when our evening service would start. There was a tremendous presence of the Lord during these meetings. People would spend hours on the floor under the power of the Holy Spirit, we would see healings and deliverances happen. People were rolling around on the floor laughing just like on the day of 'Pentecost' when the Holy Spirit of God fell on the church in Jerusalem.

One of our team was a social worker and had previously worked in hostels and was quite familiar with all the regulations, which was a great help at times. We began to tighten up in general around the place, we began to clamp down on the residents' trips into town, after one or two were caught trying to sneak drink and drugs into the place. It was quite amazing how the Lord would always let us know what was happening, his hand really was on the place whilst we were there. But we needed to run a tight and disciplined regime if we were to succeed with our mission at the Potters Centre.

After a while this proved to be successful and we began to see real fruit for our efforts, the men responded to what we were doing. We started to build links with the prison service and other bodies taking referrals from them.

After a short while all the empty rooms were filled and the finances were on the up, but the money was still going to Mr Williams. We contacted him to see what was holding up the signing over of the charity, he insisted he would get on to it.

As time passed we began to see changes in the men, one man whom we baptised called Stuart left the centre to get re-married after being reconciled to his wife, he got a full time job as a travelling salesman and was also doing voluntary work with a Christian organisation in the Blackpool area. His whole life changed and turned around after six months at the centre. He had previously lived on the streets as a wino, but Jesus' love changed him. There are many other similar success stories.

I used to spend part of the week at the centre and the rest of the week at home and of course I was still pastoring a small fellowship.

It was around this time that I first met my friend Douglas Jarvie. Douglas was a friend of Adrian and Alison Cowell who were involved with our fellowship. He was a member of their former church 'The King's Church' in Motherwell, Scotland. Douglas used to sometimes visit Adrian and Alison and when he was in town he would pop along to our meetings. He was a bit of an oddball but I liked Douglas and knew him to have a good heart. His exterior is a bit rough and first sight of him, you think 'I'd not like to meet him on a dark night,' but underneath he's a big softie!

Douglas was around fifty at the time and had been retired early from his job as a physics teacher due to an accident at school. He was lucky to be alive after falling down stairs and cracking open his skull in a freak accident. After a year or so of blackouts he was healed. He was separated from his wife at the time and was going through the grieving process, I felt sorry for him and spent a lot of time praying and interceding with him.

The more I got to know him the more I liked him, he started to travel with me and for a time we became quite inseparable, although at times he could be very irritating (I know he will smile at that!).

Douglas started to come and help out at the Centre; he would do bits of furniture restoration amongst other things and was a real help and encouragement to me.

We continued to work with all kinds of people at the Centre, some people found it too much and didn't stick the course, sometimes leaving within a few days of arriving. We took people off the streets giving them a hope as well as a home; we showed them we cared and that made the difference. One day I was driving up to the centre, it was a really beautiful day, the sun was shining as I drove through the hills, I was praising and thanking God. Everything in my life was going well, I was thinking about the work when the Lord spoke:

"This is what's important to me, I am pleased with the work you are doing at the centre, it is more important than just sitting and singing about love in a church, you are showing love in action."

"Thank you Lord" I said encouraged by this word.

Over the next few days I continued to contact Mr Williams about the signing over of the charity and changing trustees, it seemed to be dragging on and on.

"Yes, I'll get on to the solicitor" he said, "How are things going?"

"Very well" I answered,

"Have you got any more foreign trips planned?"

"Yes I'm off to Israel in a couple of weeks" I replied.

"Oh well, I'll be up to collect the rent money on Thursday, keep up the good work" he added before hanging up the phone.

As time passed it became patently obvious that Mr Williams had no real interest in people and seemed only interested in collecting his now quite substantial income. It was also becoming clear that he was in no rush to sign over the charity now that everything was up and running smoothly.

Yet despite this the Lord continued to move powerfully within the centre.

When another new resident arrived I was reminded about how someone could be brought up in a Christian home and yet not know Jesus. We had a lad called Terry arrive at the centre, he was in his late thirties and was a former soldier. He had a drink problem and had fallen on hard times. He was a very pleasant guy, whose parents were Christians. During our morning sessions he used to say to me:

"Davey, how is it that you and the lads hear Jesus speaking, but I never hear a thing?"

"I don't know, Terry," I replied "have you given your life to him?"

"I didn't know you had to," Terry answered.

"Yes of course you do," I said "No-one's born into Christianity."

"But my parents are Christians and I was christened!" he said "doesn't that make me a Christian?" he asked.

"No" I replied "you must personally invite Jesus into your life. You must ask him to forgive your sins and accept him as your Lord and Saviour, no-one can do it for you, it must be your choice."

"Oh then I had better invite him into my life" he said.

I led Terry in the repentance prayer and prayed for the baptism of the Holy Spirit, but nothing seemed to happen. He said that he felt peaceful, but that was all.

For many days afterwards, we kept praying over him, but nothing happened and he became quite despondent and frustrated. Day after day, we'd ask him if there had been any change but there was nothing until one day.

I arrived at the centre about midday Terry was waiting at the gate for me, he had a huge smile on his face and was visibly glowing.

"Davey, Davey you'll not believe what's happened," he said very excitedly.

"Why, what's happened?" I asked.

"Jesus woke me up at three o'clock this morning and he sat talking to me on my bed."

"Wow, what did he say to you?" I asked excited at this development.

216

"He told me that he loved me and cared about me and that I was precious to him."

"So what did you say?" I continued.

"I said 'Lord I need a cigarette to calm my nerves, you won't disappear will you?'"

"You said what?" I laughed at him trying to picture the night's events "So what did the Lord say to that Terry?" I asked trying to get a handle on things.

"He said it's okay Terry and then he sat talking about how he sees me and then he baptised me in the Holy Spirit. Look Davey, I can speak in 'tongues' like you now!!" he said before railing off some words in tongues eager to show me his new gift.

"Hallelujah, praise the Lord" I shouted, this was incredible.

Terry was a totally different guy after that, he became very enthusiastic to learn about the Christian life but now he had a permanent smile on his face. We received quite an amazing confirmation about this. Douglas rang us from Motherwell later that day, apparently he had been at an all night prayer meeting at the King's Centre and at 3am one of the intercessors had a vision of the Potters Centre, she said:

"I can see the house, there are a ring of angels above it and the Lord is in the centre of the ring and he is commanding darkness to keep off the building."

This was at the exact same time that the Lord turned up in Terry's room. I told Douglas the story Terry had told me, "Wow, this is incredible!" he said in amazement.

A few days later I boarded the plane for Israel, this was to be my third trip to the Holy Land and this time I was going with my pal Joash, who sadly has now gone home to be with Jesus, I miss him dearly.

We flew into Ben Gurion Airport, Tel Aviv and after clearing the airport security checks we headed into downtown Tel Aviv, to our accommodation 'The Gordon Hostel' where I'd stayed with Ed Gibson. After checking in we headed off to the beach to chill out and get some sun. We spent a couple of days on the beach before doing some sightseeing visiting Jerusalem and the Dead Sea area. The heat at the Dead Sea was unbearable, as the doors of the air-conditioned bus opened at Ein Gedi it was like walking into a wall of heat.

We had landed in the middle of a heat wave and the temperature was up to around 48 degrees Celsius almost 120 degrees Fahrenheit.

So I spent most of the afternoon stood under the canopy of the communal showers that are dotted around the edge of the salt sea. I had a couple of brief excursions into the sea itself but they were brief as I had a couple of cuts on my back and the salt was causing them to sting. It is a really unusual experience being in the jelly like waters of the Dead Sea, you cannot sink! You try to put your feet down and they just keep on rising back to the surface, it is a really queer phenomenon. We stayed for a couple of hours before boarding a bus back to Jerusalem and then back to the hostel in Tel Aviv.

The next day we took a bus over to Jerusalem and went for a walk around the old city visiting all the sites, before going to the 'Garden Tomb,' which is located just behind the bus station near the Damascus Gate.

Just behind the bus station is the famous skull rock, which I and many other people believe to be the true site of the crucifixion, rather than the traditional site in the old city. Skull Rock and the Garden Tomb fit the biblical description perfectly, plus excavations at the site over recent years by Archaeologists Ron Wyatt and Simon Gray have produced amazing evidence of this being the actual site. After a three year dig they found much evidence including finding the stone that was rolled from Jesus'

Tomb and also the post holes where the crosses were placed during crucifixions.There is much evidence which has been covered on film and in books to authenticate the site and I would definitely encourage you to visit the site if possible.

You can view Skull Rock from the garden. There is a beautiful peace in the Garden, the presence of God is everywhere. It was a tearful and emotional moment for me as I approached the tomb itself. On the door of the tomb is a sign, the contents of the sign I can confirm are true for I am a witness to His resurrection, it simply says as it does in Matthew 28 verse 6:

'He is not here, for He is risen!'

28
The African Adventure Continues

I was quite excited as August drew near; things were going well on all fronts. The church was doing well; we were making real progress at the rehabilitation centre and seeing a lot of fruit for our efforts. I had been invited to speak at the 'Move On' convention in the Nyayo National Stadium in Nairobi, Kenya by Apostle Harry Das. I was looking forward to the trip and would be accompanied on the trip by Douglas Jarvie and his son Paul.

Douglas had made the flight arrangements for us. He said that it was very difficult to get a direct flight to Nairobi on the dates we wanted, as it was the height of the holiday season and all the flights were full.

However, he had managed to get us on a flight to Nairobi that was going via Egypt, Yemen, Tanzania and that we might have a short stopover in Aden!

We were due to fly out from Heathrow Airport so the day before we were due to leave we headed south. Our friend Jonathan lives practically next door to the airport in the Middlesex village of Harlington and he very kindly agreed to put the three of us up for the night.

The following day we all trooped round to the airport to catch our flight to Nairobi, we found the ticket desk which belonged to a Yemen airline company, picked up the tickets and headed off to the check-in desk.

A couple of hours later we were flying over the English Channel en route to Egypt, the first stop on our journey.

After a short time on the runway at Cairo International Airport we were off again this time we were bound for Yemen and this is where the confusion began.

We were informed that we were not going to Aden but to Sanaa and that our short stopover had turned into a three-day delay, everybody was furious. The helpless cabin crew took the brunt of most people's frustration, it wasn't their fault, but they were the only ones available to complain to.

On landing in Sanaa the frustration was transferred to the airport manager, a grubby little man who took it all in his stride as he puffed away on an endless supply of foul smelling cigarettes. We tried to reason with him, we were booked to speak at a conference in Nairobi, we had to leave the following day.

"No, no, no not posseeeble" he answered shooing us away like flies.

"Look I have to get to Nairobi" I protested "When is the next flight to Kenya."

"No flights to Kenya till Saturday! Only plane leaving here is for Addis Ababa tomorrow."

That was that—we were stuck! It was early Thursday morning by this time and we needed sleep. In my mind I considered the options, I suppose at a push we could have got the flight to Ethiopia and hoped to get a connecting flight to Nairobi, but it seemed that nothing was guaranteed and I did not want to get stuck in Ethiopia.

"Don't worry" the manager assured us "I send you to nice hotel."

We eventually reached the San City Hotel. The 'nice' hotel that the man had promised turned out to be an Arab version of 'Fawlty Towers'—we were not happy campers!

We decided to make the best of things and had a communion service up in our rooms asking the Lord for chances to share our faith, which was totally illegal in Yemen. We would have been in trouble if we'd been caught with our Bibles, not to mention the hundreds of

Gospel testimony booklets in my suitcase, it all added to the excitement.

We began to share our faith with the other passengers, one in particular was a veteran marathon runner from Manchester en route to a marathon in Kenya. The guy's name was Mike and he was very chatty and interested in our testimonies about God.

"I need a miracle to get to my marathon now" he said quite despondently. "My ticket was only to Dar es Salaam, I had a connecting flight to Nairobi which leaves tomorrow."

"Don't worry we'll pray about it" Douglas said to encourage him, "Our God is in the miracle business!"

The next couple of days were spent witnessing and giving out testimony booklets. We decided to depart from our hotel's dismal surroundings and headed off to the plush Sheraton Hotel which, for a small fee, would allow us to use their facilities including health club, gym and pool. Saturday eventually came and we were at the airport once more, the scene was chaotic and resembled a cattle market. Soon we were on the plane again our destination Dar Es Salaam, Tanzania. By now Mike the marathon runner was sweating, everybody on the plane knew his circumstances. Dar Es Salaam was to be Mike's final leg on his current ticket, he badly needed a miracle if he was to get to Nairobi for Saturday afternoon which would enable him to compete in Sunday's marathon. The problem was, there were no scheduled flights to Nairobi that day.

As we prayed I felt the Lord say, 'expect a miracle' and so we continued to pray. Douglas suggested that Mike explain his circumstances to the captain so they spoke to the stewardess who in turn went to speak to the captain. A few minutes later she returned and told Mike that the captain would speak to him and so Mike disappeared into the cockpit of the aeroplane. The whole plane waited with baited breath and then it happened! Mike came through the door with a big smile on his face, the captain had told him that he could fly from Dar es Salaam to Tanzania on the captain's personal ticket and he would clear it with the airport authorities in Dar es Salaam. If it was ok with them then Mike could stay on the plane to Nairobi instead of disembarking in Tanzania—everyone gave a big cheer. 'Your God has done this' Mike said, punching the air. He was so excited by the developments that he ran around the plane handing gospel tracts out to everyone and giving testimony. It was 2 o'clock in the afternoon by the time we reached Jomo Kenyatta Airport, Nairobi and the conference at the Nyayo Stadium had been in full swing for four days and there was to be more drama at the airport! The sun was blazing as we disembarked and made our way across the tarmac and into the terminal building. Our problems began when we reached immigration and they demanded to see our vaccination certificates. We all had our vaccination records, but Douglas did not have a yellow fever certificate and they were not going to allow him into the country. I began to pray, Douglas assured them that he had been vaccinated and but had not known that his certificate was needed. The airport official was quite adamant over the point—no certificate, no entry. At this point I was wandering round praying in tongues desperately seeking the Lord's voice. As I glanced through the window in the immigration office, I could see Pastor Daniel Gitau and another couple of ministers who were obviously waiting for me in the arrivals hall. They were dressed smartly in suits and I could see their conference badges and rosettes.

I felt the Lord say 'take authority' so I marched up to the desk and said "Look, we are Christian ministers here in your country to preach the gospel at your National Stadium. If you look through that window, you will see a number of men of God who are waiting to pick us up.

We are men of truth and integrity and do not tell lies, this man has had his injections, now let us through." The man looked up and said, "I believe that you are men of God" and to our amazement he stamped our passports and let us through.

After picking up our luggage, and passing through customs, we made our way into the arrivals hall where the small group of ministers were waiting for us. Daniel stretched out his hand to greet me. "Davey, where have you been?" he asked, "We thought you were coming on Thursday, did you get lost?" "You do not want to know, Daniel!" I replied, "We've been stuck in Yemen for the past three days"

"Ok Davey, we are going straight to the stadium now, the Apostle is waiting for us there." There were two large vehicles waiting outside to take us into the city, which was a half hour's drive or so away.

We could see the huge floodlights of the stadium looming in the distance as we entered the suburbs of Nairobi. The sun was still shining, I looked at my watch, it was nearly four o'clock, the day at the conference was almost over. When we arrived, the stadium was still full of people and as we made our way up into the executive offices we could see hundreds of people receiving prayer ministry. The apostle was waiting for us in the function suite of the stadium, he greeted us with a warm smile and affection. He was wearing a white suit with a black shirt and tie "Eventually you arrive," he said. "We were beginning to think you weren't coming!"

"You would not believe the trouble we have had getting here" I replied.

"I am so glad you are here, we had you advertised in the programme to begin on Wednesday, so I am very relieved to see you! Tomorrow is the last day and we want you to share as much as possible.

"You will be staying at the Chrisco guest house, which is five minutes drive from here, and tomorrow you preach."

He then went on to introduce me to other senior ministers within the Chrisco work and also gave me an opportunity to see some people I had met on my first trip to Kenya.

After a buffet meal we headed off to the Chrisco guesthouse where we were to be looked after by Sister Margaret and her team. On arrival Margaret showed us to our rooms and I went off in search of a much-needed shower! I could see the runway of Wilson Airport from the bathroom window and watched a procession of small planes take off as I enjoyed the refreshing coolness of the water. Paul and I slept well that night, but Douglas seemed to spend most of it on the toilet with an upset stomach.

After breakfast the following morning we were picked up and driven the short distance to the stadium. We were amongst the first to arrive, the atmosphere was gentle and peaceful. I wandered around by myself praying in tongues and enjoying the warmth of the morning sunshine. Gradually one by one other ministers began to arrive and so we made our way to the stage that was set up in the middle of the stadium. I continued to pray and prepare myself for my sessions, every so often I would lift up my eyes towards the stands, the stadium was starting to fill up, excitement was growing in my stomach.

The atmosphere was highly charged as I got up to speak, this was by far the biggest venue that I had preached at to date and I was in a state of awe at the size of the event. There were thousands and thousands of people in the stadium and at first I was quite nervous at the prospect, but Apostle Das put me at peace as he introduced me to the sea of faces. He shared how we had met and about the times he had visited my home, he rounded off by saying that I was a man who moved in five-fold ministry, anointing and blessing and that "We have some funny characters in the Chrisco work in other countries!"

I in turn introduced Douglas and his son, Paul and invited him to share a little of his testimony about how he had escaped the perils of freemasonry, which went down well with the huge crowd. Then I got up for the first of my sessions and preached on the power of binding and loosing, then in the next session I gave my testimony. This posed quite a problem as my interpreters understood 'English' but had great difficulty with my Geordie accent and so we went through five interpreters before we found one who could decipher the Tyneside version of the English language!

Not only was I in awe of the event, but I was in awe of how much God had changed me and my circumstances. I could scarcely believe it, at times it seemed like a dream. No one in their wildest imaginings could have predicted the path that I have walked and now here I was in Kenya's national stadium preaching to thousands and thousands of people.

Nobody special, just a villain from the West End of Newcastle upon Tyne—who would have believed it!

I finished off the day by preaching on healing and then gave an altar call to repentance. I invited people to come and receive Jesus as their Saviour, I also invited people to come for deliverance and healing. It started as a trickle at first but soon hundreds had made their way forward to receive salvation and a touch from God. After this I left the stage and began ministering to the lines and lines of people, praying for the baptism of the Holy Spirit, praying healing prayers and casting out demons. The presence of God in the stadium was totally overwhelming and was unlike anything I had experienced in Britain, the closest was probably the renewal meetings at Sunderland. All over the stadium people were being healed and set free from the demonic. As I moved along the lines, people collapsed under the power of God, the anointing at times was very thick and tangible. By the end of the afternoon I was exhausted though I still managed to take part in the march around the stadium at the end of the conference. I was disappointed that we had only made it for the last day of the conference, but we had made a terrific impact and the newspapers were waiting to interview us.

Kenya's leading national newspaper, the Daily Nation did a colour feature on me which was a little bit exaggerated, the reporter let his imagination run away with him but nevertheless got the message across and made me instantly recognisable wherever we went in Kenya!

Douglas spent most of the night dashing back and forwards to the toilet with an upset tummy. We decided it best to have a deliverance session after we found him crawling on all fours and growling at us.

"Come out in the name of Jesus Christ" I shouted.

There was a bit of a roar and Douglas made a charge for me, but ended up on the floor like he had just hit an invisible wall!

After an hour or so the demon left with a scream and peace returned to Douglas, he lay on the floor for a while before we helped him to bed and I headed off to bed myself. I looked at my watch and groaned, it was 3am!

The following day Pastor Gitau and Pastor Wambete came and outlined my preaching itinerary for the next three weeks—it was a hectic schedule with two meetings a day and very little time off, but it was a privilege and a challenge I looked forward to.

Douglas looked a lot better and was back to his normal self, he gave me a big toothless grin.

"Where on earth did that come from?" he asked scratching his head, a bit embarrassed.

"I have no idea" I answered "But you're definitely a few passengers lighter now"

"What happened?" he asked.

"We cast a demon out last night" I replied.

"I had deliverance years ago when I first became a Christian, I thought it had been dealt with" he said quite shocked.

"I thought a Christian couldn't have a demon?" he said in amazement

"Now you know the truth" I said, "I think it came in when you had your accident."

"That's probably why you kept having the black outs" I continued.

"Do you think so?" he asked.

"It's possible, let's just thank God for the fact that it's out. Now let's look at the itinerary" I said trying to change the subject.

We were to begin in Nairobi, then travel to Dondori and Nakuru, after that we were to travel up to Kakamega. Next we were to go to Kisumu before travelling back to Nairobi, then fly down to Mombasa on the coast for a week of meetings before returning to England.

Later that day we spent time with Harry Das and then went for a meal in a restaurant in the city centre before going to the Nairobi Odeon where Apostle Das was recording his weekly show for Kenya Television. Once again the old man was delighted to see me and took my hand, walking and talking with me like a father to a son. The wisdom that came from him was precious, every time I met with him I took something from it, he would pray for me and heaven would open. Each time he prayed I felt as though something was being added and the anointing was increasing.

The next day I began a week of preaching in the capital, the first event being a lunchtime meeting at the Odeon. I was amazed as nearly a thousand people attended—quite a lot for a lunchtime meeting, I thought!! Our evening engagements were spent preaching at various churches around the city. Each morning I would spend hours in prayer and the Lord would give me a different message each day.

The people in Nairobi really took a shine to us and we made a lot of new friends. At the time, life in Nairobi seemed to be quite difficult. During our week there, we experienced many power cuts and the water supply was often off so people had to buy barrels of water from mobile dispensers. It was also very hot and humid and by the end of the week we were glad to be heading north to Nakuru.

Over the next few weeks we travelled extensively, ministering to thousands of people at a number of different locations including Nakuru, Dondori, Karecho, Kisumu and Kakamega.

The time we had in Kakamega was unforgettable, it became the highlight of the trip for me. The people in Kakamega were so wonderful and loving. What a privilege it was to be in a meeting where the Mayor was dancing and praising God, hand in hand with a Provincial Commissioner (the equivalent of our Government Cabinet Minister). It was a joy to be in a place where the people worshipped for two hours before the service began. These simple folk can teach the world a thing or two about praise and worship.

However, there was to be a backlash as we left Kakamega. Douglas, who had been under heavy spiritual attack and plagued by bouts of sickness and diahorrea suddenly began to suffer from dehydration. Over the previous days he had lost quite a lot of bodily fluid and was in real danger as we drove from Kakamega to Kisumu. As the journey progressed, Douglas's condition became worse and the groans from the back of the car got louder and louder.

We were headed for the presidential compound in Kisumu, to the home of the Provincial Commissioner, but that was over an hour away. Douglas' condition was deteriorating by the minute and drastic action was needed. I decided to seek the Lord's help.

At the time Douglas was suffering from food poisoning and Malaria but we were unaware of this and both were potential killers. As we approached a village I asked Richard to pull the car over. We carried Douglas from the car and laid him on the ground, then Richard, Mabel, Paul and myself joined hands. Many of the local people were now out wondering what was going on and came to watch the spectacle. I began to lead prayers, once again casting out spirits of sickness and infirmity. We started to declare and decree prayers of healing over Douglas and for half an hour we battled away, praying in tongues. I felt that we were battling for Douglas's life. We prayed and prayed until I felt that we had the victory and I felt an assurance in my spirit that God, in His mercy, had spared Douglas' life.

We got Douglas back in the car and continued on our journey to Kisumu.

An hour or so later we could see Lake Victoria as we approached the outskirts of the city.

On reaching the presidential compound, the Provincial Commissioner had Douglas taken straight to hospital where doctors confirmed our suspicions—Douglas had not only eaten some infected food, but had contracted Malaria. We continued in prayer and then God performed another miracle and healed Douglas instantly. No one could believe it, but within a few hours his condition turned around 180 degrees. Immediately his colour and strength returned to him and after a few hours rest the doctor discharged him from hospital!! The doctors were as astounded as we were and we continued to rejoice and thank God.

At a house meeting that night, Douglas was back to his old self, jumping around praising the Lord as though there had been nothing amiss. I sat in awe of the Lord as he gave testimony of his remarkable healing, here was a man who had literally been at death's door only hours earlier and now here he was, the life and soul of the party!! Our God is awesome.

For the next few weeks we travelled all over Kenya, finishing off in the coastal holiday resort of Mombasa where we conducted a series of meetings. We then spent some time relaxing, swimming and enjoying the sun on Mombasa's beautiful beaches.

The trip had been a success; we had made a lot of new friends and had a real adventure. I was now looking forward to going home.

However, I was not looking forward to the stop over in Yemen! The thought of that hotel in Sanaa filled me with dread, but once again there was to be a twist in the tail and the Lord moved sovereignly. After an amicable word with the airline representative, he decided to change our accommodation to a luxurious five star hotel with all expenses paid, where we generously indulged ourselves at the airline's expense!

On returning from Africa a shock was waiting for us! We found we'd lost the rehab! Mr Williams had done a u-turn, greed had filled his heart and he pulled the plug on everything. I was totally devastated after all the time, money and hard work that we'd put in to building the place up, but there was nothing I could do, we hadn't been able to sign any contracts. I had also just purchased a minibus for the centre. We were heartbroken, all our hard work up the spout! But it was the lads that I felt sorry for, they were left high and dry, we had shown them a love and care that many of them had never experienced. We had encouraged them, built up their self worth and self esteem, giving them a fresh start, a purpose to life, now everything was gone.

I sought the Lord in prayer to see what was going on and he said to me "This is Ananias and Saphira" in reference to Williams and his wife, greed and corruption were at the bottom of it.

Looking back now I can see that it was part of my training process, God was teaching me how to rehabilitate people, it was a new aspect of the work that I hadn't done before. There are too few places like this in our nation, Britain has horrendous addiction problems and the Government has no clue how to tackle it! I know this was a part of the vision he had shown me and I know in the future it will become an important part of my life establishing many rehabilitation centres such as these.

The Lord said to me, "One day I'll bring you another place like this, you won't have to look for it, it will find you!"

29
Revival in
the Indian Ocean

I began to feel quite worn out as 2000 drew to a close. I had done quite a lot of travelling during the year, with two trips to Africa, a third trip to Israel, as well as a trip to Cyprus. Also the experience with the Potters Revival Centre had left me drained, so by the time a crusade at Seaham Harbour was over, I was ready for a break. I badly needed a holiday but didn't have a great deal of finance and so we started to pray, asking the Lord to open a door. I didn't hear anything immediately, but I thanked him, leaving it at his feet.

I did a couple of follow up meetings at Seaham Harbour where we picked up a few more new converts bringing the total to over 70 conversions, which was quite amazing as Seaham was spiritually very dark and challenging. The Lord had blessed the time we were there with a very powerful anointing and the people were lovely.

The story of how the crusade came together was another bit of 'Divine' inspiration! The Lord had told me at the beginning of the year that we would have a crusade in Seaham Harbour. I was approached later in the year by a group of churches in the area who came to me with an unusual tale.

For a while things had been getting spiritually dry in the area, church attendance was dropping and the leaders of the local churches were becoming despondent. They started to pray and seek the Lord about what course of action to take in their 'Churches Together' meetings. Incredibly, when they came together they all had the same answer with the conversation going something like this:

"Well, I feel that we should have a crusade and I've got somebody in mind to lead it" Jimmy from the Lighthouse Fellowship started.

"I agree" said Colin from the Independent Methodist Church "I've got someone in mind too."

"That's what I believe too" said the Salvation Army captain." I don't know who you've got in mind, but I believe that the Lord wants us to have Davey Falcus come and lead it."

"Wow, that is amazing, because that who I was thinking of!" said Jimmy excitedly.

"Me too" said Colin "I've had a leaflet about him put through the door."

"Have you? I have as well" said Jimmy.

"So have we, a couple of guys were posting them through doors!" Colin added.

"Well, that settles it, I'll get in touch with him" said Jimmy.

To this day we do not know who the men were who posted these leaflets—perhaps they were angels?

Whoever the men were, the crusade was a success and the church in Seaham was thriving when we left.

A few days after our last meeting Douglas phoned with an interesting offer:

"Davey would you like to go on an all expenses paid holiday to Sri Lanka?" Douglas asked.

"Say that again Douglas" I said not believing my ears.

"Davey, you sound knackered and I believe that the Lord wants me to take you to Sri Lanka! Do you want to go?"

"Too right I do" I replied with excitement. "Amen, thank you Lord! When are you thinking of going Douglas?"

"On the second of January… is that okay for you?"

It was only two weeks away.

"Yes that's fine by me, Douglas, thank you very much."

"Okay then, I'll book it, see ya then " said Douglas and hung up.

I jumped up punching the air "Yessss!!"

Just what the doctor ordered a couple of weeks in the Indian Ocean I was ecstatic.

The Christmas period came and it was nice to spend some quality time with the family, which is difficult at times when you're in full-time ministry, as your time is often taken with other people. This can often result in neglecting those closest to you, so it was a nice relaxing time with them.

Eventually the second of January came and we were off.

A couple of hours after take off I began to nod off when the Lord started to speak to me about the trip, it was very encouraging for me as he was speaking to me in a very light hearted and amusing way.

He told me I was going to Sri Lanka mainly for rest, but that he had a 'few interesting little tasks for us to do!'

I must say the Lord has wonderful sense of humour and he is sharper than anyone! Some of the best one-liners I've heard are from God—but after all, who gave us the gift of laughter? So I lay back and looked forward to the adventure ahead with a contentedness in my spirit knowing that God had all in hand. I started to laugh as we hit some really bad air turbulence over Bahrain. The whole plane was shaking as we began our descent into Bahrain to refuel. People started to scream as the plane began to plummet, but I was not shaken at all, my trust was in the Lord, after all he had just told me I was going to Sri Lanka! Eventually the drama ended and we landed safely.

After a brief time in Bahrain we set off again and after five hours we landed in Colombo, Sri Lanka's capital.

The sun was shining, the atmosphere hot and humid as we disembarked the plane. On clearing customs we set about the task of finding some accommodation, we approached the tourist office to get some advice and a very helpful gentleman arranged for us to stay at a hotel in Mount Lavinia, which is a suburb of Colombo, next to the sea. The very helpful tourist officer Mr Ghouse also arranged for a driver to take us to the hotel.

Colombo is a typical capital city with many high buildings, including the huge United Nations building situated in the city centre. Colombo is very densely populated, the streets packed with traders and people going about their daily business, there was also a heavy military presence due to civil unrest in Sri Lanka.

After forty minutes or so we finally escaped the hustle and bustle of the big city, as we drove through the less busy outskirts of the city. I caught a glimpse of British Colonialism, with many buildings being left from the days of the 'Raj'. I was also struck by the number of temples and religious idols, which were literally on every corner. Eventually we reached our destination, the 'Tropical Reef' hotel.

As soon as we got into our hotel room I bolted into the bathroom in search of a shower, I was saturated in sweat, my clothes sticking to my body, and tiredness had begun to creep in after the long gruelling journey.

I opened the bathroom window and stood for a while leaning on the window sill peering down into the street below. At the end of the street I could see the crashing waves of the Indian Ocean, it was absolute bliss as the cold water from the shower hit my body, bringing a refreshing coolness, I closed my eyes enjoying moment.

After showering we got unpacked and went to the hotel restaurant in search of food, I was so tired that at one point during my meal I fell asleep with my face collapsing into my food! After this we slept for almost a full twelve hours, exhausted by our long journey.

Early the next morning we headed down to the beach, which was a hive of activity, the local karate school were doing their morning workout and the fishermen were dragging their nets out of the sea, which were full of shiny little silver fish. We sat for a while watching what was going on then headed back to the hotel for a prayer time and breakfast.

During the prayer time the Lord spoke to me and said that we should contact Douglas' friends Abraham and Mercy Pooniah who ran a children's orphanage in Colombo.

Douglas telephoned them and they came straight over to the hotel, then we all went for lunch in a beautiful Chinese restaurant.

Abraham and his wife Mercy were natives of Sri Lanka and had been Christians for many years. Abraham was a tall, thin, balding man, Mercy a short stocky woman. At the time Abraham and Mercy were in their late fifties, they were real prayer warriors and had pioneered many works in Sri Lanka, often in the dangerous northern areas of Sri Lanka where there was a lot of terrorist activity. After the meal we went to their home, which wasn't far from the new Parliament building.

After showing us around the work Abraham asked me to share testimony and minister to everyone.

Afterwards Mercy said to me:

"David, I think you should meet our friend Brother Raja, his story is very similar to yours, he runs a rehab work near Galle, in the South of the Island, would you like me to set it up?"

"Yes, if you feel it's the Lord's will, we were planning to head south anyway" I replied.

"Okay, I'll ring him, where were you planning to go?" Mercy asked.

"We thought we'd go down to Hikkaduwa, the beaches looked great down there."

"Brother Raja has a place in Hikkaduwa as well!" Mercy said excitedly "this must be the Lord! I'll get a driver to take you down, it's a three hour drive, have you got a place to stay?"

"Not yet, we need to pray about it" I answered.

"Okay, well if you can't find a place let us know" she smiled.

We returned to our hotel and began to pray about our accommodation in Hikkaduwa. We had a book with a list of hotels. We felt the Lord telling us to book into the Sunils hotel, so Douglas phoned them and made our reservation.

The following morning the driver turned up and we set off for the south of the country. The drive was a pleasant one and it gave us a chance to see some of the Island. The road was situated next to the sea all the way down and I noticed that the further south we went the clearer the sea became, it was a beautiful blue/green colour. On the other side of the road was the jungle, it reminded me of the early Johnny Weismuller 'Tarzan' films.

Life here looked hard but laid back, the scenery was breathtakingly beautiful as we passed many villages and fishing communities. We caught a glimpse of the world famous stilt fishermen perched on their stilts waiting to spear fish.

Eventually we reached our destination, The Sunils Hotel.

We unpacked and headed for the hotel pool and spent a couple of days chilling out in the peaceful paradise-like surroundings.

After a day or two we were contacted by Alic and Shane two young men from Raja's team, they had a community house nearby in which they held their spiritual school. We hit it off immediately with the two lads both ex-drug addicts, they told us that Abraham had phoned Brother

Raja and that he was excited about meeting us. Also he wanted me to lead the Sunday meeting at the rehab centre in Galle. I said that it would be a privilege and as it was only Wednesday I had ample time to prepare for it. Douglas told the lads that I was there for rest but would be happy to do a few meetings if required.

I spent the next couple of days resting and seeking God, the temperature was in the thirties but was not humid like it had been in Colombo, there was also a nice gentle breeze. The boys turned up to spend some time with us almost every day. On a couple of occasions Douglas went off with them to do a little teaching at the spiritual school, leaving me to recharge my batteries in the glorious sunshine.

There were some beautiful sunsets to behold. In the evenings I would sit on my balcony and watch as the sun went down over the sea. This huge orange ball of fire would disappear, slipping down behind the distant horizon, like an actor leaving the stage. It was a moment to savour as I listened to the gentle melodic strains of 'Going Home,' the theme tune from the film 'Local Hero,' performed by Mark Knopfler of the band Dire Straits.

On Saturday Alic and Shane turned up at the hotel with another fellow who was slightly older, his name was Vivien. Vivien had been a top DJ in Sri Lanka, he had also worked in England, but had fallen from grace with a serious cocaine problem. He had been in the centre at Galle for nine months where his addiction had been broken after meeting Jesus. He became a 'born again' believer and had recently moved into the house in Hikkaduwa.

Vivien suggested we moved to the bigger Coral Rock hotel up the road and that he would get us an amazing deal as the owners were friends of his.

So we moved to the 'Coral Rock' which was much better all round and cost us very little in comparison to 'Sunils.'

The owners were pleased to have us and showed us great respect.

We had a great time witnessing to the staff about the love of Jesus, many of them were genuinely interested in what we had to say. Hikkaduwa is a small place and news soon got around that the 'Men of God' were in town. Everywhere we went we were greeted with a "Hello Father!!" or "Greetings Father."

"Davey will do just fine" I would answer, quite amused at their assumption that I was a Catholic Priest! We also had a visit from a Pastor who had a church in the jungle. He asked if we would be willing to preach there, and we agreed.

We did have a few irritations however, which came in the form of the local mosquitos. We had a running battle them, swatting them with rolled up newspapers and whatever we could get our hands on! Going to the toilet at night time was like entering 'Ambush Alley', you would just get yourself settled and you'd hear a little; 'Buzzzz' and one would fly up from behind you, so you'd jump up to try and wack it! Some nights were quite entertaining, I would lie back on my pillow under the mosquito net listening to Douglas chasing mosquitos in the toilet, every now and then a triumphant shout would arise as another mosquito shuffled off to the place prepared for flattened mosquitos! Also every so often a little Gheko would peep out from its hole and make a mad dash back and forwards across the ceiling!

On Sunday morning the lads came to the hotel to pick us up to take us the short train journey down to Galle to meet Brother Raja. The train was packed with people, some were sitting on the roof, others hanging on the sides of the train it was just like I had seen in Richard Attenborough's film 'Ghandi.'

There was an assortment of animals on the train with

their owners—goats, dogs, chickens etc and we were offered all kinds of different 'wares and tares' as well as various foods by vendors who wandered through the packed carriages. The platform at Galle Station was packed solid with people as the train pulled in. We disembarked and squeezed our way through the crowd. Alic went in search of a ' Tuk, Tuk' one of Asia's favourite forms of taxi.

(A 'Tuk Tuk is a type of three wheel motorbike with a large seat and canopy on the back.)

We passed the famous Galle lighthouse and cricket ground as we made the ten minute journey from the station to Rummasala Hill, where the 'New Life' Centre is based. The centre is situated high on the hill overlooking the beautiful Galle bay.

We were met at the entrance to the centre, by a man called Moses. Moses was one of the resident pastors and greeted us with a big smile before ushering us in to the office to meet Brother Raja.

Brother Raja looked about fifty years old and had a long beard, he was dressed in a long white flowing gown. He got up from his desk to come and greet us with a big radiant smile on his face, with hands clasped together in a typical Indian greeting, there was a real gentleness and humility about him.

Unfortunately he did not speak English but Alic translated for us and for an hour or so we exchanged our stories. We found that we had a lot in common not least that we were both ex gangsters and had both spent time behind bars. Rajah joked that the prisons in England were more like hotels than the prisons he'd been in. In one prison he had spent time waist deep in a pit filled with water! But all that was past now, he had met Jesus in prison with another man who had a vision for rehabs all over Sri Lanka, a bit like the vision God showed me. However, the man died leaving Rajah to fulfil the vision, which is what has happened. Without any government help Rajah had started the work, the Lord had provided miraculously and since then Rajah has seen hundreds of people set free from drink, drugs and crime.

The Government who were at a loss as what to do with the current drug epidemic invited Rajah into the prisons, where he and his team continue to work, rehabilitating prisoners and their families. It is a real ministry of love they also look after the children of long-term prisoners.

Rajah then sprung a surprise on me.

There were currently two hundred people living within the centre, fifty or so needed baptism. "Would I like to baptise them in the sea before the service?"

Would I not! What a wonderful privilege.

So we all trooped off down the hillside to the bay, it was quite a sight to see.

The bay at the bottom of Rummasala Hill is breathtakingly beautiful, the waters are crystal clear, there is an array of tropical fish in the waters as well as the giant sea turtles. Scuba diving and snorkelling there is an incredible experience. There were a few tourists on the beach when we arrived and they were interested to see what all the fuss was about.

We had a short time of prayer on the beach, then the centre inhabitants began to sing praises to God.

Then Rajah, Douglas, Alic and myself entered the water to start baptising as the nominees for baptism formed an orderly queue. Rajah had a team taking pictures and filming the whole event.

I felt like John the Baptist at Aenon as the procession of nominees trooped into the water one by one. It was a perfect venue for baptism. Alic introduced each person as they came in, with Douglas and myself doing the baptising as the crowd cheered on from the beach. After each baptism Rajah would embrace them with a big encouraging hug and a cheering round of applause would go up from the shore. The power of the Holy Spirit hung heavy over the proceedings and one man was set free from paralysis as he entered the waters of baptism! It was an awesome and incredible experience to be involved in. At the end Douglas had counted 62!

As the afternoon wore on, my shoulders, which had been exposed to the sun for a while became sore. As I came out of the water Rajah asked me to baptise them all in the Holy Spirit, so once again they all lined up and one by one they started to collapse all over the beach! The tourists must have wondered what an earth was going on as they were certainly taking an interest in proceedings! Some of the lads went off to witness to them.

There were bodies everywhere as the Lord poured out his blessings on us.

After eating Sunday lunch in the jungle, another rare experience, I led a service at the centre baptising over a hundred in the Holy Spirit and giving communion to another two hundred. It was a very busy but very rewarding day.

We were on a total high as we travelled back to Hikkaduwa thanking and praising the Lord for the day.

As the days wore on the favour of God continued to fall on us.

At the leading of the Holy Spirit, Alic, Shane, ourselves and members of the Hikkaduwa church went to specific points around the town. At these points we would praise, worship and take communion, we poured oil on the idols situated at the gateways to the town and we commanded the spirits behind them to depart.

It was incredible, the spiritual atmosphere changed immediately, it suddenly became easy to witness to people, everyone wanted to know about Jesus. People started to get saved—barmen, waiters, the under-manager at the hotel… Tracts were going out everywhere, families started to turn up at the hotel looking for us. People came looking for us to pray over them, it began to look as though we were going to have a revival on our hands!

One family had travelled down from Colombo for a day out; they heard about us through someone giving them one of my tracts in a restaurant. They felt led to seek us out for prayer. Suddenly I was casting out demons by the hotel pool and seeing people set free from darkness, being filled by the power of the Holy Spirit.

We had an amazing time in Sri Lanka we built relationships with the people and saw God do a tremendous work. I thanked him and praised him for my rest and 'interesting little tasks!!

On the second last day of the trip I was at one end of the pool enjoying the peace and the sunshine, Douglas was doing the same at the other end, the Lord spoke to us at exactly the same time, he said: "I want you to go to Cancun."

I sat up and looked at Douglas he had a big grin on his face and simply said: "Cancun"

"Woooah, party on!" I shouted in excitement.

We decided to travel back to Colombo so we would be fresh for the plane the following day. Once again we looked to our guide book for accommodation in the capital. We decided on the YMCA as it had quite a good write up. So we said our goodbyes to Shane and Alic, deciding to take the train from Hikkaduwa up to Colombo. It was a slow but pleasant journey up the coastline passing the many towns and villages with their Buddhist temples. The journey gave me time to reflect on the trip, it had certainly been an adventure but now I was ready for home and looking forward to spending time with my family. I gazed lazily out of the window, watching the sun glistening on the sea and the palm trees gently swaying in the slight breeze. Once again we passed rows of stilt fishermen who were waiting patiently on their perches looking to land their catches.

We arrived at the Central Station in Colombo around three thirty in the afternoon it was already packed with commuters and so we had to battle our way through the crowd to get out of the place, once again I was struck by the humidity.

On leaving the station we hailed a 'TukTuk' that took us to the YMCA, which was situated across the road from the United Nations Building and the Colombo Hilton Hotel.

The YMCA turned out to be an old one that had seen better days, it had obviously been a glorious building in its day, being built by the British Colonials in the late nineteenth century, but now it was showing its age. We were given a room on the top floor of the building, it was basic but clean, I had a brief glance round and was disappointed to see there was no enamel left on the bath. I looked out of the window and saw we were right next door to the army barracks.

After a brief shower we had a meal with Abraham and Mercy and then headed back to the YMCA for a good night's sleep.

I awoke the following morning to see Douglas peering out of the window, he was looking down into the barracks with concern on his face.

"What's up with you?" I asked.

"Oh you're awake now" he said.

"How on earth have you slept through all that?" Douglas asked with a look of wonder on his face.

"Slept through what?" I asked totally clueless, as I rubbed the sleep from my eyes.

"Davey there have been bombs going off and machine gun fire for half the night, how on earth have you slept through it all?"

"Why what's happened?" I asked him still not compos mentis

"The Tamil Tigers attacked the barracks last night and there has been absolute mayhem down there, how have you not heard it?" Quick as a shot I fired back, with tongue in cheek:

"Well Douglas, those who fix their mind on the Lord will be kept in perfect peace!" I quipped.

After getting up we decided to go for breakfast, deciding to swap the cuisine at the YMCA for the breakfast bar at the Hilton Hotel, it proved to be a profitable move. We sat in the palatial surroundings discussing the trip and looking forward to the adventure that lay ahead in Cancun. After that Abraham took us to the airport to catch our plane home, one quite amusing thing happened at the airport.

After checking in we went into the departures area, which was packed solid with holidaymakers. On entering the area I saw they had a special room set aside for 'Clergy'.

"Okay Douglas let's go and sit in there" I said anxious to get a sit down and put my feet up for a while.

"Why not?" he said

We entered the little room and sat down on some vacant seats. There was a man and a woman sat in the room, I nodded politely to them.

They were both smartly dressed and looked to be in their late fifties, the woman looked me up and down then said:

"I'm sorry but this room is for clergy only!" the tone of her voice was peppered with snobby disapproval.

"I'm sorry madam but I am clergy!" I replied sharply.

"No you're not!" she insisted, looking at my tattoo-covered torso.

"Yes, I am" I said again.

"He is" Douglas chipped.

"I don't believe it" the woman snapped quite rudely.

"Right" I said reaching for my bag and wallet. I pulled out my cards and showed them to her.

"There you go" I said thrusting my cards at her "What does that say?"

She looked down at the cards with my name on and she gulped and said:

"Oh I'm so sorry, Reverend!"

"It's just that… err… you don't look like a minister!" she carried on.

"You shouldn't judge a book by its cover should you?" I said.

"By the way, are you Clergy?" I asked.

"Err….no we're not" she said looking very sheepish "Oh dear, I've really put my foot in it haven't I ?"

"Yes you have" I said and for a joke I said to her:

"You'd better get out of here!"

"Oh yes, we'd better" she said looking very embarrassed.

"Just stay where you are, I'm only joking with you, missus!"

"Thank you, thank you, I'm so sorry" she repeated.

Her husband sat chuckling away to himself "How many times have I told you not to stick your oar in?" he laughed!

30
The Town of Transformation

"If my people who are called by my name, shall humble themselves and pray and seek my face and turn from their wicked ways; then will I hear from heaven and will forgive their sin and will heal their land."

2 Chronicles 7:14

Not long after returning from Sri Lanka I received a call from Douglas asking me if I would speak in Glasgow's notorious Barlinnie Prison. I jumped at the opportunity to share my testimony behind prison walls again and so we fixed a date for the visit, 6.00pm, Wednesday 21st February 2001.

Bill McGibbon head of the prison fellowship was waiting for us as we pulled up at the entrance of Barlinnie. Bill was a man in his late forties at the time, he had been an inmate of the prison himself years before, but was now a totally reformed character after meeting the Lord. He was now a 'Born Again' Christian and was standing with a group of various workers from the prison fellowship, awaiting our arrival:

"Hi Davey, glad you could make it, I've been looking forward to this" Bill said as he vigorously shook my hand.

He then led us all through to reception and after a series of security checks led us through a number of gates into the prison yard. It was a dark and bitterly cold night, the familiar sights and sounds of prison life came flooding back as we stood in the yard waiting for an officer to open up the chapel. I looked up at the lights burning in the cells of the old Victorian building, thinking that this could well be any prison yard, they all looked the same.

We sat waiting for a while in the chapel as group after group of prisoners filed into the chapel. I thought I recognised one or two faces amongst the group.

Bill opened the meeting with prayer and then we sang a few choruses, which seemed to last forever. I was chomping at the bit to get started, eventually my time came and I jumped up launching straight into my testimony pulling no punches. I only had twenty minutes or so but I piled more in to that twenty minutes than most put into a two hour sermon. The lads took the bait instantly and were very receptive of me, then I went for the kill and invited them to repent. One of the lads who I thought I recognised suddenly jumped up and said:

"All of this is true, I know this man, I used to drink in his bar in Newcastle, I know his reputation and the firm he grafted with, this has got to be real for him to be here like this!"

He then said:

"Davey I need to repent and give my life to Jesus" he came forward and received forgiveness for his sins. I then prayed for the Baptism of the Holy Spirit, immediately the air became thick with God's presence and the man collapsed under the power of the anointing. Then another jumped up and said:

"This man is no mug, he is a pal of my brother and I'm having some of this, Davey pray for me!"

He came out and repented, then he collapsed under the power of the Lord's presence! This started a near stampede as five came out, then ten, then twenty, suddenly everyone was repenting even the real hard cases were being slain in the power of the Holy Spirit. It wasn't only the cons that were being slain by the Holy Spirit the officers and the visitors group started to get whacked as well, soon there were bodies strewn all over the floor. The SO (Senior Officer) was jumping up and down in excitement, others running around praising the Lord, it was a wonderful sight to behold. The presence of the Lord was awesome. It was like Pentecost as the Glory of God hit the Barlinnie Chapel, everyone in the place received a blessing from the Lord, a huge fellow called Tam said to me:

"Davey I was sceptical when you started talking and doubted what you were saying, but now I really know it's true, I want to thank you!"

Bill and the team were ecstatic, the SO took me on the wing and started opening up cells for me to pray with people! It was an incredible experience.

"When can you come back?" he kept asking.

"When the Lord allows" I answered.

"You're welcome here anytime" he said as we were leaving. "Come back and see us soon!"

"Wow, thank you Lord, what a night" I shouted as we left the prison.

Jesus Christ is the only answer to Britain's current crime/drug culture and I was soon to get a first hand glimpse of what can happen when God comes to town, as we visited a place that had no crime, a place where the community had been transformed, a place where the scripture of 2 Chronicles 7:14 was a reality.

A week or so later we were on a jumbo jet headed across the Atlantic Ocean, our destination was Houston, Texas. We were to stay there for a few days before carrying on our journey down to Cancun in Mexico.

We checked into a motel, then hired a car and spent a few days touring around Texas. We firstly drove down to the beach at Galveston, passing the Bible School in Le Marque where my pal Dougie March had spent a short time. Texas is a huge state. Next we drove over to the state capital Austin to visit some friends of Douglas' who ran a church there.

The following day we drove down to San Antonio, visiting the famous "Alamo" scene of Davey Crockett's famous last stand against the marauding Mexican army, which had been the subject of a film starring John Wayne, another favourite American icon.

As we were entering the building I heard someone preaching on the street, I just caught a few words but it was enough to whet my appetite, I decided to go and listen.

A short stocky man in his late forties was preaching the gospel, Douglas and I stood watching for a while, then I decided I'd get up and have a go, it was a while since I had done any street work. The guy was quite happy to make way for me and so we stayed with him for an hour or so preaching to the crowds visiting the Alamo. It turned out to be quite an interesting day, we prayed with the guy and exchanged details, he was a lovely brother in Christ.

Then we drove back to Houston and flew on to the Mexican holiday resort of Cancun.

We arrived smack in the middle of the American 'spring break', the place was full of young Americans 'sowing their wild oats!' Hotel accommodation was in short supply, but we managed to find a place. It was two o'clock in the morning as we departed the airport and boarded the transfer bus to the hotel.

The bars and clubs were packed as we came into the resort centre, people were spilling out on to the pavement, as we passed en-route to the hotel. Some were falling around drunk, others were throwing up, there was a lot of shouting going on, there was obviously one long party of drink, drugs and immorality going on. For a brief moment I wondered if we'd got on the wrong plane and landed in Ibiza, or Sodom!!

The following morning we awoke and started to pray, asking the Lord why he had sent us to Cancun, as the place looked a real den of iniquity. After a while I felt the 'still small voice' telling us that we were to only spend a short time in Cancun as our real destination was the town of Almolonga in neighbouring Guatemala, the place I had seen on the 'Transformations' video, the place where they grew carrots that were over a foot long!

The Lord suggested that I phone Kath and ask her to send an email to Pastor Harold Caballeros at the 'El Shaddai Church' in Guatemala City, the man who had introduced the world to the work at Almolonga. I was to mention Samuel Kaniaki and a few other ministers whom we were involved with, by way of reference. Then we were to pray and wait for an answer.

Within a day or two we had the green light to go, Pastor Caballeros responded to our email and invited us to visit him at his church complex. So we made our flight arrangements and flew into Guatemala City Airport.

We checked into a hotel that the Pastor had recommended in the heart of the city and then made the journey to the very impressive El Shaddai Church complex. We were met by Oscar Benitez, the second in command at El Shaddai, before meeting the head honcho Harold Caballeros.

At the time there was quite a building programme going on to help accommodate 25,000 plus congregation at the church. Oscar gave us a guided tour of the site, showing us the new arena and TV/Radio studio that was being built. Afterwards we went back to Harold's office where he shared about the work that had been going on in Almolonga, also that he had arranged for us to stay in a hotel on the outskirts of the town. Unfortunately Pastor Marianno Rischaje, the minister of the El Calvario Church where it all had started, was away in the USA but his family were happy to look after us.

"Would you like me to arrange car hire?" he asked picking up a phone.

"No thank you, I think I'd like a rest from driving" I answered.

"Are you sure? Okay there is a coach that goes from here to Quetzelanango, which is about three kilometres from Almalonga, I'll get someone to pick you up from the bus station."

Pastor Cabelleros then prayed for us and made arrangements for us to go by coach to Almolonga, which we were informed, was a four hour drive north of Guatemala City.

We thanked the Pastor for his help and left for the next stage of our journey.

We boarded the coach at the City's bus station, the coach seemed a bit rough and looked as though it had seen better days. The driver looked like a film extra from 'The Good, the Bad and the Ugly' with a big toothless grin. People were boarding the bus with all sorts of things— goats, chickens, the lot! We sat in the front seat next to the driver.

"Aaayyy okay" he laughed, banged shut the door and we were off on an unforgettable journey!!

It was a totally surreal bus journey. I had never seen anything like it, it was like being on the set of a 'Carry On' movie. Every now and then the bus would stop and people would get on, they would pay the driver in a variety of different ways, some gave him meat filled taco's, others bottles of pop, some pretty girls paid nothing, allowing him to fumble with them and pat their backsides!

Douglas and I stared in disbelief as the whacky journey continued. I lost count of the near misses we had with other vehicles. He simply was not paying attention to the road, he seemed more interested in eating and chatting to the various people who were stood next to him.

I was beginning to wish that we'd hired a car and it was to get worse!

As we got high up into the mountains, there was mist as well as low-lying cloud, which only added to the drama!

There were no crash barriers as we got higher and higher up. The driver seemed oblivious to it all as he would swing the bus round the sharp bends, there was a sheer drop of hundreds of feet at times, how we didn't go over is a mystery to me! The ending of the film 'The Italian Job' came to my mind, where the bus is perched hanging over the cliff, was that to be our fate?

The driver howled with laughter as we skirted the bends, narrowly missing the plunge!

"Do you think we'll get there in four hours?" Douglas asked optimistically.

"We'll be lucky if we get there at all, Douglas!" I replied quick as a flash.

I began to wonder if this was to be the final journey of my life! I half expected Jesus to come wandering up the bus and say:

"C'mon Davey it's time to go home!" just prior to the bus doing an impression of an Acapulco cliff diver.

It was one of the longest four hours of my life and I think we prayed in tongues solidly till we reached Quetzelenango, sweat pouring from my brow!

Mercifully we arrived at our destination still in one piece! We had a short time to wait before we were collected at the bus station by Pastor Rischaje's son, Oscar.

At the time Oscar was twenty one years old and he had never known anything in his life except Revival. There was a real peace and gentleness about him, also there was a visible glow that I was to see in many of the town's inhabitants—they were shining with the 'Glory of God'.

Oscar checked us into a hotel on the outskirts of Almolonga, then we went for a meal with him. Oscar chatted about the visitation of God which was currently in its twenty-sixth year. Thousands of people had given their lives to Christ in the town where miracles seemed to be an everyday occurrence.

Before 'Transformation' the town had been a real hive of immorality, it was a typical small town of 20,000 people or so, with all the familiar social problems, drink, drugs, domestic violence. At the height of its problems Almolonga had four jails on the go, with overflow prisoners bussed to other places.

Witchcraft and idol worship were another of the town's problems, generation after generation had worshipped a wooden statue called Marchemon. The spirit behind the statue had held the people of Almolonga in spiritual bondage for many years and the Gospel did not prosper in the town at all.

Fed up with life in the town Pastor Marianno Rischaje and his small flock from the El Calvario Church began calling out to God. For months they prayed and fasted. Then breakthroughs began to happen, miracle healings started, and Revival broke out after the town's people broke ranks with the deity Marchemon. The Holy Spirit moved into town cleaning up its image; people began to see the power of God moving in their community. They started to abandon the pubs and clubs for church, preferring to be filled with the Holy Spirit rather than alcohol. One after one the pubs closed, the violence stopped as did the crime figures and in 1996 the last of the towns jails closed. Then the promise of 2 Chronicles 7:14 became a reality, transforming Almolonga's poor arid land into rich and fertile crop-growing land making it Central America's vegetable garden!

After our meal Oscar took us for a guided tour of the town and their incredible vegetables.

The sun was shining as we drove down into the

picturesque valley surrounded with hills on all sides. Ahead of us we could see miles of neatly laid out fields with various crops, all different shades and colours, it resembled a huge patchwork quilt. Now that the land was free from curses it started to produce properly. Vegetables of huge size and dimension began popping up, huge cauliflowers, beetroots, turnips, and carrots as long as your arm! It is an awesome spectacle. Oscar shared how they get up to three harvests a year after God gave them the wisdom of how to work the land properly!

Experts come from all round the world and scratch their heads, amazed at what God is doing.

He showed us the swimming pool in the midst of the growing fields, before taking us to meet Roman Siquina the town's mayor.

The market was in full swing as we drove through the town. I got my first glimpse of the huge carrots as one woman walked past carrying a massive bundle of carrots on her head, many of them way over a foot long!

As we pulled up outside the town hall I noticed a small man watering his garden in an adjoining building, I recognised him from the 'Transformations' video, it was Donato Santiago, the town's chief of police.

Oscar introduced us to him. He was very pleasant and happy to chat to us, I asked if I could have my photo taken with him.

"Yes, but wait till I find my uniform" he said and disappeared into his cottage.

A few minutes later he appeared with his uniform, he was beating the dust off it, the uniform obviously had not been worn for some time due to the lack of business! We had a photo together before being led into the mayor's chambers.

Roman Siquina, a short stocky man in his early fifties greeted us with a warm smile, he was delighted to meet us and share what the Lord had been doing in his town. He shared about the many miracles that had happened, he also told us that when he had taken over as mayor the town's finances were in bad shape and that they had had a huge debt.

One night the Lord woke him and told him to go into the town to a certain rock and drill into it! Intrigued by the Lord's strange request he got up, went to the rock and began to drill into it. He was totally astounded as water started to come from the rock!

Today thousands of gallons per day pour through that rock, it is bottled, sold as spring water and has paid off the town's debt, such is our Lord's wonderful provision! Praise his name!

We spent an hour or so with Roman as he went into detail about future plans for the town and then he asked me to share my testimony in the Sunday Service at the El Calvario Church the following day. Then he invited us to go swimming with him and the church members the following morning!

"We swim outdoors!" he said with a bit of a grin and wagging his finger.

"We'd love to" I said thinking of the pool in the middle of the fields.

"Okayyy" he said clapping his hands, "We see you tomorrow!"

We were glad to get back to our hotel for a good night's sleep it had been a long exciting day and we thanked God before drifting off to sleep.

The following morning the sun was blazing again as Oscar picked us up to go swimming. Once again we drove down into the sun kissed valley, people were milling about everywhere in the town. Many were carrying Bibles and were making their way to one or other of the town's twenty-two churches. There was a beautiful fragrance about the place, the 'Glory of the Lord' visible in people's faces, many of them waved to us. I was quite surprised as we drove straight past the community swimming pool in the harvest fields. Oscar saw the puzzled look on my face:

"Swim?" I asked making paddling motions with my arms,

"Yes, but not here, we go up in the hills" he answered in broken English pointing up to the mountain range ahead on the horizon.

"Oh God, what have I let myself in for?" I thought as I gazed up at the mountains with their low-lying cloud, "It'll be freezing up there" I thought.

I looked at Douglas he had probably had the same thoughts as me and obviously did not relish the prospect of an icy refreshing dip:

"I hav'na brought ma shorts" he said in his thick Scot's drawl.

"I'll lend you a pair, Douglas" I shot back annoyed that he was escaping some icy peril.

"No No, I'll just watch you enjoying yourself" he said looking quite smug and turning away to look out of the window to avoid my gaze!

We met up with fifty or so members of the El Calvario Church at a pre-arranged rendezvous point up a hillside, fifteen miles from Almolonga. The people were in deep intercession as we arrived, they were praying over a town in the valley below. The mayor was there and he showed us that on the mountain opposite witches were gathered at a cave high up the hillside and they were raining down curses on the town below.

"We are here to pray against them" he said.

"Every now and then one of them gets saved and comes over to Jesus. We are praying for them and also for success in our evangelistic campaign in the town, we aim to take this town for Jesus, we have many people living there!" he said with the assertiveness of a man who means business.

So for a while we stayed praying with them before we all set off to go swimming. Up and up we went into the mountains, it started to get chilly.

However, we were in for an unexpected surprise as we reached our destination, apparently the swimming pools in the hills were huge, hot, pool-sized springs! It was an awesome surprise to see these huge naturally heated swimming pools. The place was packed with people from the church,

"Hallelujah, thank you Lord" I shouted as I jumped into the pool. Douglas' face was a picture and he stormed away off muttering he was going to pray over something or other!

The water temperature was just right, it was like being in a nice hot bath, but it was over fifty metres long and about twenty metres wide. This was definitely another example of God's blessing and favour on this community.

After our swim the mayor took us for Sunday lunch at a big restaurant in Quetzelenango, before taking us to the family service at the El Calvario Church. The church quickly filled up to its twelve hundred capacity, the atmosphere was highly charged and the air thick with God's presence. There was a very powerful time of prayer, praise and worship before Douglas and myself got up to share testimony.

I shouted out to the Lord; "This is what Britain needs!"

"Lord transform our land" I cried out desperate for the Lord to move.

"Please pray for Britain" I asked the people of Almolonga.

People started to cry out to God on behalf of Britain, they really took a shine to us and went for it in prayer, the heavens were open and the manifest presence of the Lord was heavy within the church. There was an incredible feeling of love and joy as well as holiness in the atmosphere, God's presence was everywhere in the town. Afterwards we had a time of ministry, the major and the towns elders laid hands on us, as Roman prayed for me I felt as though God was stretching my spirit. For over an hour I lay shaking on the floor as I felt my spirit being filled and filled and filled. In the finish I felt so full of the spirit that I could not breathe properly, it was an unbelievable experience, I have never experienced an anointing like it, I was in absolute bliss! I thanked God for the privilege of coming and spending a fantastic weekend with these amazing people. They showed us what happens when the people of God dwell together in unity, they were lovely and very gracious people. There are twenty-two churches that co-exist in this small town and there is no trace of division, jealousy or competition in them, which speaks volumes in this age.

The next day the mayor and the town elders saw us off, putting us on the coach that was to take us back to Guatemala City. So we said our goodbyes to them and set off on yet another hair-raising four hour bus journey, the bus driver much in the same mould as the previous one.

Early the following morning we caught our plane back to Cancun, neither of us said very much. We were still stunned by the experience, it had been one of the most incredible adventures I had been on.

We spent a few days relaxing in the glorious sunshine of Cancun, I found time to do a bit snorkelling in the beautiful clear blue waters of the Caribbean. It was a nice relaxing end to the mission.

We left Cancun for Houston once again but we had an unpleasant surprise when we reached there. We went to the airline ticket office to check on our pre-booked seats for our flight home. They told us that we no longer had our pre-booked seats for the gruelling nine-hour journey to Manchester. We had booked bulkhead seats with plenty of legroom for the return part of our journey, now we were told that this was not possible. No matter how hard we tried we were told—"no way".

"Not possible, Sir."

Annoyed and frustrated we headed off to the check-in desk. There was quite a queue of people at the desk when we arrived. By now I was quite resigned to the fact I was not going to get my desired seat, tired out by the heat and the day's events I decided to sit in a wheelchair that had been discarded near the check-in desk.

All of a sudden an airline official came round from the counter and started to push me past the counter!

"Come on sir, I'll check you in!" she said.

"Is anyone with you?" she asked, assuming that I was a disabled passenger!

"Yes" I said absolutely stunned.

"That gentlemen over there is with me," I said pointing at Douglas who had a huge grin on his face!

"Come on sir, I'll book you in together, give me your passports."

I felt "Don't say a word!" come into my spirit! "Not a word!"

Then she turned to me and said; "Bulkhead seats okay for you?"

"Yes, that'll do just fine," I answered with a big smile on my face.

Douglas also nodded in agreement not believing our luck!

She then said to an airline steward: "John, can you take this gentleman through to board his flight!" slapping our boarding passes in his hands.

"Have a nice flight home Sir!" she said giving me my passport back.

"Yes, thank you I will" I answered quite tongue in cheek.

"You just hold on tight there, buddy" the man said in his thick Texan drawl, and with that we were off! Straight through customs, down a procession of corridors and onto the plane, where the man very kindly helped me to my seat!

"Y'all have a nice day now!" he said as he departed.

"We sure will partner," I answered giving him a wave!

Douglas and I laughed and laughed and laughed all the way back to England.

31
Miracles in Lanzarote

"For I have prepared good works in advance that you should walk in."

Ephesians 2:10

By the middle of December 2002, I was whacked out, it had been a busy year for me, planting and establishing new groups around the region. I was weary, exhausted and getting close to burn out, I had given out so much spiritually and I now needed to receive myself.

My friend Nigel Tree informed me that the evangelist J.John would be speaking at a Hexham FGBMFI meeting. It was years since I had seen J.John when he had prayed for me at the Sunderland renewal meetings, so I felt the prompting of the Lord to go and let John minister to me.

We arrived early at the meeting and had a few words with John, he remembered me from Sunderland and was excited to hear all that had happened to me in the five years since he had prayed the Baptism of the Holy Spirit for me. I have enormous respect for this brother who simply is one of the best communicators of the gospel I've ever met. He is witty and funny, as well as being a very anointed man of God and is a joy to be around. J.John is based at St Andrews Church, Chorleywood.

After the meeting we spent a while chatting and praying for one another. It was a really powerfully anointed time and I felt the Lord filling me up afresh as John prayed for me, it was like going to a garage and being filled with petrol! My gas tank had long had the reserve light flashing and was desperately in need of a top up! The following day I went to the 'Together in Christ' Tyneside leaders/pastors group and asked them to lay hands on me and pray for me. It was suggested that I took a break, I agreed.

So we decided that I needed a break away somewhere and started to pray about where to go. Kath was very busy childminding so it was obvious that she and the children would not be coming with me, much to my disappointment, so I asked Mick Malone, one of the guys from the fellowship, if he fancied accompanying me, and he agreed.

So we began our search trawling through the TV teletext pages looking for bargains in 'Sunny Climes.' I saw some great deals for the Dominican Republic, Egypt and the Far East, but every time I tried to book, I failed. This was the last week that I could go before the Christmas period started as I had meetings that I needed to be back for, which meant I had to leave within the next three to four days and time was running out.

After ringing five or six numbers and getting nowhere I began to suspect that God had something planned. With every number we tried, either the bargain had gone or the flights were the wrong day, wrong place etc. So we started to pray, asking the Lord to either open or close a door, which he did. All of a sudden a deal came up for Puerto del Carmen in Lanzarote, we phoned and 'Hey Presto' we were booked. Problem was, we had to get to the Leeds/ Bradford airport for seven o'clock the next morning and it was now ten o'clock at night so we had a mad dash to get packed and ready, also we needed someone to drive us to the airport.

But the Lord provided and our friend Eddie Gibson agreed to take us there, which was a real blessing at such short notice. As usual there was a bit of drama on the way to the airport. A thick fog descended on the A1 as we came into North Yorkshire, which slowed us right down. Neither Eddie, Mick nor myself had ever flown from

Leeds airport and we didn't know where it was. We took a wrong exit off the motorway, got lost, and ended up in the morning rush hour traffic in Leeds!

Panic began to set in as seven am turned to eight am and then eight thirty and we were still miles away from the airport. The devil started to batter my head with the inevitable thoughts: 'Ha ha you're not gonna make it!' 'You'll be too late to check in.'

I was praying like mad and rebuking the thoughts. I was thinking 'We must be going to have a good time if the devil's fighting hard to resist us going out there.'

Enthused by this positive thinking I prayed all the harder.

Then we got onto the right road, the airport came into view and few minutes later we were running through the airport terminal looking for the ticket desk.

We collected our tickets and ran to check-in, which we managed just in time. I gave a huge sigh of relief as the girl at the desk tagged my luggage and put it on the conveyor belt. I watched my suitcase as it travelled the course of the belt, disappearing through the hatch and into the unseen world of the baggage handler.

Before too long we were sat on the plane and off to Lanzarote. I peered out of the window as we were taking off, glad to be leaving the mist and fog behind, and thanked the Lord. During the course of the flight I chatted to the couple sitting beside me—a bank manager and his wife from Bradford. They were a nice couple who chatted on about all sorts of things and as is usually the case on these flights, I managed to have a good witness to them. A plane is a great place for witnessing as you have a captive audience!!

They were very interested in the work I was doing, the lady had a Methodist upbringing and seemed quite switched on. Dave the husband was a bit more reserved but asked me some good questions, it was obvious to me that he was very open, and was searching for some answers to his existence, which I hope I answered for him.

The sun hit me straight in the face as we disembarked the plane at Arrecife airport, the glorious warmth of the sun cloaking me as I walked across the tarmac. I began to feel better immediately and the cold of Britain was now a distant memory.

After a pretty quick clearance at the airport and a fifteen minute transfer we arrived at our Hotel, 'The Green Oasis' in Puerto del Carmen. By this time I was quite exhausted and ready for a rest.

We were allocated a nice little apartment situated right next to one of the hotel pools. We unpacked our gear and then went in search of food and drink. After being fed and watered all I wanted to do was crash out.

I slept like a log for the remainder of the day, then got up, went to the restaurant for our evening meal, then headed straight back to the room and sleep.

The following day we awoke to the familiar sound of wind and rain, for a glancing second I thought I was back home. So for most of the day we continued just to rest apart from spending a time praying and seeking the Lord. For the next couple of days the weather was pretty much the same but each day I felt a little bit better and each day our prayer time increased to the point that we were spending all day in prayer and meditation.

It was wonderful to be able to do this away from the phones and everyday hustle and bustle, just to spend the time in God's presence feeling his closeness. There is no better place to be than in His presence.

During the holiday the Lord impressed on me the importance of following his plans for our life. He tells us in Psalm 139 that he has written the days of our life and in the book of Ephesians chapter two verse ten, he tells us that he has prepared good works for us to do in advance. They are already there for us to walk in, it is amazing! You must believe me that God has already prepared a wonderful adventure for you, all you have to do is claim it on a daily basis, when you do this, amazing things start to happen for you.

A while ago the Lord said to me:

"Davey, just let me do the thinking."

"What" I said surprised at this statement.

"It's already laid on," the Lord continued.

"Laid on?"

"Yes, it's already been prepared."

Then he said to me: "Imagine we are on a raft flowing down a river, when you make the decisions we bump into rocks, but when I do.... we flow freely."

"Okay Lord I've got it, you make the decisions," I said.

'Amen' said the Lord.

God provided manna, quails and water for the 'Children of Israel' every morning and night for forty years in the wilderness. The manna could not be stored overnight and had to be eaten that day, so that they had to rely on God daily for their provision, they were utterly reliant on him.

In the same way he wants us to go to him on a daily basis to claim the good works that he has prepared for us in advance, but we must be prayed up and tuned in to hear his promptings. God showed me afresh how his plans are minute perfect just as he showed me at Keswick—you need to be in the right place at the right time or you can miss what he has for you—and he has a lot for you!!

The key to this is spending a time in worship before praying, which attracts God's presence, then claim what he has already prepared for you, bind yourself to God's total will and claim the fullness of your inheritance.

To illustrate this point, Mick and myself had spent all

day praising and worshipping God, then we went for our evening meal, afterwards we went up to the main bar where the evening show was underway.

We sat for a while watching the show and having a couple of drinks, then I felt the Lord prompting me to go up to the snack bar at the other end of the hotel complex. So in obedience I got up and walked up to the snack bar. I got myself a hamburger and a drink, found a table and sat down to see what transpired. Almost immediately an elderly lady and her grandson asked if they could join me due to a lack of free tables. I said yes, wondering if this was my first divine appointment of the trip.

After a minute or two, Mick joined us and we sat talking about the usual things, the hotel, weather etc. It turned out that the woman's name was Val, she was about sixty years old and was on holiday with her twelve year old grandson David. They were from Stockport in Cheshire. Val shared that she was a Jehovah's Witness and that she had recently had an operation on her stomach and was convalescing in the Canaries. It quickly became obvious that Val was in a lot of pain and desperately needed help, in my spirit I was praying like mad, hoping the Lord would give us an opportunity to pray with her.

I felt the Lord leading us to share testimony with her, so Mick shared some testimony first, which encouraged her to respond. She was retired, but had worked as a probation officer in the notorious Mosside area of Manchester. I mentioned a couple of names of people I knew and her face lit up a bit, I decided now was the right time to give her one of my short testimony booklets that I carry with me.

She sat motionless as she read through the tract and then lifted her head with tears in her eyes, she said:

"This is marvellous."

She had been moved by my story, so I started to tell her

more, I told of all the healings that I had seen the Lord perform through me, she was absolutely gobsmacked, especially when I shared the story of Eric's healing in Whittington hospital, she knew the hospital.

I could see that we were reaching her and that cogs were starting to turn in her mind.

I began to share about salvation, she told me that she had been a Jehovah's Witness for many years but had grown disillusioned with it and had stopped attending their meetings. Mick and I explained the Christian viewpoint on the JWs

Then I said to her; "You know Val, I believe Jesus can take that pain away that you're suffering now."

She looked at me with pain in her eyes and said, "Can He really, love?"

I replied "Val, Jesus gave up his life on the cross for you, because he loved you, he has a wonderful plan for your life, would you like to meet him? Would you like a personal relationship with him?"

"Is this possible?" she asked.

I said "Yes, it is possible. If you want to give your life to him now, all you have to do is say a prayer of repentance from your heart, and invite Jesus Christ to be the Lord of your life, I promise you Val it's the best move you will ever make and you will never look back."

"Okay" she beamed, "I'll give it a go."

To cut a long story short, Val gave her life to the Lord and I prayed healing prayers for her, the pain left her body immediately. Her countenance and facial features completely changed before our eyes as she received her healing and the Baptism of the Holy Spirit. The pained expression turned to pure joy as she was set free from darkness. We prayed and broke all curses over her, and she renounced being a Jehovah's Witness.

As the joy of the Lord filled her she began to run around

celebrating, prior to this Val had been unable to lift her arms above her head, now this sixty year old woman was dancing around like a teenager, her face was radiant and was shining.

"This is awesome," she cried.

Then she said, "Do you think God can heal David's asthma?"

"I know for a fact he can" I replied.

"David, would you like to give your heart to Jesus?" I asked.

"Yes, I really would, look what he's done to Nan" he said as he watched the continuing transformation of his grandmother.

So I led him in the prayer and then commanded the asthma to leave his body which it did, with a bit of coughing and spluttering. Then David also was filled with the joy of the Lord. It was a truly amazing spectacle to watch and a wonderful end to the day. Another work the Lord had prepared for us to walk in had come to pass. Mick and I rejoiced as we returned to our room, thanking God and giving him the glory for what had taken place.

The following day we were sitting at the breakfast table when young David shared with us that he had been running all over the place and that he had no chest pains whatsoever and that he was breathing perfectly. Amen, praise the Lord.

Not long after breakfast the sun came out, so we decided after our prayer and praise time to head off down into Puerto del Carmen. We took a casual stroll down to the seafront and for the first time since we arrived, I got a glimpse of the island. The thick cloud now dispersed and this meant that I could now see some of the volcanoes in the distance. Apparently there are a lot on the island. In the past there had been a lot of volcanic activity leaving the landscape resembling the moon.

For a while we searched our way through the endless array of gift shops, buying presents to take home with us, before heading off to McDonalds for a cup of tea and a rest. We sat for a while discussing the previous night's events with enthusiasm, wondering what was going to happen next!

As we left McDonalds and began to head back along the front I heard a voice calling to me from one of the bars, it was the couple who had sat next to me on the plane! I knew that this was another divine appointment, so we joined them for a drink and waited to see what developed.

Dave had one hundred and one questions for me. It was obvious that my discussion with him on the plane had given him food for thought. For a couple of hours we sat and shared testimony with him and his wife Janet, who was from Mick's home town, Stockton on Tees. I answered as many of Dave's questions as I could and firmly believe that he will be saved. I felt the prompting of the Lord to suggest that they pay a visit to the 'Abundant Life Church' in Bradford where they lived, which is a big church that is very switched on to things of the Holy Spirit.

On the way back, the Lord once again demonstrated the importance of listening to him for the promptings and how his plans are minute perfect.

I suggested to Mick we go for a Chinese meal, but as we went to step into the restaurant, I felt an emphatic 'No' in my spirit.

So we tried one a little further down the road, but once again 'No'.

We tried a third, a fourth and a fifth with the same results!

After the sixth occasion I gave up and decided to head back to the hotel, the Lord obviously did not want us to eat in any of the restaurants.

As we walked back into the hotel the Lord said: "Go to the hotel dining room."

So we went into the dining room, the lunch session was nearly finished and a few people were still in, I went to pour myself a drink of orange and was joined at the pump by a dark haired Irish woman, who looked to be in her mid to late fifties.

"Oh there you are" she started. "We've been looking everywhere for you."

"Oh, have you?" I asked, looking a bit confused. "What for?"

"Well it's my husband Tom, he was in a serious car accident a while ago, he can't walk without help and has all sorts of things wrong with him, we heard… about Val getting healed and we wondered if…..you know, you could….." She said looking at me with a desperate look on her face.

"If I could pray with him?" I said finishing her sentence.

"Yes" she said with relief. "Would you?"

"Bring him up to our room after lunch and we will pray for him," suspecting that this was why the Lord had wanted us back at the hotel.

So after lunch we headed back to our room and started to pray fervently, this bloke had a lot wrong with him and we would need a miracle to sort him out…but that's the business we are in!

It turned out that the woman's name was Jerrie, Tom and Jerrie! I began to think it was a wind up as it was definitely starting to move into the realms of Mickey Mouse!!

I asked Jerrie if she believed in God.

"Yes, we're Catholics, I pray to Mary every night,"

"Have you ever invited Jesus Christ into your life to be your Lord and Saviour?" I asked tactfully. "Do you have a personal relationship with him?"

"Not really" Jerrie answered looking a bit confused.

"Would you like to have a personal relationship and a closer walk with God?"

"I would," she said.

"Okay then Jerrie, I am going to lead you in a prayer of repentance, you're going to hand your life over to God and I promise something will happen right now, so close your eyes!"

Jerrie committed her life to Jesus there and then. There was an overwhelming presence of God in the room as Jerrie gave her life to Jesus, she was immediately filled with the Holy Spirit and collapsed in a heap on the settee with a huge grin on her face. She spent a long while just lying in His peace, her face had been transformed and was shining radiantly.

Tom was totally bowled over by what he was seeing and needed no persuasion to follow suit.

Tom was also filled straight away by the 'Spirit of God', so we set to work on the mammoth task of praying for all his ailments. The accident had left Tom in a terrible state, he had died on the operating table and had felt himself going down a tunnel, then he heard a voice telling him "It's not your time yet son!"

After surviving a number of operations he found himself brain damaged, unable to walk unaided, he also had a number of metal plates in his head and body. Tom's hips had been knocked out of place and his left leg was three inches shorter than the right one!

I felt led to pray for his hips first and commanded them to realign in the name of Jesus Christ. I commanded all the bone, muscle and tissue to submit to the name of Jesus Christ and cast out spirits of infirmity.

Miraculously as I prayed I felt the hips realign in my hands and felt them come back into the place they were meant to be! Next we prayed for his legs, everyone looked on in total amazement as Tom's leg grew three inches in my hands, it was awesome, we could visibly see it grow. It grew to the point that it became slightly longer than the right one!!

The expression on Tom's face was priceless, he just sat there saying:

"This is unbelievable! How is this happening?"

Next I got him up to walk, for the first time in over a year he got up and walked unaided, his face radiant with joy, it was a wonderful sight to behold. We all started to jump up and down celebrating and praising the Lord. We were ecstatic, I felt the Lord say to me:

"This man's life has turned around today." I felt as time goes on God is going to heal every area of his life and bring restoration. Jerrie now had a lovely smile on her face, I felt led to pray for her and once again she keeled over under the power of the Holy Spirit, collapsing on the settee. "Pray only to God and not to Mary" I said.

Then the hotel bedroom became like a doctor's surgery as others turned up for prayer!

On the last morning we were packing, ready to leave the hotel when there was a knock on the door, it was young David with a girl of about ten or eleven years old. They were both dripping wet and had just come out of the pool.

"Davey, this is Emma she's not well. Will you pray for her please? I told her about how God has healed me of asthma."

"Listen Emma, I will pray for you if it's okay with your parents, where are they?"

"My Mum's over there" the little girl said pointing in the direction of the pool "I'll go and get her" she added and dashed off to bring her mum over.

Her Mother came, looking a bit confused by what was going on. I explained that I was a Christian Minister and the Lord used me a great deal in healing. Emma's mum

Carol was an attractive lady in her early forties, she agreed to me praying over her daughter, she told me Emma had an ulcer which caused rectal bleeding. I decided to pray outside, next to the pool in full view of everyone.

I led a prayer of repentance and asked the girl if she believed in God, she smiled nervously and nodded, did she believe God could heal her? Again she nodded.

A small crowd gathered to see what was going on, I felt the presence of God with me so I started to pray, rebuking the ulcer and the symptoms. Emma then collapsed under the power of the Holy Spirit, the crowd gave a little gasp and there was a momentary look of concern on her mother's face. But that disappeared and was replaced with joy as her daughter stood up with a big smile and said "The pain's gone mum, I feel great."

We rejoiced and thanked God, I then felt led to pray for her mother.

As I spoke to her she shared that a lot of bad things were going on in her life. I told her Jesus could help her and shared a bit of testimony. Would she be willing to give her life over to God and allow him to sort things out?

"Yes, I need his help" she said with tears in her eyes and then gave her life to him.

I prayed over her and prayed for the 'Baptism of the Holy Spirit' she immediately dropped under the power and we laid her down by the pool, where she bathed and rested in the Glory of the Lord. This sparked a few people to begin shouting out that they needed God!

It was amazing, one woman shouted:

"I'm an alcoholic, can God do anything for me?"

"Yes he can, give your life to him and he will heal you and set you free!"

"Right, I want to give it to him now" she cried.

So I led her in a prayer of repentance, cast the demon of addictions out of her and 'bang' she went out like a light, then another shouted and another, it was incredible—a mini revival was kicking off in this hotel! Even as I boarded the bus to head for the airport, people were stopping me and asking for prayer! Just as I was leaving, little Emma came up and said to me: "Davey, I want to thank you for praying for me, until today I didn't know if God was real, now I really know, thank you so much."

"Don't thank me Emma, thank Jesus, talk to him every day and he will start speaking to you!"

"I will," she said.

As the bus took us to the airport, Mick and I thanked God for this wonderful time, for all the salvations and healings. I felt fit, refreshed and ready for the new season with the inner peace and satisfaction of knowing that God has already prepared the good works that are yet to come.

32
Prayer Mountain

Christmas came and went peacefully enough but for a short while both Kath and I had felt an unsettling in Killingworth. Then we received news that the church building we were using was earmarked for demolition. God had stopped adding people from the Killingworth area to our small fellowship, although he was increasing people from the Ashington and Wansbeck area of Northumberland.

I had held a couple of meetings in Ashington and seen some remarkable healings. A friend asked me to go to the home of a man called Ken who had excruciating head pain. At the time Ken was taking eleven different medications and was having daily injections to help cope with the unbearable pain. His wife Cath thought he was dying. The Lord gave me a few words of knowledge. I prayed and the pain left him immediately, the Lord completely healed him! Praise the Lord!!

Media attention continued and I was asked to take part in a number of radio and television programmes, including an appearance on 'The Jerry Sadowicz Show' on Channel Five which also featured London Gangster Dave Courtney—the man who organised Ronnie Kray's funeral. I appeared on a number of shows for Christian TV, I particularly enjoyed doing the 'Battle for Britain' show on GOD TV as Dougie and Douglas were also on it with me. I also recorded some more 'Thank God it's Thursday' programmes on BBC Radio, which were great fun with Francis Wood and Peter Cordell.

In February I was invited preach at a number of events in Uganda by Apostle John Mulinde including his annual summer camp meeting at which there would be youth from 20 nations attending. The events were to be held in August—could I come? I accepted the offer with joy. I had met John at the launch of the 'Transformations 2' video at Birmingham in 2002, the amazing revival in Uganda and John's work are featured on the video, he is an amazing man of God. Apostle Das had also invited me to speak at the Chrisco Annual Conference at the Nyayo Stadium in Nairobi, which was to be held in August. All the dates coincided so I would be able to do both on the same trip.

But in March our time in Killingworth came to an end, we had felt unsettled for a while and had felt God was getting us ready to move. Our landlady needed to sell the property, but we felt no leading to buy it and knew in our hearts it was time to leave.

Killingworth had been our home since 1995, it was a place we loved and cared about, it was the place where we'd been saved, and we would be sad to leave. In the time we'd been there we'd seen the physical transformation of the town, we know our prayers had played a major part in that (much of the spiritual warfare will be covered in my next book).

But we didn't know exactly where God was leading us, so we called the church to prayer to find out what the Lord had in mind.

After a few weeks of prayer the Lord revealed we were going to Ashington, which I suppose was logical since we had some people from Ashington in the fellowship.

So after a few more weeks of prayer God led us to lease the vacant Methodist Manse in the mining town of Ashington in Northumberland. It was not somewhere I would have chosen to live, but the house was nice and had a wonderful view of the countryside out the back. We were told we could have the house for a couple of years at least as the Methodist Church had no plans to appoint a new minister.

So we moved in on April 1st and for the first few weeks spent some good quality family time. Kath was not working and it took a few weeks to get the kids into school so we were able to spend some precious time chilling out together having days out enjoying the beauty of Northumberland.

For about six months we did very little other than continue to seek the Lord for why we were in Ashington. Around the July time we started to hold a few meetings in the local YMCA, which was run by our former landlady Liz! I no longer believe in coincidences!

God began to add a few people to our little group but the venue was not ideal and so we continued to seek the Lord for His plan.

As we came into August it was time to head off to Africa once again. Mick Malone was to accompany me on the mission to Kenya and Uganda.

At the end of July we left England for the start of our five-week mission, which was to begin at the 'Move On' Convention at the Nyayo Stadium in Nairobi.

Once again we were met at Jomo Kenyatta Airport by our friend Daniel Gitau after our twelve hour flight from Heathrow.

"Bless you my brother, we are so glad you're here!" He exclaimed embracing me as we entered the arrivals hall.

"Yes, it's good to be back. I wonder what the Lord has in store for us?" I answered with equal enthusiasm "I believe we shall see some amazing things on this trip!"

"Amen" he agreed.

The sun was shining again as Daniel drove us to our accommodation at Unfangomano Guesthouse near the Presidential Palace in Central Nairobi.

"The Apostle would like to meet with you tomorrow

at his mission house, he is very much looking forward to seeing you" Daniel said.

"Yes, I am looking forward to meeting him again, it's been a long while since I've seen him" I replied, looking forward to my meeting with the man I consider to be my spiritual father in the faith.

"He is very busy, we have a lot going on and many people are here from different nations to see him, but he always likes to see you" Daniel continued.

"Yes, I have a lot to share with him and I need him to pray with me over my itinerary."

"Yes, it's very important to have his prayers over you" he agreed.

After dropping us at the guesthouse, Daniel headed off with the promise to pick us up the following morning at 9.00am. Mick and myself were both shattered and headed off to our rooms and crashed out after our long journey.

I awoke to birds singing and the sun streaming in the windows, I lay there for a moment gazing up through my mosquito net at the ceiling. I retrieved my Bible from under my pillow and began to pray in tongues.

After a while I heard Mick moving about so I got ready and went down to breakfast. Soon afterwards Mick joined me.

As we were finishing off our breakfast Daniel turned up with David Githinge, the Chrisco National Presbyter.

"How are you my friend?" he said greeting me with a big smile. "Did you sleep well?"

"Yes, thank you," I replied as I got up to embrace him.

"The Apostle is waiting for us, he's looking forward to seeing you."

We then got into the car and headed for the Mission House where the Apostle was waiting for us. It was good to see him again, and he was delighted to see us, warmly greeting us and inviting us into his Nairobi home.

For a couple of hours we sat talking over all the recent developments in our ministry. Harry was able to give me sound words of advice, praying over me and encouraging me. We talked about my forthcoming itinerary and what it would include, as I was due to travel to Uganda first to fulfil my programme with Apostle John Mulinde before returning to Kenya and a heavy four week programme of daily meetings and conference speaking. The Apostle prayed over me and gave his blessing over the forthcoming programme. As we were leaving his house I saw queues of people waiting to see him. I always enjoy the time I spend with him for he really is a true statesman and ambassador of the Kingdom of God. He looked very tired as he had just returned from Guyana where he was standing as a candidate in the national presidential elections and the months of campaigning had left its' toll on him. I prayed that God would give him times of rest and refreshing although I knew it would be difficult as he had many obligations in Uganda, Congo and Angola. A massive door was opening for him in Angola after leading the president of the nation to Christ. Along with Pastor Kaniaki he was setting up a massive rehabilitation programme that would help millions of people, and I prayed that the Lord would give him strength. Shortly afterwards we took a short flight to Kampala, Uganda where we were met at the airport by Apostle Mulinde's representative. As we were flying into Ugandan airspace I really felt the presence of the Lord in the atmosphere, it was an unusual time. Uganda is a very beautiful country, it is known as the pearl of Africa. It has also known some very hard times under the dictatorships of Milton Abote and of course Idi'Dada'Amin. During the days of Amin's reign he had outlawed Christianity declaring Uganda a Muslim state. The Christians had to meet in the swamps and forests of Uganda under fear of death. Many people disappeared from their homes in the middle of the night, ending up in the torture chambers of the dreaded Nakasero State Research Bureau. Even Uganda's Archbishop was murdered by Amin. There was a rumour that the Archbishop had been eaten by Amin in a depraved cannibalistic frenzy. The faithful continued to pray from the swamps for the day when God would deliver them from the tyranny of these dictatorships. Eventually the prayers of the righteous arose like sweet incense before the nostrils of God and God moved. Uganda came under the rule of General Yoweri Museveni, a God-fearing man whose wife Janet was a committed born again believer. Museveni brought stability to Uganda and the church emerged from the swamps, holding massive crusades and prayer events before nationwide revival broke open. Apostle John Mulinde was among the leaders who organised these huge events and it was he who had invited me to Uganda to speak at his annual camp meeting. I was also to speak at a huge event on Prayer Mountain, an eighty-acre mountain that had been given to the churches of Uganda by President Museveni and at a massive evangelistic rally being held in Parliament Square in Kampala. The German ambassador and Bishop Robert Kayanga from the Miracle Centre Cathedral were also on the same programme with me.

John's team had booked us in at a nice hotel that overlooked Lake Victoria, we arrived just after dark and headed straight to our room, we unpacked and got our heads down for the night.

I awoke early the following morning and headed down for breakfast at the hotel restaurant. As I walked the short distance I suddenly became aware of the beauty of our surroundings. I stopped dead in my tracks as I reached the balcony just outside of the hotel restaurant. For a long while I stood gazing over this awesome spectacle, drinking in the beauty of it. The sun was just up and there was a slight haze of mist lying over Lake Victoria. It was one of those perfect moments, when the beauty of creation left me totally in awe and I will never forget it.

Later that day we were in the university grounds for the camp meeting where I was informed I would be speaking to the youth from twenty nations!

The whole thing was a complete privilege.

That night I stood on Prayer Mountain leading thousands in worship, it was one of the most memorable nights of my life. The event had opened with the American Ambassador, but now the cloud of the Lord's presence was thick on the top of the mountain, it was an awesome experience. As I gazed out at the sea of people in front of me, tears filled my eyes. I said 'Thank you' to Jesus for allowing me to be part of this amazing spectacle.

For over an hour I shared testimony and the word with the masses before giving the altar call, many came forward to receive salvation as I made the appeal. As I ministered under the anointing many were slain in the Spirit, it was a very emotional experience for me. Once again I just thought, 'Lord how amazing you are to get me here from where I came from'. That night it felt as though we were sleeping on clouds!

The following day I was invited to go to the British High Commission to meet the Commissioner.

There was a little party of us who were invited and we were greeted warmly by the Commissioner who said to me:

"It's good to meet you Davey, I've been looking forward to meeting you!!"

"Have you?" I asked, puzzled that he should know about me.

"Yes, I've heard all about you! You've got quite a story haven't you?"

"Yes, but how do you know?" I asked.

"Ah well, one of my staff is an ex-CID officer from Newcastle!" he laughed.

"He's filled me in all about you, keep up the good work!"

"I will" I said quite surprised by this revelation. He was a nice guy and we chatted for a while before moving on to our next event in the Parliament Square.

Thousands were gathered as we arrived at the square. John Mulinde was there to greet me with a big hug. They had erected a stage but were having some problems with the sound system but eventually it was sorted out. John introduced me to Alex, the German Ambassador and to Bishop Robert Kayanga another major player in Uganda's revival.

I was surprised when Alex, the ambassador, got up and sang "He's Got The Whole World In His Hands!!" — not something you see everyday, a politician leading a Christian chorus!

The crowd loved it and joined in with the singing, there was a real presence of God's love and favour in the atmosphere

Next was Bishop Robert Kayanga who led a very powerful talk on the miracles that had been happening inside his Miracle Centre Cathedral. His church had grown from a small handful of people to 50.000 in a short space of time. There had been a number of spectacular miracles including people healed of AIDS and even people raised from the dead!

I got up next and once again shared my testimony and the word with the thousands that were gathered in front of me. By now the sun was going down, it was a beautiful sight to behold. I started to round off my message and make the call for salvation. Once again many streamed forward to receive salvation and prayer.

It was pitch black by the time we had finished ministering

and that night I crashed out as soon as my head hit the pillow, exhausted by the day's events.

The following day we left Kampala and headed out to Mbale on the eastern border of Uganda, where we were to stay for a week with Pastor Otim and his family. Pastor Otim is a Chrisco minister who oversees a number of churches in that area, including two churches in the dangerous North Eastern area, where rebel forces are currently terrorising the local inhabitants, with rape and murder commonplace.

En-route to Mbale we crossed over the River Nile at its source just outside Kampala, the same river that had carried Moses to Pharoah's daughter some thousand miles or more north of here in Egypt. We passed through Jinja and many other exotic locations, always with the reminder of how beautiful Uganda is, the scenery breathtaking and spectacular in places.

I had first met Pastor Otim a couple of years before when he had visited us in Killingworth with Harry Das. Pastor Otim had organised a week of meetings in local churches and also hospices where I was to pray with AIDS patients. Throughout the week we saw a powerful presence of the Holy Spirit in the meetings and many people were touched by His presence and were blessed.

A week later we were back in Nairobi, Kenya preaching to the thousands in the Nyayo Stadium at the 'Move On' convention. The conference was powerful and was very much an equipping one. Harry Das and other ministers prayed over me. I had given out a lot on my mission into Uganda and was feeling tired. Praying over thousands of people can be a draining experience so it was good for me to receive a spiritual top up before I continued on my Kenyan tour. It was good to see my friend Pastor Kaniaki once again and also to meet Apostle Das' son John.

I ministered with Apostle Das as we anointed over

a thousand people to go out as missionaries to various countries. We also anointed many thousands for other aspects of Christian work.

I was asked to do some television programmes for KBC with John Das, which were great fun, I also gave interviews for a number of newspapers, so once again the testimony was getting out there!

After the conference in Nairobi I headed out into the country for another three weeks of meetings. I travelled once again to Dondori and Nakuru with Pastor Daniel before moving onto Molo, Kerecho, Kisumu, Kakemega and Eldoret.

It was good to be back in Kakamega with Pastor Richard and sister Mabel once more. They were excited to see me and informed me that everything I had prophesied on my first trip had already come to pass. They had their new house, they had also acquired land next to the church building and the church had massively increased. I had prophesied a huge event also to be held on that land and much more, this had all come to pass! Praise be to God!

We spent a lovely week there ministering, it is one of my favourite places to minister in the whole world! The people in Kakamega are so humble and gentle, they have a real love for the Lord, there is an innocence about them and the worship in that place is an awesome experience. I love the people there, they are dear to my heart and it is always a privilege to minister and worship with these folks.

We had an equally good time at Eldoret with Pastor Boniface Mutisso. Boniface oversees some twenty or so churches in that region. God TV have a small office in Eldoret and they came and filmed some of the meetings. One of the programmes was broadcast over Kenya and there were many reported healings and miracles as I prayed and asked the viewers to come and touch my hand on the screen at the leading of the Holy Spirit. I had seen Benny Hinn do this on occasions but I had never done it before, but as I prayed in my spirit I saw many healings taking place as the people touched their screens. Faith often takes that single act of reaching out to touch the hem of His garment, that simple act of faith brings healing, as in the case of the woman who had the flow of blood for 12 years. The word says that all who touched His garment were healed (Matt 14:36, Mark 6:56).

Later when Boniface visited us in Britain, he told us of all the reported healings and miracles that had taken place through that programme. I was so humbled and blessed that the Lord should use me that way.

On leaving Eldoret we flew down to Mombasa for the last leg of our five-week trip. I was shattered and badly needed a rest.

It was hot and humid as we disembarked our plane at Mombasa, a complete contrast from Eldoret where it had been quite cool.

We were collected at Mombasa airport by Pastor John Nzinga and his wife.

"Yeah, you need to chill out and rest," Pastor Nzinga told me. He could obviously see how shattered Mick and I were.

"One of our ladies is manager at one of the large beach resorts here" Mama Nzinga chipped in, "I will contact her and see if you can pop down there for a few days."

"Pastor Davey I've made Shepherd's Pie, I know you like it!" Mama Nzinga said, "I remember from last time!" she said with a little chuckle.

Mick and I gave a little cheer! It would be a welcome change after the weeks of rice, chicken and ugali! "Excellent, just what we need sister! Good old Shepherd's pie!" I replied with great enthusiasm.

I slumped back in the car seat and drifted into snooze

mode as we continued the journey to their home near Mombasa beach, letting out the occasional snore from time to time. Over the next few days we rested and recuperated at the Beach Resort enjoying the peace, tranquillity and beauty of the surroundings, another successful African mission over!

33
Tsunami

I returned from Africa in the middle of September the trip had been quite exhausting but very rewarding. It was good to spend some time at home with the family chilling out. For a few months I did very little apart from organising our 'Transformation Prayer Events'. These were the all night prayer meetings that we held in many towns and cities across the north of England. From Edinburgh to Humberside we clocked up many miles inspiring and encouraging believers to take a stand and fight in prayer for their communities. We started in Newcastle in 1997 and pretty soon many were catching the vision of things such as 24/7 prayer initiatives that we had pioneered. Out of our 'Transformations' events came things like Prayer for Tyneside and Prayer for Middlesbrough, Together Northumberland Leaders Group, Northumbria Prayer Net and many other initiatives. I travelled thousands of miles the length and breadth of the country with many, many nights of travailing and crying out on behalf of the nation and also praying for Israel. We saw the answers to many prayers as we prayed for many different social issues in our communities and this is an ongoing work.

In January 2004 we started holding meetings at the local St John Ambulance Centre and Ashington Family Church was born. God began to add people to our little group and as usual there was a powerful presence of His Spirit in the meetings. Sometimes people would just fall down under the presence as it was so strong and many healings took place! It says in 2 Chronicles 5 that the priests were unable to stand when the Glory cloud filled the temple— I know that feeling and there is nothing like it!

To know the Lord is the greatest privilege man can have, He truly is so wonderful. Over the years people have noticed a mellowness and maturity in my character, I am more at peace both with myself and others now, I have learned the faithfulness of God and how to trust him in all situations. When you are in the midst of a storm there is no safer place to be than in God's hands. Over the years the Lord has protected me through many trials and tribulations and when God says 'I will never leave you nor forsake you', He is true to His word. He knows the pitfalls and dangers that are up ahead for us and this is why we must stay close to the Him. An example of this occurred in November 2004 as I made plans once again to return to Sri Lanka. For a while I had been looking for a break. We had recently moved out of the Methodist Manse and into a farmhouse on the edge of Newbiggin by the Sea, half a mile from Ashington. The workload had increased as our small fellowship grew and we often had people coming to the farmhouse for healing and deliverance. For a while we had an 'open-style' house where we used the farmhouse and facilities to their max. The rooms at our house were often full of people who needed intense prayer ministry and whilst this work is very rewarding it is also quite tiring.

During this period we saw many amazing healings take place and one in particular springs to mind.

I had been asked by friends to go and pray with a chap called Chas who had bowel cancer. Doctors had warned Chas that there would be a fifty/fifty chance of survival after they removed the tumour that had developed in his groin area. The problem was, the tumour had grown to the size of a cricket ball! Chas was in his late seventies at the time and was quite frail, but boy did he have faith in the Lord! So before he went for the op he decided to come to us for prayer. I spent a good while praying over him and then left it in the Lord's hands. I didn't see him or hear anything for quite a while after that. But one day I was preaching at Unity Christian Fellowship, a church based in the west end of Newcastle and there was Chas with a big grin, sitting at the back of the church shouting:

"I'm still here Davey."

I got him up to testify, eager to hear the outcome of his story.

He said: "After I came to you for prayer I went back to the hospital for my operation but they couldn't find the tumour, it had disappeared!! They kept X-raying me time and time again but could find nothing! Then they said 'You can't be the same man!'"

"So, what did you say Chas?" I asked, marvelling at the old man's tale.

"I said 'Of course it's me! Jesus has healed me!'"

The church erupted with cheers at that point!

Encouraged by Chas' testimony a lady called Norma came out for prayer. She had been in tremendous pain for some twenty-three years due to osteoporosis and was desperate for a breakthrough. She was taking a number of different medications for the condition and found movement very difficult.

"Do you believe Jesus can heal you, Norma?" I asked.

"Oh yes, Davey" Norma replied in her soft Scottish accent.

"Okay then Norma, just close your eyes and imagine you are the woman in the crowd, pushing your way through to touch the hem of Jesus' garment."

Norma closed her eyes, there was a real hush around the church. I anointed her head with oil and laid hands on her.

"In the name of Jesus Christ of Nazareth I command the spirits of pain and infirmity to leave this body and I command healing to this body now!" I shouted.

Norma immediately hit the floor under the power of the Holy Spirit!

She spent over an hour on the floor, but when she got up she had no pain in her! She was rejoicing with a huge smile and tears in her eyes!

"I know I'm healed!" She cried and gave me a big hug. Once again the church went into rapturous applause!

I returned to the same church six months later and there was Chas and Norma going on strong in the Lord! Norma looked totally different. She had lost weight and was a lot happier in herself, she was dancing away at the back of the church. Later she told me that she was doing things that she had been unable to do for more than twenty years!

By early November I felt that I needed another break and one afternoon I was visited by my pal Dougie March. Dougie is always ready to go off anywhere at the drop of a hat so I asked him if he fancied a break, which inevitably he did!

We switched the TV on and started trawling through the various offers that were advertised on Teletext. True to form we quickly realised we were getting nowhere fast and decided to pray about our destination, the Lord obviously had somewhere in mind for us.

After praying for a short while it became clear the Lord wanted us to go to Sri Lanka! So we prayed for the confirmation and 'surprise, surprise' the next advert on teletext was for Sri Lanka! I had a further confirmation of this when I rang the holiday company. The deal turned out to be for the Kogalla Beach Hotel, less than 5km from Brother Raja's work in Galle. It was also the same hotel I had stayed at with Douglas on a previous trip!

They were offering some great prices, especially over the Christmas period and so we decided that was the best time for us to go. I was just about to book those dates when the Lord urged us to bring the dates forward, travelling from the end of November and returning a week before Christmas. I didn't realise the significance of this until a month or so later!

Later the same day Douglas phoned me from Greece to say he would be home for Christmas and that he would like to come to see us. I then informed him that Dougie and I were heading off to Sri Lanka and did he want to come?

"Yes, I'd love to" he said laughing "give me the details and I'll ring the holiday company and see if I can get booked on with you two."

"Okay then Douglas, I'll speak to you soon" I said.

He later rang me to say that he'd be on the same flight but not the same holiday package and that he wanted to spend a little time travelling round Sri Lanka, joining us in Galle for the second or third week.

I contacted Brother Raja to let him know that I was coming and would be excited to see how the work had progressed since our last visit.

The following day we received devastating news from our landlords that they needed the farm back as they were bringing forward the development of that land! This was a crushing blow to us as we had been told that we could have the place for up to five years or so. We were also trying to raise money to buy it so that we could convert some of the barns and farm buildings into healing and respite care centres. As I said earlier the rooms at the farmhouse were always full and we had a constant stream of hurting and damaged people coming for prayer and respite.

This hit us like a bolt out of the blue! We had not been expecting it, we felt angry and let down, we began to pray and ask the Lord what was happening. It was the Potters Revival Centre scenario all over again! Here we were doing an amazing work of love and once again we'd had the rug pulled from under us, so we kept praying but there was nothing forthcoming.

To make matters worse they said we needed to be out by January 2nd, which was just after Christmas and I was to be away for most of December, so I would have little or no time to help find us a new home!

We pleaded with them for an extension of tenancy, but they refused to budge. If I'd known that this was to happen I would not have considered going on holiday and decided to cancel the trip. However, I felt a prompting in my spirit not to cancel the holiday but to put my trust in God and see what would develop! So at the end of November, Douglas, Dougie and myself set off on our trip to Sri Lanka.

It was a long flight and I was glad when we landed at Colombo Airport. I tried to put the turmoil of the previous weeks out of my mind. We parted company with Douglas at the airport making arrangements to see him later on the trip, then we boarded our transfer bus which was to take us the four hour journey down to Galle in the south of the Island.

For a few days Dougie and I just chilled out enjoying the sun and the sea, resting from our long trip. The hotel is very laid back and stretches for nearly a mile along the beachfront.

After a few days of rest we went along to see Brother Raja and the work at the Nawa Jeena Centre which is located at Rummusala Hill overlooking the bay at Galle.

We were greeted with such love and affection by Raja and the team. The work had grown quite considerably since my last visit and they were excited to show me all the new developments. They had acquired their own land and had constructed a number of buildings. They were currently working on a new main building for the centre! They had treated more than five thousand people on the rehabilitation programme and had been given an award by the World Health Organisation as the best rehab work in Sri Lanka and they now had eleven centres scattered around the island! Many of the boys whom we had baptised and taught had gone on to run and establish some of these centres. We were so blessed it brought tears to my eyes. Here was a real work of love in action.

Raja informed me that the Lord had told him to put a meal on at a hotel and invite many of the local church leaders to it and that I would speak to them when I came.

I started to laugh, quite surprised at this revelation from Raja. He looked a bit confused so I explained that this was what I had been doing at home—trying to bring leaders together, promoting love and harmony within Christ's body of believers by setting up leadership groups and other Kingdom building initiatives.

Dougie and I spent a few days around the centre teaching and encouraging those on the programme at rehab.

I was blessed to see my dear friend Ravi who is the Pastor at the rehab centre and to hear the outcome of another miraculously answered prayer.

On a previous visit to Sri Lanka I had prayed for Ravi's wife Shira who had her womb removed due to cancer. The young couple were desperate for children and began to petition God, encouraging others at the centre to pray and fast also. They knew I was coming to the centre and had prayed that when I visited God would do a miracle. I was totally unaware of all this, but when they informed me of all this I agreed to pray for Shira. I felt a weird sensation travelling through my hands as I laid hands on her stomach and prayed, something was definitely happening! As I prayed I asked the Lord to put a new womb within her and miraculously He did!! We got an assurance that the prayer was answered and the work had been done!! How awesome and wonderful is the Lord!

So on my return visit Ravi and Shira shared the amazing news that Shira's periods had started again!

"Praise the Lord" I shouted "When are their children coming Lord?"

I was so overjoyed at this news it was yet another tremendous testimony of God's love.

Then Raja said: "Apostle Davey we have many new converts for baptism would you please baptise them whilst you are here!"

"Of course Raja, it would be a privilege" I answered him.

The following day I stood before a gathering of fifty or so leaders and their wives at a hotel next to the beach in Galle. We had a wonderful time of love and fellowship. After dinner I shared my heart with them encouraging them in love, reconciliation, fellowshipping and working with one another.

It was a wonderful sight to see as Anglicans, Methodists, Pentecostals and others embraced one another, repenting of their doctrinal differences. There were tears of joy and laughter, as the ministers reconciled themselves with God and with each other, it was a moving time.

At the end of the night Raja and myself washed all their feet before making a covenant with them to work towards one church in Sri Lanka! The presence of the Lord was heavy in the atmosphere, His love was overpowering as our praise and worship rang out across the sea and into the darkness that blanketed the bay.

The following morning I stood in the crystal clear waters of the bay as we gathered to baptise the fifty or so new converts in the beautiful waters of the Indian Ocean. The sun was shining high in the sky and there was such a peace and tranquillity in the air.

A big cheer went up as each new convert came up out of the waters of baptism their countenance shining radiant with the 'joy' of the Lord.

After the service I went diving in waters that were populated with an array of beautifully coloured fish and turtles. I love diving and the sense of peace that exists in the sea. Once again I marvelled at God's awesome creative abilities.

After lunch it came to me to ask Dougie to take some of the lads out onto the streets to hand out tracts and witness about God's love to people. As the day wore on I felt a prompting of the Spirit to get thousands of my testimony tracts printed and then get them out as quickly as possible. At the time I didn't realise the urgency of it all but looking back now I realise why the Lord was hastening this. On the back of my testimony is the sinner's prayer—the 'Ticket to Heaven' and we were only a few days ahead of what was to become the biggest natural disaster of recent times—the Tsunami and we were in the place that was about to take the brunt of it—Galle!

We had thousands of leaflets printed and Dougie took the lads out distributing them everywhere around Galle and the surrounding areas. I hope that some day when I am in heaven someone will come up to me and say they were saved through saying the prayer on the back of that tract—what a privilege that would be!

Like the rest of the world I sat absolutely gobsmacked in front of my TV set on 'Boxing Day' 2004 as the full horror of the Tsunami was broadcast to the nations. Galle had been massively hit, thousands were dead. I tried to contact Raja but the lines were all down, we kept seeing images of devastation around the bay where only a few weeks earlier I had been baptising people in the calm lush sea. Eventually they made contact with us by email and let us know that none of our people had been killed.

They had been preparing for the Sunday morning service when the wave hit, mercifully everyone was up the hill at the centre, all two hundred and fifty of them! Our churches and Prayer Networks went straight into prayer, I desperately wanted to go back over and help but felt the Lord say 'No'.

Raja and the team went straight into action, taking in several hundred people who had lost their homes and families, ministering love to many, many people. I could do nothing but watch; I felt totally helpless. We sent what financial support we could, but that was all the Lord would allow us to do.

We were reminded how the Lord had told us to change our dates, otherwise we would have been there! Our hotel had been completely destroyed, as it was a beachfront hotel. I shuddered as I watched the pictures, reminding myself my life had once again been spared thanks to His love and mercy.

A few weeks later we moved out of the farmhouse into yet another property in the area, but the Lord has promised us a permanent one in the future—we wait in anticipation!

34
Cocooned in His Love

I am updating the writing of this as of September 2006 and I have continued to see many, many amazing miracles take place. I would like to draw a line and finish this book here, though there will be other books following with more amazing stories and testimonies, as well as an in-depth one on discipleship and prayer warfare.

But before we go I just wanted to share where I am and what's happening in my life at the moment.

At the time of writing we are still in Ashington in Northumberland leading Ashington Family Church. Over the past year or so since the Tsunami I have continued to travel the world having many great adventures with the Lord, going into many different and unusual places.

During July 2005 I was invited to go to the Lord Chancellor's Prayer Breakfast in the House of Commons. It was just days after the '7/7' bombings in London and the whole place was in a state of high alert when I arrived for the two-day event, which was being held in Parliament for the first time. It was yet another new experience for me, I was meeting lots of new and influential people, well-known people, politicians, Peers of the realm—so different from the ones I'd met in the past! I was talking to the Lord as I wandered around the place saying "Lord, how on earth have you brought me from Durham Prison to here?"

One afternoon I was sitting in my office when the phone rang. It was a lady from the BBC. She told me they wanted to feature my story on their TV programme 'Songs of Praise' and asked if I would like to do it.

I was completely bowled over by her request. 'Songs of Praise' had been my Gran's favourite programme! I told her I would be very happy to do it and put the phone down!

"Wow, Gran would be over the moon" I thought. I sat chuckling as I remembered sitting watching it with her when I was a young lad. At the time it was not 'my cup of tea' and I would never have believed that I would be featuring on the same show years later!

In July 2006 five of us headed out to Israel for our annual trip to the Holy Land. The small group consisted of two ladies from the church—Dorothy and Deborah, Deborah's son Adam and another guy from the church called Gordon.

We started our tour in Tel Aviv at the good old Gordon Inn where I stayed with Ed Gibson and later Joash. Kath and I had also been there the year before with a small group.

On arriving at Ben Gurion Airport we picked up our hire vehicle—a nice air-conditioned seven seat MPV. We headed straight to the Gordon Inn, arriving at 1.00am.

The following morning after breakfast we drove up to Caesarea and spent the day looking at the ruins before heading to the beach for a bit of sunbathing—'Factor 4' ministry!

The following day we were booked into the Prima Hotel in Tiberias next to the Sea of Galilee.

The drive up to Tiberias was nice and relaxed. We drove across the Meggido Plain and up through the hill town of Nazareth.

A while later we descended into Galilee. The sight is breathtaking as you drive down the hill into Tiberias, with the sea in the background and the lush rolling hills. As I drove down I felt the Lord urging us to drive straight to the hotel and check in. I thought this unusual as it was only just midday, but 'No' the Lord was insistent on it, go to the hotel and check in!

So we headed for the hotel where the staff were happy for us to book in early.

We took our bags straight up to the nice, spacious rooms.

"We'll get changed and head up to Capernaum" I said.

"Okay" everyone answered enthusiastically.

We had only just unpacked and hung up our clothes when the room was rocked by a large explosion! I was lying on the bed waiting for Gordon and Adam to finish unpacking when the door burst open and Deborah ran into the room in a state of distress!

"What's happening?" she shouted, obviously shaken by the explosion.

Gordon and Adam came in looking very shaken by the experience.

I felt I had to take control of the situation and keep a calm head before the whole thing got out of hand.

It went quiet outside for a while and that gave me a chance to pray for everyone.

Then there was another bang, and another! Explosions were happening all over the place! We later learned they were Ketusha rockets fired by the Islamic 'Hezbollah' group from inside nearby Lebanon. When we went downstairs we found there was a state of panic and everyone was being taken to secure rooms in the basement. All around people were praying, but I did not feel troubled at all and asked if I could go out and use the hotel swimming pool!

"What!" the hotel manager exclaimed "Are you crazy?"

"No, no, no," he shooed me, "Go down to the basement room."

So under protest we headed down to the basement room, which was full of other guests, many were crying, some were praying. I asked our little group to start praying and we soon felt the presence of the Lord putting us at peace and at rest. Again I prayed for the others who were

301

quite shaken by the whole experience and not as battle hardened as I was, though Dorothy was putting up a brave front!

After a couple of hours we got the all clear and were told that we could go back to our rooms.

We were on the top floor of the hotel and had a simply splendid view over Tiberias and the area in general. Outside we could see a procession of police, army personnel and ambulances racing all over the town with their lights flashing and sirens blasting. Many cars were heading out of Tiberias as people began to evacuate the town.

I decided to lie on my bed and pray for a while, Gordon and Adam did the same. A little later I turned on the TV and there we were on CNN. Full reports were being broadcast, it was quite an experience being in a war zone and watching yourself on the TV at the same time!

I decided to turn the TV over and watch the film which had just begun, to take my mind off things. I'd just started to get into it when suddenly an enormous explosion rocked the building! The whole room was shaking and then there were more explosions in quick succession, the windows nearly coming in! Gordon ran into the room in a state of panic and then Deborah and Dorothy ran in also. I continued to lie there in a state of peace I felt totally enveloped in God's love! They were amazed at my calm, but I was cocooned in His love, totally at peace! I think the expression is 'as snug as a bug in a rug'.

As the rockets continued to whizz past the windows I asked the Lord what course of action to take. I felt him say:

"Davey you need to get packed and take them back to Tel Aviv, they're very frightened!"

Then he added: "Go back to the Gordon Inn, but baptise Adam on the way!"

"Right okay, let's get packed everybody, we're heading

back to Tel Aviv" I announced to the gathered group who were waiting expectantly, everyone looked relieved and rushed off in different directions.

"Adam are you still up for baptism?" I asked.

"Yeah, definitely" the young lad said looking quite surprised.

"Okay, let's do it then!"

It didn't take long to pack. I was quite disappointed that we were leaving, I love Galilee and had really been looking forward to spending a few days here. I gazed out of the window again at the peace and calm of the lake and then down to the chaos that had erupted on the streets below, what a contrast it was! I took one final look, grabbed my case, slamming the door behind me and made my way down into the hotel reception area to check out. Many of the other guests had already left we were almost the last.

I felt the Lord say to me:

"Davey you need to ring the Gordon Inn."

"Okay, I'll do it on the way" I thought.

"No, do it now!" the Lord insisted. "The north of Israel is on the move and you need to book now! Many will head for Tel Aviv looking for accommodation," He continued.

"Okay Lord, I'll do it now," I said.

The duty manager was a really nice man and agreed to ring the Gordon Inn for me, which was just as well as the lady on the other end of the phone only spoke Hebrew! I handed him the phone back and after a few minutes the man smiled and said:

"Your reservation has been confirmed."

"I am so sorry you have to leave," he added, looking quite apologetic.

"Thank you, but it's not your fault," I responded. "Maybe we'll come back some other time."

"Yes, that would be nice, have a safe journey," he said.

I grabbed the case and headed out to the car where the group were standing looking quite nervous.

"Right, let's go!" I said jumping into the car and quickly starting the engine.

The steets in Tiberias were now totally deserted apart from the odd police vehicle, which screamed past with its lights flashing and sirens wailing. We headed south out of the town towards the Yardenit Baptism site, which is situated at the point where the Sea of Galilee flows into the Jordan River, only a few Kilometres outside Tiberias.

When we arrived at Yardenit the building was closed.

"Okay, we'll head up the river a bit" I said not put off.

We got back in the car and headed along the river looking for a suitable spot.

The scenery is quite beautiful, it is lush and fertile, the water in the Jordan a beautiful emerald green.

Eventually we found a nice spot and pulled the car over. I looked at my watch. It had just turned six o'clock but the sun was still shining and it was still quite hot.

We got changed into our swimming shorts, and then I read some verses from the Bible referring to Jesus' baptism by John at the same spot some two thousand years or so before. After a few prayers we noticed there was a strong presence of the Lord and a lovely peace in the atmosphere.

Then we headed down the riverbank and into the water. The water was just the right temperature, nicely cooling us.

I then invited Adam into the water to be baptised.

The young lad clambered down the bank and into the water.

"Are you okay?" I asked.

"Aye" he said.

"Okay then Adam, do you renounce Satan and all his works?"

"Aye" he said.

"Do you believe that Jesus Christ of Nazareth is your Lord and Saviour and that he died on the cross for your sins?"

"Yes I do," he said with conviction.

"Okay then Adam, I baptise you in the name of God the Father, Jesus Christ of Nazareth and the Holy Spirit, your sins are washed away!" then I ducked him under the water.

Miraculously, as he came up out of the water a white dove flew over our heads, bang on cue!! It was absolutely staggering! What a privilege for the young lad!

We spent a while in the water, Gordon and I renewed our vows to the Lord, rededicating ourselves. I could feel the presence of the Lord in the water as I went under. I felt totally cleansed inside and out, it was a beautiful feeling reminiscent of my baptism at Longbenton years before.

As I swam around, my mind went back over the past ten years of my life. It had been an incredible journey with many memorable moments! God had done such a massive work in my life healing me of so many of my hang-ups and hurts. He has dealt with the rejection I felt in my life by saturating me in His love. He has used me as a vessel of His love and compassion to reach others who are hurting. He has taught me how to forgive people who had hurt and offended me. He released me from a twenty-year alcohol problem and a fifteen-year drug problem. He has released me from 25 years of cigarette addiction as well as setting me free from anger, bitterness, hatred, fear, paranoia and a life of crime and violence.

I thought about how blessed I am to know the Lord the way I do. No-one in their wildest dreams would have believed my life would have turned out this way! God has been transforming me in every type of way! The job is not fully complete yet and I am still a work in progress but I am truly grateful for all the Lord has done and continues to do for me.

I thanked God for those who had played a part in my life in showing me the way to God, laying seeds in my life. My adoptive parents, Derek and Joan, who knelt down by my bed at night, teaching me to pray the Lord's Prayer. Auntie Wynn, my Godmother who had faithfully taken me to Sunday School week after week and of course Hannah, my beloved Gran who never stopped praying for me till she saw the fulfilment of God's promise.

As I watched Adam swimming around I hoped that he would have a close relationship with the Lord and an adventure-filled life. The Lord wants the very best for us, he has an individual plan for each of us—but it's up to us whether or not we want it. It's not easy at times but it is definitely worth it!

It's not how you start the race, it's how you finish it. If you give your heart to Jesus and follow His leading and guiding, who knows where you'll end up? I am having the adventure of a lifetime and would not swap this for all the money in the world! At times it is like walking through the 'Twilight Zone' as I have seen such incredible things!

I have found God's plan and purpose for my life, my real vocation in life. Have you found your plan and purpose yet? All my life I felt as though I had a piece missing from me, I tried everything to try and fill that void—drink, drugs, sex, money, power, success but nothing worked. You see, only God can fill the missing part you are searching for, without God you are incomplete. I felt whole when God filled my life, filling that missing piece! Heaven and Earth will pass away with riches and material things but the things of God are eternal.

The best this world has to offer is nothing compared to

the things of God! There is no real peace and joy outside of God. I know I have tried just about everything!

For me there is no other path, I searched and searched for the truth to my existence and for a true lasting peace in my life. All I know is that on 16th August 1995 my search ended as I met 'My Lord', 'My Saviour', 'My Friend'—I met 'My Jesus'!

Have you met Him yet? If you haven't you need to, for He is truly awesome!

May God bless you richly and may you find your plan, your purpose and destiny. Don't take my word for it try it for yourself, I promise you won't be disappointed!!

Salvation—
The Sinners Prayer

"Unless a man is 'born again' he will not see heaven!"

John 3:3

I was on my way to a lost eternity in Hell! It is God's wish that no man should end up there and he has provided a way for us to be spared. By calling on the name of Jesus Christ of Nazareth the Bible says we shall be spared. Nobody is born a 'Christian' and even though we may have been christened or confirmed that does not necessarily make us Christians.

The Bible says 'The decision is ours alone'. We need to make that decision for ourselves and personally invite Jesus into our lives, asking His forgiveness for our sins, this starts the salvation process. Next we need to connect with other Holy Spirit-filled Christians for fellowship and teaching. We need to seek 'Baptism' and 'Baptism in the Holy Spirit.'

So let's now prepare our hearts and get ourselves into a right relationship with the Lord by saying the sinner's prayer.

> Father God, I come to you this day to ask
>   forgiveness for my sins.
> Father, I come in the beautiful name of
>   Jesus Christ of Nazareth.
> Father, the 'Word of God' says that You sent
>   Your Son into the world to save sinners
>   and Lord I recognise myself as a sinner.
> I acknowledge, Jesus, that you are the

Messiah, the Holy One of God and that
you died on the cross of Calvary for my
sins and the sins of all mankind.
I now repent of my sins and invite the Lord
Jesus Christ to become Lord of my life.
Come into my life as My Lord, My Saviour
and My Friend.
Teach me your ways Lord and help me walk
daily in Your plan for my life.
Lead me by the power of Your Holy Spirit
this day and always.
Amen!